Leaving America with Erica

How to Travel and Set Yourself Free

ERICA DERRICKSON

D0376923

Copyright

Difference Press

Copyright © Erica Derrickson 2020

All rights reserved. No part of this book may be reproduced in any form without permission in writing from the author. Reviewers may quote brief passages in reviews.

Published 2020

ISBN: 9798679215825

DISCLAIMER No part of this publication may be reproduced or transmitted in any form or by any means, mechanical or electronic, including photocopying or recording, or by any information storage and retrieval system, or transmitted by email without permission in writing from the author. Neither the author nor the publisher assumes any responsibility for errors, omissions, or contrary interpretations of the subject matter herein. Any perceived slight of any individual or organization is purely unintentional. Brand and product names are trademarks or registered trademarks of their respective owners.

Cover Design: Cassandra Smolcic

Back Cover Design: Erica Derrickson

Cover Photo: Selfie in India by Erica Derrickson

Editors: Natasa Smirnov, Luke Maguire Armstrong, and Erica Derrickson

Author's photo courtesy of Matt Rentz

Hummingbird photo courtesy of Randy Wilson

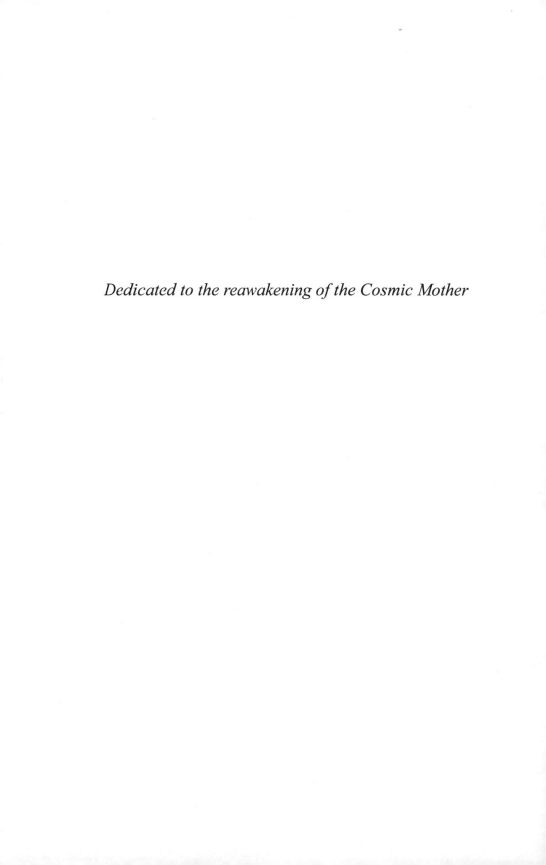

Dedicated to the reawakening of the Cosmic Mother

Table of Contents

And what does your heart say?

Foreword

By Luke Maguire Armstrong

Seven minutes after meeting Erica, she asked permission to cry in my arms. I acquiesced, and she crumbled into a pile of tears—tears of joy, of pain, homecoming tears, tears of elation. These were the tears one cries after finding out that, while the Easter bunny and Santa Clause aren't technically "real," the magic that created them is and available to anyone who dares to believe.

As her sobs wet my chest, I knew this was going to be the start of a deeply enriching friendship, or that I'd need to call the police to remove her from the premises of Karuna Atitlan, the artist residency I'd just opened of which she was resident número uno.

She turned out to be my kind of crazy—the kind of passionate wild that leads people to new heights of possibilities. The sort that dances beneath a thunderstorm wearing only a bar of soap while shouting Disney songs. She's the type of community member who releases a swarm of bees into our kitchen because she just took a beekeeping course and her heart felt so much love for bees it told her to feed them our honey (and then she gets stung in the face: http://bit.ly/EricaGotStung). Erica is a wildling—an uncompromising seeker and someone whose own journey has helped many others begin theirs.

Witnessing her living in my community here at Karuna Atitlan, I can say that she is a sincere, seeking, striving woman who's found a piece of heaven within her own heart that has transformed her world into a place of joy and discovery. She's found a healthy balance in the face of life, which sometimes feels like dancing on a blazing teeter-totter with a venomous snake in one hand and a glass heirloom in the other, all while a playground full of punk kids spit cutting remarks. Life isn't always easy, but it can always be beautiful.

Erica's overriding message is that when you find yourself on life's teeter-totter, don't give up. Hold the course. You got this. If pain is a teacher, healing is its lesson. She breaks down the mysterious process of finding yourself at the right place at the right time doing the right thing into steps. "To achieve a certain result," she writes, "one must follow certain steps, like baking a cake" (Chapter 2). Even with all the right ingredients, you could still end up with a mess. If you throw the eggs at your uncle Vinny and powder your hair with the flour and use the butter as deodorant, you will not get a cake. And uncle Vinny's feelings will be hurt. And you'll be all sticky and floury. So it's important to do things in a way that will achieve the result you want. Erica's discovery of this in her own life is now available for you to understand and apply to your life. She offers an intimate glimpse into her world, and a sincere sharing of what she's struggled with, how she's overcome these, and what she needs to continually maintain her health and happiness.

It's Erica's ability to be honest, vulnerable, candid, and hilarious that has led to her large online following. And that's what she offers a full dose of in her book. Just be careful, following your heart and living out your bliss IS habit forming, just like chocolate cake.

I watched Erica from my perch as facilitator of my Writing Your Dreams True Writers Retreat (IG: @WritingYourDreamsTrue) as she first birthed the pages of this book into life—birth being the operative word. Every morning Erica would greet me with bloodshot crazy eyes. The sort of maniac eyes of someone who has been up all night composing a masterpiece symphony or hunting possums. She was fulfilling her dream of writing this book and it took every bit of her energy to do. She woke up at 4am every day to cram in extra writing sessions. She showed up fully each day for the task with full courage and heart and the result is the guidebook in your hands. A guide to open your heart, unearth your sincerity, and let these lead you to where your happiness will reign king or queen over the minions of doubts and despair that are ever trying to dethrone you from your highest bliss.

Her book is a testament to asking, "What would it take for you to stop believing all those reasons you repeat like a mantra for why you 'can't' do it?"

"It" being your deepest purpose on earth, that which will cause you to bloom into the fullness of what you're capable of being and doing with your life. She writes in Chapter 9, "Let go of the shores of everything that feels comfortable and familiar and be willing to be taken by the flow of life." This is the invitation her life and book extends to you—the invitation to be more than just an amused follower of her life on social media—a summons to be the star of your own empowered life.

You'll have work to do to get there. And Erica's supportive example is proof that you can do this. "If you allow yourself to let go and become an empty cup," she writes, "life will respond by sending you all sorts of new wonders."

In my own journey of empowered freedom living as a struggling writer on the road, I cannot help but agree wholeheartedly with that statement. In my case, the discouraging voices said things like "Get a real job!" And my soul was like, "Excuse me, I'm too busy building a real life where my soul will sprout wings and have free rein of the sky to sing." If you're in a place where you don't want to be, the only way to get out of it is to "Start really listening to and be willing to get really honest with yourself" (Chapter 10). I think anyone who reads this book will have a hard time avoiding listening to that pleading voice of truth within. And that's where the true power of "Leaving America with Erica" lies—in activating the potential in you. The bad news is no one can help you, not Erica, or me, or your priest or pastor or rabbi or guru, not a library of self-help books, uncle Vinny, or the clerk at the store who asks, "How can I help you?"

"You can't!" you'll have to tell him. But the good news is YOU can help you. You have the power to bring yourself from places of pain and misery to shimmering heights of unencumbered bliss. And it starts with surrender. And it sparkles with gratitude. And this book in your hands or on your device is here to help you begin. "Learn to recognize how you hold yourself back," writes Erica. Her heartfelt book asks you to do a big thing: to own yourself, your dreams, and despairs and to take steps to walk away from the latter to reach the former. You don't need to worry if it sounds daunting. You got this, because "Magic is real, joy is possible, and there are unseen forces in this reality that we will entirely miss when we stay rushing around at the level of the mind."

- Luke Maguire Armstrong

FB: Author Luke Maguire Armstrong

Nonfiction Travel Adventures:

"The Nomads Nomad" (2015)

IG: @LukeSpartacus

www.TravelWriteSing.com

A Note to My Dear Readers

What you are holding in your hands is a work of my heart.

The inspiration for "Leaving America with Erica" first arrived in May 2009 out of a period of darkness. At that point, it was a travel TV show that would teach people how to travel the world on a shoestring budget, and essentially liberate a new generation of American travelers. This idea gave me the courage to drop out of college in NYC and move to LA. However, things didn't go as I planned and after that "failure," I stopped believing it was possible. Sadly, I put my dream away. But life had other plans for me, and now here it is, ten years later as a book backed by a story told on social media.

A few things, before we embark on this adventure together:

I've prepared a music soundtrack to accompany the mental, emotional, and spiritual journey you'll potentially experience in the following pages. You can listen to it on Spotify here: bit.ly/LAWEmusic

I reference moments of my story in videos I made along the way. If you're reading this as an ebook, you can click directly on the links provided. If you're reading the paperback book, you'll need to manually type the links. In order to access the correct links, make sure you type them *exactly* as they appear in the book, with respect to capitalized letters.

If you want to see the full playlist of my videos from my original six-month journey to India, you can start here: bit.ly/ComeWithMeToIndiaPlaylist. The first video you'll see "Come With Me to India" was filmed in my photography/acting studio at Foundry24, directed by the visionary filmmaker Ben Proulx.

If you want to give me feedback on how I can improve future editions of this book, or if you have questions you'd like to ask me, please use this form: https://bit.ly/LAWEFeedbackForm. I can't get back to everyone individually, but I will take everyone's feedback and questions into consideration.

In the future, I plan to offer retreats, travel experiences, online classes, workshops, and other offerings. If you would like to be on my email list to receive information about these opportunities as they become available, please use this form: https://bit.ly/EricasEmailList

Lastly, if you want to show some love for this work, please direct that energy towards helping the children of the Integral Heart Family, a kids charity I support in Guatemala. There's more info about that at the end of the book. All donations and support go towards educating and feeding these kids experiencing generational poverty who otherwise would not have access to such privileges. I fully believe in this work, so if you love me, please love these kids too.

Okay, grab some snacks and put on your seatbelt...

THE ADVENTURE BEGINS...

Chapter 1: My Story

"In the beginning was the Word and the Word was God."
– John 1:1

I often feel confused about where my story actually begins. Does it begin the moment my heart broke open when my sister told me she was pregnant, and I knew then that I could not keep pretending everything was okay? Or maybe it began with my head down on my desk at work, lamenting my life and this job I hated that kept me docile and domesticated with the paycheck I received every two weeks that barely covered my living expenses.

The Cracks in the Mountain

When a landslide occurs, all the rocks and boulders go tumbling down the mountain, wiping out everything in its path of destruction. Although it may seem like it to the onlooker, this doesn't actually happen in one instantaneous event. No, sometimes it takes days of rain, weeks, months, and years of subtle cracks within the foundation of what seems like an immovable mountain. That's what it was like for me. My life seemed like this immovable mountain, but slowly over time, almost imperceptibly, cracks began to form. One day, the pressure and tension were enough for something to break, and it did. But what people often fail to see is that *destruction* is also an act of *creation*.

People look at my life now and they are quick to call me "lucky," and understandably so. They look with what I imagine to be wide and envious eyes as I travel to exotic beaches in Thailand and picturesque rice fields in Bali. They see me boarding planes to go explore the pyramids of Egypt by camelback or to find myself working at Granja Tz'ikin, a permaculture farm in magical Hummingbird Valley in Guatemala. Seeing me do these things on Facebook, Instagram, and Youtube, they must think I'm rich. I've got it easy. That I just sneezed and my life settled into this configuration with the same ease that mist settles. Well, let me tell you outright: that is a trick of the mind that keeps one trapped in a state of victimhood, a kind of "They can do it, but I can't" mentality. But I digress, we'll get there. Let me tell you what happened, first.

2012 was the best of times and the worst of times because that's when I did the scariest thing possible: I quit my job. I had been miserable for a year under the whip of an emotionally abusive, passive-aggressive boss, working as the Assistant Creative Director at an event design company in Massachusetts. I was spending my days working for this woman who did not respect or care about me, coming home exhausted with no energy or vitality for anything else except just getting by to do it all over again the next day. For some insane reason, I was convinced at this time that this was the "correct" or only way to live. But little by little, the tension and pressure of my misery strained my "safe" foundation, and finally the cracks in the rock became so profound that the mountain came crashing down.

I don't know what I did that day to summon every ounce of courage I had to walk into her office and quit. It was terrifying. I barely had a backup plan, except to work in real estate with a strong woman whom I respected and admired. But even that plan was flimsy at best. I'll never forget the scene leaving the building that day, feeling like my heart had fallen out of my chest and was beating limply in my hand. My stomach was all over the floor. I had to pick it up like a dying animal and carry it in my arms out to my car. That was the moment it started raining as hard as God can make it rain. I slammed the door to the car, white-knuckling the steering wheel, tears streaming down my cheeks. I raised my eyes to the sky and cried out, *"What have I done?!"* As you can imagine, it was very dramatic. I laugh now at the drama of it all, but at that moment it felt very real and very scary. I was facing the Great Unknown with no life raft or safety apparatus. I was devastated.

Fast forward. Slow down. Pause. Rewind. What did I really want at that time? For years I had been quietly harboring the dream of becoming an actress. Since I was a child I remember having this dream inside of me, but I was afraid. I was afraid of telling people because I thought they would reject me and my dream. So I put my dream away in that small dark quiet place inside of me where I know better than to look because I might find something there that might disturb me. So I shoved my dream of being an actress down in that shadow space, closed the door, pulled the rug over it, and pretended everything was fine. But of course, it was not. In fact, the more I shoved the things I didn't like or want to look at in that dark place, the more that darkness grew in power. And when that unexamined shadow space becomes full and gains too much energy and pressure, something is bound to explode. And let me tell you, it's not pretty. And yet an overwhelming darkness can actually be a major turning point in our lives, if we use it as an opportunity to get honest about what's really going on inside and what we really want and need. For this reason, *the dark times are important*.

A Butterfly Grows its Wings in the Darkness

One of the most important spiritual teachers on my healing path who I met on the island in Thailand, Seulki Koo, always said "All data is good data." By that I think she meant that any information we receive is useful. When we feel stuck in those dark places - in situations, relationships, and emotions we don't like or want - it gives us the opportunity to dream about what we *do* want.

I know those dark places well, and now I appreciate that I get a lot of good data from those places. When I'm not in alignment with myself and my truth, everything feels off. My body tells me by being tired all the time and having weird pains. My stomach gets funky. My emotions become depressed or numb. Essentially, I experience a kind of "system failure" where things aren't working quite right inside me, and I can feel it. *Oh, can I feel it.* And what I've learned is that those feelings are actually my internal guidance system trying to get my attention - and that's good information. When things don't feel like they're working, this is a good space to observe and reflect. Taking the time to recognize that I am out of alignment with my truth is the first step to making a change and doing something different. That's what I realized in 2012. I was so out of alignment with myself that I could not go on like this, working that job I hated and living each day with such misery and discontent. This was not the way I wanted to live my life. "There has to be a better way," I thought. *"But how?"* I had no freakin' clue.

I am learning to believe that there is no such thing as "good" or "bad." In fact, I think that kind of dualistic worldview is part of our cultural programming, a system that is designed to keep us trapped in a loop of shame, guilt, and fear of not being enough if we don't do things "right." When we become sensitive to shame and guilt through that kind of mindset, then we as humans become easier to control and manipulate through fear. Whether we're talking about relationships, experiences, emotions, outcomes, etc., thinking in terms of good and bad, right and wrong, heaven and hell - it's either *this* or *that* - is just a judgmental mindset that limit us.

Rather than judging things as good or bad, I like to think more in terms of inputs and outputs. If I eat foods full of toxic chemicals (input) it will harm my overall physical health, not to mention my mental and emotional wellbeing (output). If I put myself in a situation where I give away my power to someone who doesn't really care about or respect me (input), I will likely feel depressed (output). If I take drugs or drink alcohol (input) for the momentary relief it gives me from the discomfort (output), but at the cost of my integrity, my sleep, my health, and so many other variables, I won't feel good later (output). It's simple. And it's neither good nor bad, it's just a certain outcome which is the result of my choices. If I don't like the outcome I'm experiencing, it's time to wake up and recognize the patterns of thinking and behaving that are responsible for the outputs I experience. If I don't like those outputs, then I need to make the decision to change my patterns around my inputs. But I digress, come back, where were we?

What happened to me?

Doing the Scary Thing

Let me just say I was afraid. No, "afraid" doesn't even begin to touch the depths of my fear. It was more like "absolute terror." I was terrified to quit my job, but something deep inside me knew I had to do it, that there *had* to be a better way, even though at that moment I had no idea what it was or how to get there. The only thing I knew for sure was, at that moment, my heart's deepest desire was to become an actress. I had always wanted to do it but I had never dared before. In fact, there were so many voices in my head screaming at me why I couldn't or shouldn't do it; I hadn't done theater in high school, nor in middle school, elementary school, nor in my mother's womb, and therefore these ideas seemed like very convincing reasons I thought I couldn't do it *ever*. But if there's one thing I had that was valuable above the rest, it was willingness and courage. I was willing to face my fears and walk through them, and I did. I quit my job, I conveniently ignored my rent payment while I knew my landlord was out of the country for a few months, and slowly but surely started connecting the dots to find my way into the acting world in Boston, lovingly known as "Hollywood East."

Finding Answers Through Meditation

It was around this time I was driving to a real estate appointment in Worcester, MA, that I passed by a Transcendental Meditation Center. However, at the time when I was driving by and swerved to a sudden stop, I didn't know that's what it was. All my thinking mind knew was that the sign outside the little house read "Jerry Seinfeld does TM." I wasn't a Jerry Seinfeld fan, nor did I know then what TM meant. But something inside me that I did not understand perked up, my foot hit the brake, my arms turned the wheel onto the side of the road, and next thing I knew I was following my body into a little office just as an introduction to Transcendental Meditation was beginning.

I listened with awe as the science and mystery of this ancient meditation technique unfolded before me, and I just *knew* from inside my bones that I *must* learn. But that's when they told me how much the program cost, and I might as well have started crying then and there for how I felt on the inside. You see, I was broke, or nearly broke. I had quit my job, said goodbye to my paycheck, and was flailing around in real estate hoping to catch onto something as a drowning person thrashing in the sea hopes to find a piece of driftwood. Or perhaps in my case, a piece of the ship onto which I had myself planted the bomb and exploded it into pieces, casting myself into the water.

But let me assure you, where there's a will (and a focused desire) there's a way. I knew I was led to this meditation program at that moment. I could feel with something my thinking mind didn't understand that this was important to me. Oh, and my mind, did that sucker protest. You see, the mind loves structure, control, security, predictability, and to put everything into clean little boxes that are neatly labeled and easy to understand. And yet following my mind and her need for security and control was what led me into the prison I had found myself in. She was the one who put me there and turned the key.

So everything I was doing at this point was in direct contrast to what my mind wanted. It was like we were at war with each other, and let me tell you she was being a real bully. She would say the most awful things to me, like: "This is useless. You're stupid. You're making a huge mistake. You should be better. You're never gonna amount to anything. You should just go get a job. You're doing it all wrong. You don't deserve to be happy. You suck." So, *wow*. If any person on the outside ever spoke to me like that, I would clearly recognize that this person was not someone I wanted to be around. But this offending voice was far more clever and hard to recognize because she was inside my head, talking to me in

6

my *own* voice, starting from the moment I woke up until the moment I went to sleep. And just like a sick person needs medicine for their body, I needed to start meditating also as a kind of medicine - because there was a sickness *in my mind*. I explained my financial situation to the kind folks at the meditation center who were generous enough to give me a discount and I was able to put the course on a credit card. *I was in!*

Cultivating a daily meditation practice had far and wide-reaching implications in my life, especially since it was during meditation that I received the idea to get a camera. Although looking back I see now that it wasn't exactly an "idea" per se, rather it was a deep *knowing* that I needed a camera. It had been years since I owned a good camera. I hadn't had one since by younger days as a photographer's apprentice in 2001 in Washington, DC. Back then, I worked with and learned from an amazing professional photographer who specialized in photographing events like weddings, social gatherings, and political parties. I did this photography apprenticeship for many years through my late teens and into my early twenties, but life took me like a river takes a leaf, and over the years I had fallen away from my photography practice. But as I connected with myself through meditation, I felt something stirring within me. It was time to come back to doing photography. But *how*? I was still broke. I didn't have money to spend on a camera. I could barely buy groceries.

What About Money, Honey?

Here's the thing. People get so caught up in money, as if it's this fixed thing like a castle built of Lego pieces that have been glued together. Trust me when I say, I know *well* the fear of not having enough money and how limiting that can feel. But one of the most important things I learned during that time was that it's not a matter of the resources I have, but rather how *resourceful* I could be. The feeling I got in the meditation was so strong I just knew I needed to figure out a way to get a camera. But I had no idea how, and I struggled to believe it was possible.

Luckily, my beliefs around what was or was not possible didn't stop me from praying on it. I talked to my concept of God and the angels about it, and I chose to open myself to the possibility of owning a camera. It took some effort and intention, but I even stretched my mind to *expect* it would somehow arrive. And soon enough, my dad told me the good news: he was getting married. He had been with a wonderful Italian woman for several years and they were finally getting hitched. That's when the Universe bent to deliver me an answer: He offered to buy me a camera in exchange for photographing his wedding. *Bingo!* Thank you Universe.

To the applause of the angels watching over me, I got the camera - a refurbished Canon 60D off of Craigslist. I used it to shoot the wedding and on the day I stood on the steps of the cathedral, or whatever building it was in Rome, was also the day I found out that I was officially offered a role in the movie "The Heat" with Sandra Bullock and Melissa McCarthy. What a celebration! Amidst the darkness, the light shone brightly.

For the next year, my photography career and my acting career grew like two plants climbing up each other in the garden. If you took one away, the other would fall. They were inseparable. I built up my reputation post-by-post on Facebook and found acting auditions and photography clients. Even though I was nearly broke and cried all the time out of fear of falling to my death as I crawled across the vast and daunting chasm of the Great Unknown, I kept moving forward, finding a way to pay my rent and my bills and feed myself.

Well, in all honesty, at this point in the story I would often not feed myself very well, which is the saddest part of all to me. It was amazing how much I was able to do considering how poorly I was treating myself. But the hunger that carried me on was a hunger of the soul. That existential hunger was what fueled the fire within me - the inner fire that kept me going and taking action amidst all the fears, the obstacles, and the expenses I didn't know how I could possibly afford until the Universe said "here," just when I was about to give up.

The important thing to understand was that this was a time of building. I was building the wings of my new life even though I was nowhere near the moment I would take flight. So even though money was a big challenge and I constantly lived in fear of running out, I invested in myself as I could in different ways according to the tug of my heart.

I didn't know then that I was being led by my intuition because no one ever talked to me about what that was or helped me develop this ability. All I knew or felt inside was that there was something *I must* do. Sometimes that was to invest in an online marketing course to learn how to reach more people. Sometimes that was to get on a bus to NYC to receive a blessing from a spiritual teacher. Facing my fears and that nasty voice inside telling me I was bad, wrong, and couldn't do it - I persisted.

Day by day, I grew. I went to auditions and I landed acting roles. I started a Facebook group for actors and filmmakers called "Hollywood East Actors Group" (which as of this writing has about ten thousand members). I met actors and did their headshots to earn my bread. In the face of the darkness, I planted my flag and proceeded forward, piecing together one opportunity after another, stringing together the chances like knots on a rope that I used to pull myself across the bog of uncertainty. Slowly but surely, I found my way.

Getting Honest with Myself

Things were going well in many regards, but still a quiet discontent brewed inside me. I could feel something calling to me, though I didn't know what it was. Then one day in acting class, I connected with a truth deep inside of me, a feeling that I had once had many years ago the first time I went to India as a bright eyed twenty-three-year-old. My family lived in Singapore then (my dad worked at the US Embassy there) and the course of destiny took me on my first trip to India with a handsome young French man whom I loved dearly. I followed him to India where I spent two amazing months of my life wandering the country with him, experiencing the joy that I found at the intersection of love and freedom.

This was the most beautiful feeling in the world that somehow, over the years, had slipped away from me. It was that feeling that I rediscovered during a profound exercise in my acting class and realized - with great pain - that I still yearned for. Sure, by this point in the story I had become a moderately successful indie actress (Video: http://bit.ly/EricasDemo). I had a photography studio at Foundry24 amidst a collective of other striving artists based out of an old factory building in Charlestown, MA. I worked hard to be there, building my career inch-by-inch by following the thread of coincidence and chance that wove together to form this new life since I had quit my job. And yet, in spite of my relative success, I was still missing something.

I'll go into detail later of what happened next and how I pulled it off. The important thing to know is that I got honest with myself and fully acknowledged that I was missing something that my heart yearned for. I had become so caught up in the drive to survive and succeed in the world that I had almost forgotten a promise I had made to myself back then on the streets of Varanasi many years before, that one day I would come back to India alone and spend at least six months traveling there. I had almost forgotten this promise I had made to myself, but it didn't forget me. It came back for me, and *how*. In fact, it practically slapped me in the face and knocked me to my knees, and after that there was no longer any question what my life was missing: it was the freedom I had once felt while out traveling in the world.

Now granted, reconnecting with my desire to go traveling to India for six months was *not* a welcome realization at that point. I was just getting my footing in this new life that I had created. Paying my studio rent each month was a miracle in itself and the thought of going to India for six months was daunting and terrifying. How could I possibly afford that when I was just getting by as a struggling artist? And yet something in me knew I must do it. I *must* find a way if my soul would ever be satisfied.

Long story short, I did it, and I'll share that process in the following chapters. It was the most challenging and rewarding thing I ever did in my life up until that point. By the miracle of the divine I made the choice to go. I believed, spoke, thought, and acted my way through the darkness, confusion, and uncertainty. I made different choices about how I spent or didn't spend what money I earned, and shortly before my twenty-ninth birthday, I boarded a plane bound for India - and my life was forever changed.

I spent six unforgettable months in India having an adventure beyond my wildest dreams. I met my teacher M. I went to the Himalayas and learned about energy and started my journey with plant medicines. I learned how I would never truly learn anything as long as I was angry. I made mistakes. I had incredibly hard lessons that bruised my ego. I had awe striking moments waking up on beaches, in the mountains, sunrise on desert dunes crying my heart out over lost love. It was rich, it was full, and it was an adventure that changed me.

I came back from India and got back to work, building my photography business and taking acting roles doing the thing I loved. And yet again, something was missing. I was just going through the motions to work and pay my bills, and it wasn't satisfying my soul. And that's when I received an invitation to Thailand and started the whole process over again. And again.

As of writing these words, I've been traveling on and off for about six years. I recently fulfilled a lifelong dream and went to Egypt on a sacred pilgrimage with a group of women, and now I'm in Guatemala in a magical place called Hummingbird Valley and truly loving my life. Today I live a life that defies reality and people are both amazed and confused about how I do it. Sometimes I am too. But I just keep following the steps I'll be outlining in the coming chapters and the mystery just keeps weaving together to give me this amazing life beyond my wildest dreams, a life that I would never have thought was possible in the misery of 2012.

Back then, with my head down on my desk, overwhelmed with fatigue and depression, my world felt so small and my options so limited. But as it turns out, that wasn't the truth. It turns out that the prison I was living in was a lie I had agreed to believe without even realizing that I had a choice. It's like believing a dream is real, without realizing you're asleep. Waking myself up and liberating myself from that miserable dream was indeed possible, but it required that I finally admit to myself and face how I was really feeling inside, and start making different choices. And that's exactly what I did.

If I had listened to the original set of fears and beliefs in my mind, I never would have left. I would have stayed small, stayed put, stayed in the realm where things were becoming predictable and "safe," and yet a realm where my heart and soul were not happy. The important thing to understand is that I had to change as a person to achieve what I did. I had to reassess the beliefs I held to be true in my mind, holding each one up to the light, examining it and questioning it, interrogating it like a detective. *"Who are you and who put you here?"* I asked each suspect. The most challenging part of all was finding the ones that wanted me to believe that my dream was impossible, that I was incompetent, that I was not enough or not deserving of good things, that I was trapped and there was no way out, and "that's just the way life is," and I had to cast these false beliefs over the side of my ship like mutineers discovered on deck and proceed forward with the remaining crew.

If you're reading this and feeling the call for freedom, travel, adventure, or just a different life than the one you have, let me assure you that *it's possible*. But you will need to challenge yourself and grow as a person. You may have to do some rebelling. And that's because you do not get to have the magical new life that fills your soul with joy while holding onto the same life and old stories that fill your heart with discontent. My journey is an example of this. In the coming chapters, I will outline how I've done it. If you want what I have and are *willing* to follow these steps with courage, honesty, patience, an open mind, and a willingness to step out of your comfort zone, I know you can create a fantastic new reality like I did, and continue to do so by following this map. No one will have an easy hand, but if you're willing to make the hard choices and necessary sacrifices, then anything is possible for those who dare to believe.

"The willingness to grow

is the essence of all spiritual development."

~Bill W.

Chapter 2: The Adventure Path

To achieve a certain result, one must follow certain steps, just like baking a cake. After years of traveling and going on adventures, I believe that I have identified the steps that have worked for me, and I share these with you now in the hopes that someone out there will take this map I'm offering and run with it. Run into the bright and scary horizon of your dreams where personal legends are written. Some will see this map I'm offering and turn it down, believing for whatever perfectly valid reasons that it's not for them. And that's okay. This path is not for everyone. You must have a clear and strong desire, you must be willing to summon your courage, and you must be willing to proceed forward in the face of fear and discomfort, just like any great adventurer who ever set off toward the horizon of the Great Unknown.

Fast forward to the present day. I'm standing on a dock at beautiful Lake Atitlan in Guatemala. Before me is a majestic range of massive volcanoes elegantly perched above the pristine water sparkling in the sunshine. There's about a fifteen-foot drop from the dock to the water, and I've decided I'm not just going to jump in, but I'm going to run, jump, and dive in *headfirst*.

It feels scary standing up here, looking down at the water so far below. My heart is racing. The very idea of throwing myself from such a height into the water feels terrifying inside my body. *"But what about this is so scary, exactly?"* I ask myself. Is it the uncertainty of the free fall from such a distance? Is the fear about losing touch with the safety of the dock? Is it the risk that I might somehow hurt myself during the fall? Or is it perhaps a subconscious fear of not knowing what's waiting for me down below in the water where I can't see from where I'm standing? *"What am I so afraid of?"* I have to ask myself.

In this moment, I am so deeply uncomfortable, and yet I'm standing here looking at the water with such a longing in my heart. I *must* know what it feels like to immerse my body in this water. Amidst all the fear and desire, suddenly I sense a gentle knowing from within. It whispers to me in a voice only I can hear: *"You're not alone. I'm with you."* With immense fear coursing through my body, I take a breath, run, and jump.

Where the Path Starts

The process I offer begins with an inner pull towards something you desire. This inner pull can come in many different forms, whether it's the arrival of a sudden idea, a weird hunch, a subtle feeling, a strange curiosity, or an exciting invitation. It's some kind of *calling*. The first time I went to India for six months it was because there was an undeniable urge deep inside of me that awoke after a series of disrupting events in my life. An inner knowing was born within me that I *must* go.

My understanding and acceptance of this inner calling didn't happen all at once, like Harry Potter receiving his letter from Hogwarts. No, there was a series of fractures in my life that lead to the breaking open of this truth, and the biggest split in the mountain came when my sister told me she was pregnant. That was such a big shock to me because it reminded me that my life was passing, and it made me face my belief that once I became a mother, I would not have the freedom to travel.

To put it plainly: *shit got real.*

Sometimes life has to get real and give us a good smack in the face for us to wake up and realize what we must do. For me, I could not ignore this call to go to India if I wanted to be truly and deeply happy. In the next chapter, I will share more of my story of hearing the call and teach you about listening to the gentle whispers of your own heart.

Letting Your Heart Lead You

After enduring and examining the stirrings of discontent from within that help you gain clarity on what is calling to you - what you deeply desire - the next step is to make the difficult choice to heed the call of your heart. Let me be clear: this is not "If I have the money I'll go" kind of choice. It needs to be like what I said to myself: "Come hell or high water, *I must go.*" I must figure out a way by the blood in my veins and the breath in my lungs, *I must*. If you're waiting for life to hand your heart's desire to you, it's probably not going to happen. You need to choose from the deepest depth of your soul that this is what you want and you're going to move towards it, despite all the reasons in your mind why it feels impossible. You must set the machine of unlimited possibilities into motion by throwing the switch with a decision planted firmly in your heart. Without a decision guided by your heart, you might as well just stay on the couch and turn on Netflix. Chapter 4 discusses what it takes to decide with your heart.

Aligning Your Energy

The next step is to direct your energy toward the manifestation of your heart's desire. You must accept the belief that your thoughts, words, and actions have immense creative power. As you learn to bring these aspects of yourself into alignment towards manifesting your desired outcome, you will witness *miracles* unfold.

In Chapter 5, we will learn about energy - what it is and how to consciously direct it towards the manifestation of your heart's desire. I am of the belief that our heart's desire is linked to our ultimate destiny, our dharma path, aka our highest purpose on this earth, so deeply connecting with our heart and aligning our energy to support its desire is how we find out who we really are and why we're here (*kinda important, right?*). So this chapter is critical because learning to align and master your energy is an important part of not only manifesting your dreams, but it's also a key element in the process of realizing your own spiritual destiny and purpose on earth.

Creating a Plan

The next step is to start feeding yourself new information and to come up with a basic plan. In Chapter 6, we will cover what you need to know about traveling, like how to find places to stay, how to get around, what to eat, etc. We'll cover topics on safety, what to do once you get to there, and *so much more*. Stay tuned for some super ninja moves, kids!

Letting Go of Control

In order to achieve the dream of your heart, you must be willing to change and grow as a person to receive the way. Just know that it will not go the way you expect, and that's okay. You must be *willing* to let go of control and open yourself to the possibilities that the Universe will send your way. This is about releasing your ideas and expectations of how it's going to happen.

It's a kind of paradox between *making* it happen and *letting* it happen. You set your mind on what you want, but then you have to let go and trust what comes. You will learn to tap into the unlimited creative force of life when you surrender to the divine machinery of the Universe that knows better than you. In fact, one of the best things you can do in this process is hand the reins over to a power greater than yourself. You must learn to dance with this force and take action when the coincidences and synchronistic opportunities present themselves.

Granted, it's important to come up with a general plan - as we will do in Chapter 6 - to have an idea of where you want to go, how you'll get there, what you'll do once you're there, but then you must be willing to throw it away and go with the flow of what's happening in the moment. In Chapter 7, you will learn how to let go and embrace the steps as they are revealed to you.

Getting Out of Your Own Way

Chapter 8 is about self-sabotage and the "Obstacles to Flight"[1] that try to hold us back from reaching the dream of our heart. When these resistances arise (and trust me, *they will*), you must keep moving forward and not give up on your dream. Your mind is going to try to sabotage you with fear, doubt, and a plethora of old self-limiting patterns. You must recognize these resistances and acknowledge the familiar patterns you're running that hold you back, and you must do the work to change them.

You must learn to weed the garden of your mind daily. You're planting the seeds of your dream, after all. And like any farmer, you must keep working the fields, even when you don't see the results you want piercing through the surface yet. You must keep believing in yourself and your dream, even when people tell you you're crazy. You must keep showing up for your dream, even when they laugh at you for going out every day to water the barren soil where nothing appears to grow. When the hard winds blow inside the confines of your mind and everything inside you screams at you to throw in the towel, *don't give up*. We'll shed some light into that familiar darkness in Chapter 8. In my opinion, this is the most important (and most challenging) chapter.

Trusting the Process

You must decide to keep your mind and heart open in order to receive the way. You must learn to recognize the mysterious coincidences and take action as the path presents itself, which it will. You will never be able to see the whole staircase, but you will be able to see the next step, and then the next. You will not be able to know how it will work out in advance. In fact, you will have to be *willing* to let go of the need to know the hows of it all and switch out that ill-fitting garment for a coat made of faith and trust

---

[1] I learned this term from a fascinating book called "The Magdalene Manuscript" written by Tom Kenyon and Judi Sion. This term translates as "psychological issues" or any hindrances to reaching elevated states of consciousness.

to combat the chilly winds of uncertainty and doubt that will try to knock you over.

You will have to let go of your old life and ways of doing things, and be willing to die to who you were in order to rise as the phoenix of who you will become. You will need to connect with yourself deeper than ever before. You will have to make other people unhappy with your truth. You may have to lose some people, places, or things. You will have to be uncomfortable, like pregnant women who get uncomfortable because they are creating new life. You will have to hold your vision, surrender to the process, and trust that *you can do this*. Let me tell you now so there are no illusions - this may be the hardest thing you've ever done. But *oh,* it's worth it. In Chapter 9, we'll talk about trust.

Stepping into the Great (and Scary) Unknown

You will have to leave behind everything that feels comfortable and familiar and step into the Great Unknown. It will be scary at times, but it can also be the most beautiful, inspiring, rewarding, and empowering thing you will ever do. Sure, there are villains (like Darth Vader) hiding in the unknowable darkness of your cave, but there is also the most glorious and rewarding treasure you could ever hope to find, waiting for you ahead. Along this process, I've had to face countless fears and literally step into my own Cave of Fear in Bali (Video: bit.ly/CaveofFearBali), and that's a big part of how I earned this freedom. As Joesph Campbell said *"The cave you fear to enter holds the treasure that you seek."*

Finding Your Bliss

Once you're out there, you'll need to slow down and really listen to yourself from moment to moment. This is a process of learning to align with your truth. This is the journey you'll go on to discover what's really important to you and what you really want. You will encounter many trials and teachers in unexpected forms and unexpected places along the way who will trigger your mind and ego. At times you may experience bliss, awe, important realizations, or you might want to set things on fire. That's okay - all of it's okay. You can't get it wrong, and that's because you're learning about who you really are. All experiences, feelings, successes and (especially) failures are useful on this path of self-realization. This is all part of the process of going on an adventure of the heart to discover what lights you up and how to give yourself what you need to be happy and aligned with the truth of who you really are. I will teach you about walking the path to finding your joy in Chapter 10.

What Holds Most People Back

In Chapter 11 we will cover some of the most common reasons people will never leave home. I'll share observations I've made about how and why we stay stuck in those same old patterns that keep us playing small in life. If you really want to break free, don't miss this section.

Discovering Your Treasure

If you feel called to this Adventure Path, just know that feeling this call is often connected to feelings of frustration, fear, sadness, self-doubt, and/or confusion. But those feelings are important because they're trying to lead you somewhere. They are trying to lead you away from something that's not working and into something that is. So if you feel the call, it means you're being led into something you can't yet see or understand, and that's okay.

This is where faith is born. The sooner you surrender into your feelings, into whatever this is for you, and into the guidance of your Higher Power who will lead you to it and through it, the better. It may very well be the hardest thing you've ever done, but I'm excited for you to walk this path so you can discover what's waiting for you on the other side. It won't always be a walk in the park, but if you stay committed to the path, *you will be rewarded.*

Chapter 3: Hearing the Call of Your Heart

There's a big myth about spirituality, that it's all about light and love and this perfect image of someone completely at peace with themselves meditating in a field of flowers and butterflies. While yes, light and love are *indeed* part of a full and true spiritual path, a more accurate representation of the real spiritual path is like crawling through a minefield of sadness, sickness, pain, death, and destruction. At times, it feels like your life is falling apart. The real spiritual path will take you into some dark places, and that's because we need to go into and through those dark places in order to face our deepest selves, to find our strength, and discover who we really are.

The Darkness

The awakening process often begins in a dark place, or at least it passes through it. In fact, I like to think that the more heartache and hardship you face, the more you're qualified to reach the sunny shores of peace and happiness. Sometimes it feels like the people with the most to give the world are the ones who have had the most taken away. It's a weird paradox. But stick with me, we're talking about traveling, right?

I was in a place of quiet desperation when I heard the call of my heart (ironically enough, at that time I was also producing and starring in a web series called "Quiet Desperation" in Season 5. You can see it here: http://bit.ly/QuietD502). On the outside, things were going pretty well and I had a lot to be grateful for. At this point in my story, I had my bootstrapped and acting photography studio up and running out of Foundry24 in Charlestown, MA, and I had a fairly steady flow of headshot clients coming to me from the acting and business world. I had a place to live and food to eat. I was creating a vibrant and dynamic community flow with the Hollywood East Actors Group on Facebook, and I also had the most amazing boyfriend I could've asked for, Brad (oh, and btw, some names, like this one, have been changed, just FYI). Brad was like a super-charged car battery that never stopped running. Thanks in large part to him - his experience, his example, and his amazing energy - I learned how to be both an artist and an entrepreneur. I showed up every day at Foundry24 to work as my own boss and generally felt encouraged and supported to establish myself as an independent creative person making it happen.

Yet as good as things were going on the outside, something was not okay under the surface. That feeling that something missing was there. As much as I loved my boyfriend, something inside me knew that it wasn't meant to be. I hated that feeling, and I didn't want to listen to it. I hated that whisper of doubt and if I could have cut off its head and sent its body down the drain, I gladly would have. I wanted to feel like I had arrived and everything was alright, and I could just keep running on this track that seemed to be working well enough, despite the frequent bouts of depression I would sink into amongst all the stars and light around me.

When Everything Changed

Then the day arrived when everything changed. Brad and I went to my sister's house in Cambridge for dinner. I'll never forget the scene: the four of us happily sitting around the table in the kitchen by candlelight. Brad, in his unique and lovably upbeat temperament, asked my sister and brother-in-law "So, do you guys have any big plans this year?" They looked at each other with a knowing smile, as if they couldn't have asked for a better opportunity to share the news. "Yes," they said, "we're going to have a baby."

I don't know if I burst out crying then or if I was able to hold it together until I got to the car, but *oh* did I let those tears rip. While this was amazing news that my sister was having a baby, it was also devastating for me. It felt like a big shock because it felt like *I* was having a baby.

You see, I'm what's called an "empath," and that means I have a heightened sensitivity to other people's emotions and energies. I can feel everything, like a sponge that just takes it all in. In fact, sometimes I have a hard time knowing what   what's mine and what's not. So when my sister told me she was pregnant, at that moment it felt like *I* was pregnant, and I wasn't ready for that. There was so much more I wanted and needed to do with my life before I gave everything to becoming a mother.

So there I sat in the car, quietly sobbing as we drove home, Brad looking at me concerned and confused by my reaction. I looked at him silently and knowingly. This was not the man I was going to have a baby with. You see, the thing about Brad, and many of the other partners I had chosen up until that point (because, *here's a hint*, the people I chose to keep closest to me were all a reflection of myself and my own issues) was that they didn't like to feel their feelings. In fact, in order to avoid feeling the pain, sadness, and anger inside, in order to keep working every day to win the approval of the world, Brad drank a lot of alcohol, and together we smoked a lot of weed.

We used the weed as a way to cut off the harsh edges of facing life. While it was a great tool to help ease the stress of everyday life, I could also feel the way I was using it was hurting me. It helped me feel more relaxed, and that's great, but what was not so great was the way I was using it was to numb myself against the feelings I didn't want to feel. And that's actually a big challenge for empaths - because we feel so much, often times we just want to turn it all off, and something like weed or alcohol is an easy way to do that. But the thing is, *you can't selectively numb your feelings*[2]. So while it did help me feel less stress, it was also limiting my capacity to feel joy, excitement, and the fullness of my desires and ambitions for my life.

In that moment, quietly sobbing on the car ride home, I couldn't deny the truth within me anymore: I was not with the man I would marry, and my time was running out to do what I really wanted to do with my life. I could no longer avoid or ignore that

---

[2] *Brené Brown has some incredibly valuable insights on this subject. I highly recommend her book "The Gifts of Imperfection"*

promise I had made to myself long ago - to travel across India for six months by myself. It had to be now, or never.

The Arrival of a Fantastic New Idea

It was around this time that I went to an actor networking event where someone showed me a TED talk that would change my life. A talk given by Stefan Sagmeister, the owner of a design firm in NYC, posed a fantastic new idea that I was ready to hear. He spoke of his experience taking a sabbatical. This was time he took off to go traveling, in spite of his busy and successful career in New York City. He showed a diagram depicting a conventional model, showing how most people will work until the end of their life and then take their last years in retirement to travel and experience the world. In this fantastic diagram, I watched as that block of years at the end of the person's life was lifted out of the timeline, separated into slices, and then redistributed back into the timeline. These slices of travel were peppered throughout the working years, instead of being relegated to the very end, as it is in the traditional Western concept of the retirement years.

He went on to describe how taking a one-year sabbatical every seven years had a profound impact on his life. Everything was touched from his emotional wellbeing to his ability to create new and highly innovative designs for his company in NYC. Consequently, his business grew and he made more money than ever. However, he spoke of the financial setbacks he faced initially, because - *let's face it* - it's not easy to halt a business in motion and put everything on hold to go hang out on a beach in Indonesia for a year. He talked about the hits he took up front, but ultimately how, in the long run, it all paid off. In the bigger picture of his existence, he was far better off for having taken that time off to go be in the world and gain a new perspective on life. You can watch that transformational TED talk here: bit.ly/PowerofTimeOff.

This TED talk had a big impact on me. It was right around the time that my sister told me she was pregnant, and it was also around the time I had that profound experience in my acting class where I rediscovered that desire for freedom that I had long since castaway like Harry Potter under the stairs. It was like bam, bam, BAM. One hit after another and the mountain trembled.

Then came the unsuspecting rainy day when I was alone in my little studio apartment in Malden, MA. I was listening to a recording of Alan Watts. I remember vividly the sound of the rain pelting against the window, a perfect mirror of the way my thoughts of doubt and dissatisfaction were pelting against the walls of my mind. And there was Alan's velvety British voice asking me, *"What do you want? What do you truly want?"* over and over again. As it thundered outside, inside of me the whole mountain shook, until finally, it broke open. The truth was coming up, whether I liked it or not. I reached for my pen and my journal. Using a full page, I wrote out the words that would change my life: "I want to travel to India for six months by myself." I'm pretty sure I almost vomited.

Realizing What's Important

The thing is that *it was important to me*. It was important for me to go claim this thing, even though I had no freakin' clue how it would happen. In fact, the card deck of my life felt like it was stacked full of jokers against me. But I had connected with my heart's truth and I couldn't deny it anymore. In fact, if I tried to deny it - as I tried to pretend that I wasn't hearing those whispers about Brad - I might as well have drank poison for the effect it would have had on me. So I took a deep breath, and I made the decision I was going to India.

But *when*? Did I need a year, or maybe two years, to prepare? How much would it cost? Surely I would need time to save up money and figure out how to do the whole thing. It was around January of 2014 at this point and I was twenty-eight years old. At first I said, "Okay, I'll go for my thirtieth birthday, that has a good ring to it." But wait, wait, *wait*. Why would I put it off so long? The fighters inside me started boxing each other, one taking the side of: "We need more time, we can't afford it, it's not possible to do it any sooner, and it's too hard anyways." The other fighter, though, was fighting to *believe*.

I love this story and maybe you've heard this one, but I am of the belief that there are two wolves inside of us and they are fighting. One wolf is dark and nasty, he is made up of fear, doubt, insecurity, lack, perfectionism, and unworthiness. He is one ferocious dude! The other wolf is made out of courage, love, hope, and faith. Her fur glows with trust and divine providence. These two majestic beasts are constantly dueling within us, fighting to own us, to be our spirit animal that guides us. Do you want to know which wolf will win? Whichever one you feed more. Whichever one you give more attention to. Whichever one you nurture and stroke in your moments alone. Whichever wolf receives more of your energy is the wolf that will dominate the other, and that wolf will lead you as you approach or run from the monsters within you. So let me ask you this. Just like with any pet, which wolf have you made a practice of taking better care of?

And yet an important point is not to starve the dark wolf, for the last thing we want is for him to turn against us for completely neglecting him. Both wolves are there to protect us, but neither one can do it if we don't master them. We want the dark wolf on our side as much as the light wolf, for in spite of his shortcomings, the dark wolf has many admirable qualities like determination, tenacity, a strong will, commitment to a belief or cause, and an unrelenting nature. Qualities which can all be helpful qualities to have, if harnessed correctly.

That's when I had to stop, look at my two wolves, and ask myself the question: if I could do this for my twenty-ninth birthday, would I? I mean, if I had the money, if I *could* do it, *would I?* The answer was an undeniable *"Hell yeah!"* with both hands on the table. The white wolf howled as I realized that here was an instance where I had to challenge my belief of what was possible. At that point, my twenty-ninth birthday was about nine months away. Was that enough time? Could I really do it? The darkness inside screamed no, that it was impossible, that I was stupid and ignorant and a failure. But suddenly, from that deep well of darkness within me, something else rose like an illuminated lady of the lake. She rose upward inside me and posed a simple question, as if ringing a bell: "What if it *is* possible?"

This was the time to make my choice. If I wanted to go have this adventure in India - crazy, illogical, possibly impossible - it would be up to me to *claim it*. With tears in my eyes and my heart racing as if trying to escape my chest, I scrawled my declaration: "I am going to India for six months by myself on my twenty-ninth birthday." *[insert dry retching sounds here]*

Admitting What's Really Going on Inside

If you want to go on adventures like me, the first step is to recognize what you're feeling. This has nothing to do with luck and everything to do with choice, courage, and intention. You will need to make a conscious choice to feel what you're feeling, and decide whether you want to stay where you are or set yourself on a new course. You must listen to your heart and not the fears of your mind, who are understandably just trying to keep you safe and comfortable.

This means you must peel back the surface layers of "everything is okay" and look under the hood of your emotions. What's really going on in there? Are you fully satisfied with the direction of your life? Is there something you feel like you're missing? What do you feel in your heart would be really great to experience? *What do you really want?* And what is getting in the way of you having it? I dare you to get honest here and see what comes up. Are you genuinely excited in your soul about the things you're doing and the path you're walking? If the answer is a "*YES!*" then Goddess bless you, my friend. Keep going, keep moving in the direction of your bliss, because you're exactly where you're meant to be.

If however, you're like I was, and you know in your heart that there is something missing in your life and not having it is lashing at your soul like the Romans lashed their whips against Jesus, then it's time to make a conscious choice to give value to that messenger of discontent stirring within you. This part of the process is about you finally listening for your own deeper truth. Even if your mind screams at you that you have to stay put, that it's dangerous out there, that you can't afford it, it's not possible and you're going to die, this first step in this process is to look underneath those fears to discover your heart's true desire.

Practice Connecting with Yourself

So how do you practice this step of connecting with your heart's desire? In my experience, this part is best done alone and in silence. Especially for a highly-sensitive, empathic being like me, when I'm around other humans it can be hard to feel my own feelings and know what's mine. So if you really want to start connecting with your heart's desire, I advise you to put your phone on airplane mode and go into nature. Make the time to go quietly into the forest, to the ocean, or to any body of water where you can sit and settle your thoughts away from all the other people and their agendas. Find a good rock to sit on where you can look out at the view. Don't try to run. Just sit and breathe.

Feel what you feel, even if it hurts. If you feel like crying, let it out. Let go. It's okay. It's important that you let yourself feel whatever you feel, be it sadness, joy, grieving, wonder, curiosity, anxiety, confusion, frustration, whatever. These feelings are a golden doorway to your freedom, although it may not feel like it in the moment. Welcome them all. As Rumi would say, they are clearing you out for some new arrival.

Now, take some deep breaths and feel into your body. Scan your body for tension. With awareness and intention, release the tension you're holding. With each breath, give yourself permission to relax. Look at the trees. Look at the water. If you can, let your mind become soft and open. Don't try to solve your problems or figure anything out. Just sit quietly. Even as your mind wanders, keep bringing your attention back to your breath and the sensations in your body. When you feel more settled, envision your mind as a clenched fist or a tightly-closed flower bud. As you take some deep breaths, watch this flower bud and imagine it's beginning to slowly soften and open.

Now, continuing to focus your attention on those deep, relaxing breaths, let me ask you this (and I double-doggy dare you to admit the first answer that comes up): What do you really want? What is it that you really want to *feel* in your life? What have you always wanted to do in your life but never let yourself do? What Is the thing in your heart that you know you must do?

What does your heart say?

This Can be Scary

Let me just warn you, this part can be scary. Asking these questions and finally getting honest with ourselves opens a whole new box of secrets, demons, and angels. When we start asking ourselves about what we really want, we also need to start considering what we might have to let go of in order to get it. And that my friends, to put it plainly, *sucks*. My teacher Seulki was always talking about people coming to her for psychic readings and asking some iteration of the question "How do I get all these things I want but still keep my life and relationships exactly the same?" And the answer is: you don't. You don't get to keep everything the same and get the new life that feeds your soul - and that can feel very scary. What if wanting what I want takes me away from everything I know and love into a place I don't know? That is a highly uncomfortable feeling - and it's one of the first challenges we must face on this pathway to freedom.

Back then, when I was in that dark place and knew something had to change, I connected with the call of my heart and heard a promise I had made to myself to go to India for six months. In other years, the call, like a jury summons (but much cooler), was an opportunity to go to Thailand. Some of my friends from Singapore had built a place they called "Labracadabra," a Burning-Man-inspired artist community collective on a magical jungle island, and I was invited to the grand opening.

Another year, I was bound again for the island, back to Labracadabra. Just before that trip, I received a vision in meditation of myself with blue hair. I saw that as a sign, so I proceeded to dye my hair blue a few days before I left. I'll never forget the moment I turned around in the salon chair and saw my blue hair for the first time (See photos: bit.ly/EricasMermaidHair). The words just tumbled out of my mouth: "Oh! I'm a *mermaid*!"

Heeding that single impulse I received and then acted on sent me down an unexpected rabbit hole of unbridled possibilities, off on a treasure hunt that lead me from Thailand to the Philippines where I enrolled as a student at the International Mermaid Swimming Academy on the beautiful island of Boracay. That's where I learned how to swim like a mermaid - hot pink mermaid tail and all - and how to teach others to do the same as a Certified Mermaid Swimming Instructor. *Crazy, right?* And I never could've imagined that would happen from that innocent moment when I decided to heed an illogical nudge I received in meditation.

In more recent times, the call from my heart was to go with a group of women on a sacred pilgrimage to Egypt. In November 2019, we spent two weeks together exploring and experiencing ancient Egyptian temples and activating our divine feminine energies together. That was an experience that totally changed my life in ways I could never have imagined. By visiting these sacred places of high energy and being held by these women on their ascending spiritual paths, I was pushed into a higher frequency.

I'm still actually processing, understanding, and discovering what happened to me in Egypt. There's so much I don't understand, and now I know that's okay. I do not understand, but I accept. And that's how answering the call works. It doesn't make sense. You feel excited and terrified at the same time. It feels confusing, confronting, and yet *oh* so alluring, like a bee drawn to a flower. Does he know why? No, he trusts the calling, and goes.

The Adventure Continues

Each year, the call has been different. Some years, when I got back I thought "This is it, I'm not going traveling again." But then a new call rises within me, and I recognize it. I know that while I may not understand it rationally on the level of my thinking, doubting, fearful mind, this tug on my heart is my intuition speaking to me. I now know that my intuition is trying to guide me towards my greatest and highest good. I know now the importance of following what I feel because I'm being led towards some kind of treasure. And I've learned that to ignore this calling is a kind of self-abuse I cannot endure.

So now when I hear the call, I'm wise enough to listen and value what I feel, even if I don't understand why it's there. I've learned to let go of my need to understand (which is really a need for control) and instead I choose to trust the guidance I receive. From there we proceed to the next step, which is to decide to do something about it.

HOMEWORK:
MIND DUMP

I've mentioned several times that writing in my journal has been a key part of my journey, and that's because journaling is a wonderful way to let out what's inside. I highly recommend you use this powerful tool to connect to your inner world.
Here are my suggestions:

● Get a cheap composition notebook, the kind that you can easily get another one if needed. I actually *don't* recommend using a really nice, special, or expensive journal. In my own experience, when I had a nice journal, I didn't want to write in it unless what I had to write was brilliant or "good enough." These inner judgments of what's good enough are so deeply engrained in our psyche, which is why I recommend you get a cheap notebook that's more like a scratchpad that you can fill up without worrying about getting it right or using it up.

● On the first page, I encourage you to *make a mess*. Scratch it up, make it ugly, intentionally make it look bad. On top of that scribble, write these words: "I give myself permission to completely *f*&k* this up!" You're welcome to use different language if you prefer, because remember, this is *not* about right or wrong. Here, we are liberating ourself from our inner critic and perfectionist, and creating a container to express ourselves freely, openly, and honestly.

● Program yourself to view this journal as a place to dump out the contents of your mind. Remember, it doesn't matter if you take up space because you can always get another one. I'm really inspired by the work of Julia Cameron in "The Artist's Way" and her exercise of Morning Pages, which essentially instructs us to spend our first waking moments writing whatever comes up. I really like this technique of free form writing where there are no rules. You don't have to write logically, sequentially, or in perfect detail of what happened, unless that's what you feel called to write. Sometimes I even write a few sentences in gibberish to open my entry, and then I follow wherever my mind wants to go after that. The whole point is that you start to let out what's inside.

● Try not to judge, control, or limit what comes out. If angry words want to come, let them. If sadness arrives, welcome her. If you feel like telling a story, or describing the events of your day, or idly writing about your shopping list or things you need to do, do that. If poetry suddenly wants to flow, let it. This is a safe container to be, feel, and express yourself. All is welcome.

● I recommend making a practice of writing one to three pages in the morning when you first wake up, and/or one to three pages when you're going to bed. If you feel the need to release or express something during the day, do that. Express your feelings, thoughts, and whatever comes up. Just make it your practice to write, without caring if it's good or bad. If you don't know what to write, set a timer for 10-30 minutes and write "I don't know what to write. I don't know what to write," until you feel like writing something else or until the timer goes off. Just write. That's it. This will really help you start to move the stuff inside so you can start to connect with yourself. You might be surprised by what comes out.

● Carry this journal with you at all times. Don't worry about other people finding it and reading it - in fact, maintain the belief that you're going to burn it when you're done, so it doesn't matter what you put in it. The whole point is to give yourself the gift of free expression. No one is going to read it, grade it, or judge it. This is just a place for your mind to throw up. Use it in whatever way feels right for you…but *use it.*

● Take your journal into nature and spend time alone. Ask yourself, *"What do I really want?"* Then write whatever comes up. Get honest. No one's looking. You won't be punished for being who you really are. You're allowed to want what you want. Go ahead, I dare you to spell it out. If you feel like throwing up, that's a good sign. *Keep going.*

Also, if you haven't already, now is a great time to check out the Spotify music soundtrack that goes along with this book: http://bit.ly/LAWEmusic

Chapter 4: Deciding with Your Heart

The most important thing for me was that I decided I wasn't going to stay where I was. In fact, I realized that the pain of staying the same was *worse* than the pain of making a change. So even though I had no idea how it would happen, I made the scary decision to face my fears, dare to believe that the impossible was possible, and put out an official declaration to the Universe that I was going to India for my twenty-ninth birthday. Keep in mind, where I was at that point I could *not* afford to go traveling to India for six months. Remember, back then I could barely afford to pay my rent. If I was to do this thing calling my heart, I wouldn't be able to do it if things stayed the same. I was going to have to find a way to make it happen.

Consider this, I wasn't saying: "If I can get the money, I'll go." No, I was saying: "If I have to sell my blood to get the money I will, because *I must* find a way." Those are two very different philosophies. One says, if the external world lines up without any concentrated effort from me, then I will proceed forward. The other says, "Look out, here I come!" When I want something badly enough, I will crawl on my hands and knees through barbed wire to get it. I will claw my way through a brick wall if I have to. I will command my ship through dark waters full of sea monsters thrashing for my hide because I *will* have my prize.

You see, the Universe is listening. And it likes people who know what they want. In fact, I would say the Universe is waiting for you to get clear with yourself on what you *really* want and then dare to ask for it. That's because this infinite creative force wants to serve you. It wants to prosper you. But the problem arises when we're not clear on what we want and operate in an unconscious way. When you stay in the realm of "Oh well, I suppose I'll have what he's having," or, "Well, I'm supposed to want this because that's what everyone else has, and it's what I'm supposed to want to so I guess I'll take that because I don't know what else to ask for and (*subconsciously*) I don't think I'm allowed to ask for anything else." That is *not* the formula for your own personal joy.

Don't Settle For What (S)He's Having

Let me tell you, that's how you get into a situation that looks good from the outside. You know the one. With the car, the house, the degree, the job, and all the accoutrements of society that are *supposed* to equate with success and happiness. All this stuff on the outside that's supposed to make us happy, yet on the inside yields a curdling disposition of discontent and dissatisfaction. No wonder so many people drink.

In fact, I think that's one reason why we have so much depression, anxiety, and addiction in our society today. It's because too many people are settling for someone else's truth. Too many people are taking what their parents, teachers, churches, governments, and societies are handing them, saying "Here, take this, you want this, *this* will make you happy." And I think so many people take it without pausing to assess and question, "Wait a minute, *is* this what I really want?" Is getting an expensive college degree what you *really* want or are you doing it because you're *supposed* to? Because then you'll be "successful" and your parents will be happy? "This is a good job," we've been trained to think. And "I'm supposed to get a good job because if I don't everyone will think I'm a failure."

What Will it Be For You?

Maybe you don't really want that. Maybe what you really want is to go on an adventure out in the world, like me. Maybe your heart yearns to explore the pyramids of Egypt, to read poetry in fields of lavender in France, or to hike Mount Everest in honor of a loved one who passed away and leave their mark on the top of the mountain. Maybe you want to go work with animals in South Africa, learn meditation at a monastery in Thailand, taste wine in Italy, study marine biology on a boat floating in the ocean, go to mermaid school, or return to the land of your ancestors. Maybe you don't know what you want exactly, but only that what you have isn't entirely it. Maybe you just need to get out there where it feels like something is calling to you, even though you're not sure what it is yet. It's okay not to know what it is, only that you feel the tug of your heart calling you away into the unknown. That's what it was like for me, and I can tell you, that's the real adventure. The kind that takes you away from everything that feels familiar and comfortable. The kind that leads you into new places, exposes you to new ideas and the wonders of the world, teaches you things about yourself you never knew, and sends you home with fresh a perspective and a renewed excitement for what's possible in your life. That's the kind of adventure that nourishes the heart and changes you as a person.

If you want to go on an adventure of your heart's calling, first you have to answer the question: "What do I really want?" For me, I didn't want a life where I was just working to survive and pay my bills. I didn't want to participate in a system of economic enslavement just to pay a mortgage. I wanted to taste that delicious flavor of freedom I had known once in my younger years. I wanted to know what freedom felt like passing through my fingers as I stood courageously at the front of the ship like Jack on the Titanic. I wanted to know what it was like to be at the top of the mountain and hear the special song the birds sing there. I wanted to taste the real bread of life, the kind of nourishment that reaches not just my body, but my soul. I wanted to make my soul happy.

At that time, I was doing a lot of things that made my mind and ego happy because it looked good from the outside. I did those things because I got to look good and be liked and approved of by others. But all the while my soul was sitting in the corner unamused, quietly rolling her thumbs, checking her watch with an exasperated sigh, looking up at me asking *"What about me?"*

Flexing Your Courage

I think it's about time we talk about courage. A lot of people see my life today and they are quick call me "lucky," as if this life was just handed to me. But it wasn't. In fact, it would be for more accurate if they called me "courageous." That's because what they are really seeing are the results (output) of the very hard choices (input) I had to make last year and the preceding years in order to have this life today. They don't know the feeling of wanting to throw up facing the fear of not knowing "How can I possibly make this work?" Instead, they see the highlight reel of my life and call me "lucky." That makes me want to throw up in a different way.

You see, there's a big difference between throwing up because of something gross and disturbing versus wanting to throw up because you're pushing yourself outside your comfort zone and literally setting yourself on the track to raise your vibration and change your life (to be discussed in Chapter 10). You see, when we settle for the life that doesn't make us happy - when we sit in those feelings of worry, anxiety, and sadness - that's a very low vibration. To dare to set out towards a life that truly makes us happy is actually a process of learning to raise our vibration, which feels wildly uncomfortable to the point of nausea. Which is also why most people will never venture there. It takes a lot of courage to rise.

For one thing, courage is *not* the absence of fear. Courage is the thing you hold against your chest as you approach the scary monster. As all of those limp noodle voices tell you to run away and hide, courage is the thing that says, "No. Hold on. You can do this. There is a way. Keep going." And it's important to call upon your courage and to recognize it's a muscle that requires exercise, just like working out any other muscle. If you don't use your courage muscle, it becomes weak. And yet I am of the belief that, like intuition, everyone has courage and the more you use it, the stronger it gets.

I know a lot about *not* using my courage. I am acutely familiar with that feeling inside me that says I should speak up when something doesn't feel right. When something needs to be said, I hear the words in my mind that need to be spoken, but all my fears rush in and get in front of the screen. In so many moments like that I didn't try to shoo them away and I just sat in the fear without taking action. I think that's because something about being paralyzed by my fears felt comfortable and familiar - as if behind my fears was a safe place to hide. In fact, I hid behind my fears so many times in moments where the thing that needed to be said or done was reaching its arms out to me, asking me, *pleading* with me to take it, to say it, to stand up for myself and say no or leave, or whatever my truth was at that moment. But instead, I did not call upon my courage. No, I just sat there behind the fear, doing nothing, saying nothing, summoning no courage and just letting the moment pass, letting the person walk over me, or letting them touch me when it made me feel uncomfortable because I was too afraid to speak up. Without courage, I allowed the violation and offense continue. *Sigh.*

So courage is a muscle, it is a force connected to your heart and your truth. It is available to us all and the more you call upon it and use it the stronger it will become, like any other muscle or ability. So my friends, to approach your heart's desire and make a heart-based decision, you must call upon your courage because, *I assure you*, there will be monsters on your path. I believe there is a very real force working to keep us separated from our heart's desire, and it will do anything it can to stop us from reaching it.

I can't even begin to tell you the fears I had to face when I moved towards the decision to change. These fears repeatedly told me I can't, I shouldn't, who do I think I am? The fears rise like monsters with exceptionally convincing and seductive words that try their darnedest to keep you away from the treasure inside your inner vault. They will look and feel big and scary, like I imagine Goliath felt to David. In order to overcome these monsters and reach your treasure, you must pick up your slingshot of trust, adhere your glowing breastplate of courage, blow a kiss to your wolf of love and make the choice from your heart to show up and claim what's yours. And I know you can do it because you have love inside of you and you can summon your courage as your birthright as being a soul chosen to incarnate as human. But only if you decide to do so. As a being of free will, it is up to you to make the choice to activate and rise. You have to *want it* for yourself. It is up to you to choose, and you don't need anyone's permission, nor can anyone make this choice for you. No one can hand it to you, nor do it for you - it's up to *you*.

This is Meant to Challenge You

Let me tell you before you tell me, it's not easy. I know, dear one. I know you have challenges, whether they are physical, mental, emotional, with your family, with your finances, whatever. Your challenges are real and they have been designed and customized uniquely for you to hold you back and test you. I'm not here to tell you what to do with your challenges. I can only tell you what I did with mine.

After my first six month trip to India, I came back to America to work and replenish my funds. But after everything I had been through on the first trip, I came back feeling confused about what to do with my life after having changed so much on that trip. But instead of sitting with the discomfort and letting nature take its course, I decided to head back to India to continue learning about energy and healing with M. He encouraged me to put together a group of friends to come with me, to offer them a healing experience in India.

Knowing how much I had gained from him (which we'll explore more in the next chapter), I thought it was a great idea. And honestly, I didn't have a better idea of what to do, so I was eager in my codependent style to latch onto someone else's plan. However, things didn't go well. I didn't properly manage the group's expectations. They didn't realize what they were getting themselves into, they weren't wanting or ready for what the experience entailed, and the whole thing tragically fell apart. Just days before my 30th birthday, my friends literally abandoned ship, leaving our houseboat in Kashmir. I was devastated. Because I was so attached to things going the way I wanted them to, and they didn't, I was nearly destroyed by feelings of shame and failure.

I came back to Boston after this second trip to India resolved to use what happened as a learning experience, get my life in order, and just get back to doing what worked for me before. I felt a renewed commitment to build my photography business, to be an actress in movies, and to reconstruct my reality and generally "succeed" at life.

After a few months into the warmth of spring and onto summer, things were going well. I had a fancy new photography studio shared with some of the most elite photographers in the city of Boston. I had a cute little room on Green St. near Central Square in Cambridge, MA, a short walk from Harvard University. Things were looking good. But yet again, the seedlings of discontent were wriggling beneath the surface. Sure, things were looking great on the outside, but inside I sensed there was more to life than just working to earn money, pay my bills, and become successful according to the measuring stick my culture had presented to me.

And that was when I received the next call. It was an unexpected invitation from my dear German friend Fíne, who I had known many years before when we lived in Singapore. She gave me the good news that a group of our friends had purchased some land on the magical island of Koh Phangan in Thailand. They had been busy building a Burningman-inspired house for artists, fire spinners, and DIY makers and doers. It was a magical place they were calling "Labracadabra," and I was one of the lucky few invited to the grand opening month of December 2015.

I was floored. I wanted it, but I had just gotten back from India a few months prior and my ego was still licking her wounds. I wanted to go but in that moment my heart felt heavy, not to mention I wasn't sure I couldn't afford another trip. I had just signed on at the studio and was excited to be there. I had also just signed a new lease on my little room in Cambridge. I felt torn. The boxing match inside me began anew. I want this, but can I have it?

Can I afford to go to Thailand? Am I allowed to do this? I just got back from India. Who do I think I am? People will think I'm crazy to keep doing this. What about the studio? What about my room? What should I do? I wanted it, but I wan't sure if I could do it again. The first two trips to India were crazy enough, *but this*? I struggled to believe it was possible.

Receiving the Guidance I Needed

That's when I made the fateful trip up to Maine for the 4th of July weekend with my studio mates. Someone's family had a house at a picturesque New England lake and we were all invited up for the weekend. I hitched a ride with Eric, the leader of the pack, and his girlfriend. On the outside it looked like a bright and happy road trip with friends on a beautiful Saturday of summer. But on the inside, a battle raged about whether to go to Thailand this winter or not. I was confused, I was torn, and honestly I wasn't sure what to believe. And that's when we pulled over for gas.

As I got out to stretch my legs, I noticed a graveyard on the other side of a nearby fence. I walked up to the chain links and slipped my fingers through the holes, pressing my face against the wire. My eyes settled intensely on the tombstones. I drank in the sight of the graves and the bodies I knew to be laying underneath them, sleeping forever, the candle of their life extinguished. And so too, I recognized, was their chance to do anything anymore. And in that moment I thought to myself, "If I were to die without doing this, *would I regret it?*" Coincidentally, that was also the question I asked myself as I faced the crazy desire and decision to embark on my acting career. The honest answer was *"Yes."* If I lay dying on my deathbed and had not done this thing, I could not stand to think of myself in my final hours tasting the sour and pungent regret of the chances I had not taken while I still had time.

And if that wasn't enough, when we arrived at the lake house I happened on the chance to share some magic mushrooms with some kind friends with whom I felt safe and welcome. I went on a profound, powerful, and life-changing journey within where I had the opportunity to receive counsel from a power greater than myself. It was an energy that was wise, knowing, and unconditionally loving. It was like meeting my maker, the source of life itself, and it said to me "Erica, you can choose anything you want. We just hope you choose something amazing."

At that moment, something profoundly shifted inside of me. I deeply understood that yes, I could choose and accomplish anything I wanted. Even more, I understood that there were greater forces at play watching, waiting to see what I would do, and would even support me if I asked for help, like angels watching over me. It was the affirmation I needed to make the choice from my heart. So that's when I decided: *I'm going.* Even though I was afraid and I didn't know how, I resolved, come hell or high water, I would find a way to heed this summons and go where I was called. And it was that decision that made all the difference.

Trust the Path

Making the decision to follow your heart is about trust. Trusting that there's a way, that it will be okay, that you're not alone, and that there's some kind of a Higher Power that is available to help you, but *only if you ask.* Making the decision is a choice to face your fears and no longer allow them to hold you back. Making the choice is about making a commitment to yourself, to living the life you truly want - while you still have time. Making the decision to follow your heart's call is easily one of the most difficult and scariest choices you'll face in your life, and yet it can also be the turning point of your story. It was for me.

If you're feeling ready to make the decision to follow your heart, I invite you to make some time to get out into nature again. Maybe by now you've found a special spot that feels like a refuge. Maybe you have a special rock where you like to sit and write. Go there. I know you're probably very busy, but if you want this change badly enough, make the time. Hire a babysitter if you need to. Ask someone to cover your shift. Just find a way to give yourself this time. Don't forget to bring your journal, of course. Turn off your phone. Arrive and settle.

While the busy monkey mind spins its wheels, take a moment to focus your attention on your breath and the sensations in your body. Greet them all like a compassionate witness. Welcome all feelings, all sensations, and just focus on your breath. Seek and release the tension in your body and relish those deep, slow breaths. As you settle and slow down, tune into your heart and connect to the thing she really wants, however big or small.

Can you feel it? Is it coming into clarity? Are you willing to admit what it is? Now ask yourself, how would you feel if you were laying on your deathbed and had not done this thing? Would you regret it? And if so, are you really willing to die with the regret of what you did not do while you had the chance? If you *could* do it, if it was possible, *would* you do it?

If you want this badly enough, if you don't want the life and almost probable certain future you have, *now is the time*. Ask yourself, are you ready to do something about it? Are you ready to make the decision to change and commit to it? Are you ready to set a date by which you will do this thing calling to you?

For me, that moment came amidst a lot of pain, confusion, questions, and self-doubt. But like a ray of light that broke through the dark clouds, something became illuminated amidst the darkness. Perhaps the most important moment of my story was when I decided to reach for the light.

Declare Your Desire

So, are you ready? Are you ready to change your life? To set your ship on a new course towards heart's treasure?

Open to a blank page in your journal. Even if your hands are shaking, write out the words of that which your heart truly desires. Claim it. You have my permission to want what you want.

For me, I wrote "I am going to India for six months by myself on my twenty-ninth birthday." It was clear, it was specific, it was written in the now. It was not "*I want* to go to India," but rather

"*I am going* to India." Write the words of your Declaration of Independence. Look at them, even if it feels uncomfortable. Soak them in with your eyes, and realize, *this is it*. This is the moment you've been waiting for. *You* are the person you've been waiting for. Now, read the words aloud. Perhaps softly at first, while you're still struggling to believe the possibility of this statement. That's okay. It's okay to feel exactly what you feel at this moment. Just stay with me. Read the words aloud. Again. And again.

Each time, start to get a little louder and a little faster. Stand up on that special rock if you dare, if you want it badly enough, and shout your Declaration to the Universe. Let all the angels hear it. Get their attention. Go ahead, you don't have to play small anymore. Let that power watching over you hear you. Are you shouting yet? If you are, *good for you*. I'm proud of you. You have just done something tremendous, akin to throwing a gigantic lever that switched the track of your life. This is the first step towards freedom. By finally making this heart-based decision and Declaration of Independence, you have just called forth and activated the limitless creative force of the Universe, that same force that wishes for nothing more than to prosper you.

You've planted the seed. Now you will need to water it, which is the next step. In the coming chapter, we'll learn about energy and how to channel yours towards growing this new seed.

HOMEWORK:
A VERY SPECIAL TEA PARTY

When we declare our heart's desire and set ourselves on a new course, some voices inside us will come up to try to block us. These adversarial points of view can get into a never-ending boxing match inside of us. It can be all-consuming, and quite exhausting.

Sometimes it's a voice that says "You're not enough." Sometimes it's the voice of our mother who tries to shame us for wanting what we want. Sometimes the voice will try to make you feel guilty. Sometimes it's a voice that says you're gonna to end up poor and alone and no one will love you if you do this thing. Often times we don't want to listen to them, and understandably, we don't want to hear what they have to say, so we try to push them away. But like anything that is suppressed and ignored within us, the more you hold it down, the more it pushes back and has power over you. So in this exercise, we're going to host a tea party for the voices in our head to give them a chance to speak and really listen to what they have to say.

This is an exercise called "Aspecting" which I instinctively did once on my own, but then was further clarified by my amazing coach Reva Wild (@WildErosAwakening) and now has become a regular practice for me. This is a powerful healing technique to release the pressure within, and give all aspects of you the chance to speak fully and be heard once and for all, so you can be free.

Once you get clear with yourself about what you want, pay attention to the different voices that come up to try to stop you from moving towards your heart's desire. For me, when I started doing my shadow work with Seulki in Thailand, I was being really challenged by sadness, guilt, and shame, so I imagined them as separate characters and I invited them to tea.

Literally, make tea. Once you figure out who the main characters are and name them, you'll know how many cups of tea to pour. Keep an extra cup on hand, just in case another character wants to show up. Welcome them all and give them a place.

I recently had a situation where I was feeling really hurt by a friend and had to do this exercise around this person because the voices in my head just would not shut up while I was trying to cook dinner. While I was trying to choose and be love, there was a voice inside of me that hoped she got bit by a dog (this was a character I've known well since childhood, who I call the "Tiny Violent Tyrant") So in this situation, the voices I named and called forward were: Wounded Victim, Tiny Violent Tyrant, Inner Child, Inner Mother, and my Compassionate Higher Self.

You can also do this exercise with the energy of your mother, your father, your child, your boss, an ex-boyfriend, a bully, someone who hurt you, or anyone else you want to speak openly to and to give them a chance to speak openly to you. This is an especially helpful process if the person has passed away, and you never got to say what you needed to say to them, and vice versa. This is your chance to have a healing conversation.

When I've done this exercise, I also find it powerful to let my voice change with each character or archetype. When I spoke from my Wounded Victim, my voice became more high-pitched and whiney. When I spoke from my Inner Mother, my voice became deeper, softer, and more comforting. There was more of a reassuring aspect to it, and it happened naturally without me trying to force it. I just let it be what it wanted to be. That's the very essence of this exercise.

Don't worry about getting the characters or archetypes right. You can do multiple, or you can do just one. If you have multiple, and they say a lot of the same things, that's okay. For example, my Inner Mother and my Compassionate Higher Self sounded a lot alike. I could've chosen to just do one of them, and that would've also been okay. Just see what you feel called to, and do that. Rest from perfectionism. Whatever you feel called to do is right for this moment.

You can do this exercise sitting at a table, or sometimes I like to do it sitting on the floor. I'll arrange four pillows like a cross, with a fifth pillow in the center. Just so I can remember who is who, I'll write their names on a little piece of paper, and put one on each pillow. I also like to record the conversation on my phone or take notes in my journal, because you might be surprised by some things that come out, and you might want to review it later. When I did the exercise with sadness, shame, and guilt, I even drew a little doodle of each character as I connected with them. There's no right or wrong way to do it, just lean into what feels good for you.

The Aspecting Process:

To begin, sit in the center of the cross, or at the head of the table, and take some deep breaths to ground yourself. Now, begin to speak aloud, from your own perspective, what it is you want and how you're feeling about the situation. Notice what feelings, emotions, or sensations come up. Now, invite the different voices, one at a time, to come forward and speak.

You're going to embody the voice in your head and speak from their perspective. Think of it like acting and taking on a character. To do this, get up and go sit in their place, whether it's on a cushion or at a different seat at the table. Face the place where you were just sitting, because you're going to let them talk openly to you, and the place where you were just sitting is holding your energy. Now is the time to let this voice speak. Go ahead, let them talk. Don't hold back. What do they want to say to you?

As you go, ask them, "What do you want?" and "What do you want for me?" Don't hold anything back.

Go until they are complete, and then ask them "Is there anything else you want me to hear?"

Now go back to your place and this is your chance to speak to that voice. Tell them how you're feeling. Tell them what you want. Tell them what's important to you. Tell them what you need them to hear. Tell them what you want from them.

If needed, you can go back to their place and they can respond to what you said. Dig deeper. What do or did they *really* want? Often times, if we dig deeply enough, we may discover that these voices really care about us and are trying to protect us and keep us safe, or they are just sad and hurt and feel ignored and just want to be seen and heard.

When you feel complete, go back to your place and thank them all for their input. Tell them all that you will take all of their words into consideration, thank them for trying to help you (because, after all, that's really why they're there), and that you're in the driver's seat and you will make the choice about what you feel is best. Bow deeply to these fierce protectors with honor and appreciation.

Pour the tea into the earth with gratitude and burn the slips of paper, inviting theses energies to move onwards with love and to let you lead now.

Chapter 5 - How to Use Your Energy to Manifest Your Dream

Once you've connected with your heart's desire and decided you're going to make it happen, the next thing you'll need to do is actively direct your energy toward its manifestation. First, we need to address, *what is energy* and how do we direct it? Well, I'll give you a hint. If you spoke your desire aloud at the end of the previous chapter, if you got up on that rock and shouted it out like a crazy person, then you just tapped into and directed a *huge* amount of life-force energy.

Meeting my Spiritual Teacher in India

Nikola Tesla once said "If you want to find the secret of the universe, think in terms of energy, frequency, and vibrations." But what does that really mean, for us?

Before I went to India and met my teacher Mustafa, or M, as I like to call him, I thought energy was the stuff that came out of the electrical outlet. Or that shaky buzzy feeling I would get from drinking a Red Bull. Oh baby, was I in for a wild ride to discover a glimpse of the truth, which I hope to distill down here into something you can consume which will feel a lot better than drinking a Red Bull.

One day, about four months into my solo journey across India, I was walking through a magical and dubious place called Pahar Ganj in New Dalhi, a bustling marketplace full of wonders. Cows wandered to and fro. The smell of shit and spices rose in the air. From every angle, merchants with colorful shops were calling out to me "Hello, my friend! Come look my shop!" Like a ninja, I deftly maneuvered my way through the crowd, avoiding the merchants' hooks and happily swimming along with the current. That's when I heard a voice. For my life, I can't recall what he called out to me as I walked by, but whatever it was, I stopped dead in my tracks and turned around.

There behind me a few paces was a man dressed all in white with a gentle smile on his face. Immediately I noticed around his neck was the most curious necklace I had ever seen. It was the size of a big cookie, shaped like an elephant, and looked as if it was fashioned crudely out of golden clay. Contrasting the crudeness of the clay and elephant shape (that kind of looked like it was made by a seven-year-old), was a fantastic array of inlaid stones sparkling in the sunlight. I would later come to learn these were the bright reds of rubies, the deep blues of sapphires, and the luscious greens of emeralds twinkling and winking at me in the sunshine.

While I did not understand what was happening, the next thing I knew I was following this mysterious character into his little shop at the back of the ground floor of a hotel. I was delighted to discover a veritable treasure trove inside - precious stones collected dust in just about every nook and cranny. Odd trinkets, antique statues, beautiful necklaces made of stones, and strange exotic clothes covered every inch of the walls. It felt as if I had stepped into a crystal cave belonging to another world. This was how I met my teacher, M.

M was to become my spiritual guide, and I could write a whole book just on the experiences I had with him. Like a good mystical guide he triggered me, taught me, led me into a deeper understanding of myself, and helped me undo so much of the poison that I had been carrying inside up until that point. His methods were hard to describe, extremely unorthodox, and varied. He used a combination of methods involving special plants from the Himalaya mountains, nourishing foods, healing crystals, strange body movements and exercises (some extremely painful, like when I would sit on the floor and he would push against my back to touch my toes in order to open certain energy "lines"), working with the energy of chakras, having specific experiences in nature, and more. I proceeded to spend a lot of time in his little shop, always confused about what was going on, but somehow deeply reassured that I was exactly where I was meant to be.

He never gave me a clear explanation of anything, much to the riot of my mind that desperately wanted to understand. But no, M wanted me to learn by my own direct experience. He didn't want to tell me the name of the plant I was consuming, or why he was standing on my stomach with a stone painfully pressed into my belly button, or making me recite tongue-twister rhymes like mental riddles over and over, or why he was having me jump on one foot for what seemed like hours.

M didn't want me to rationalize and try to understand things with my mind. He wanted me to surrender into having a direct feeling experience of whatever the thing was. At the time, I rebelled and pushed back, wanting with my Western mind to have things explained and justified. But looking back, it makes more sense to me now because I was dealing with energies that could not be understood at the level of the rational mind (just like Egypt), not to mention that I was never very good at learning by being told anyway. I needed to experience it firsthand. I needed to try something for myself, fall on my face, get back up again and go, ahhhh okay, that's how it works.

Energy is Everything

Everything was energy to M. He spoke of it constantly and effortlessly. In fact, the way I talk about energy today comes from him. A person would arrive in his shop and he would ask in his thick Kashmiri accent *"What energy is this?"* The people themselves were an energy to him, or they were carrying an energy. He would talk about energy lines, not just in the body, but also in life. He would always talk about "The Good Way" versus the "Suffering Way." The "Natural Way' versus the "Chemical Way." The "Material Way," the "Special Way" or the "Animal Way." He spoke of the "Sufi Way," the "Hindu Way," the "Christian Way," the "Man Way," the "Woman Way," the "Family Way," and the "Food Way." He taught me to see the world in terms of energy and these energetic pathways we could follow, or that could become engrained in us without us realizing it.

The Doorways to Your Energy

Amongst many of the valuable lessons that I received in the crystal cave, one of the most significant for me was around the importance of eye energy. Through a series of trials and lessons, M helped me learn that one of the most powerful ways to harness and direct our energy is through our eyes. The energy that you carry comes through your eyes, and this has been a very important lesson for me. In fact, today when I'm making my videos online I make sure to really connect my eyes to the camera - to the viewer directly. That's because I'm literally giving you an energy transmission through my eyes.

Think of when people flirt - they make eye contact to "catch" each other's energy, as M would describe it. I think back now to a very handsome, charming, and seductive boyfriend I had named Alex, who had a way of looking at me that made me melt. Let's just say he caught and hooked my energy so strongly that I became willing and even eager to betray my own truth just to feel this seductive energy from him. It felt so intoxicating to receive it from him that I would do almost anything for it. In fact, I was confused to think I was in love with him. The reality was that I was addicted to his energy and how it made me feel, just like a drug.

Back in the marketplace with M, I learned that our energy doesn't just come through the eyes. It also comes through our voice and the movements of our body. He would observe the way someone entered the room and get a clear read on the kind of energy inside them just by the way they walked, how fast they moved, the way their eyes darted around the room, and finally, what and how they spoke to him. It was all energy.

When I arrived, my energy was too fast and loud. In fact, that was one of the first things M said to me during our first fateful meeting. Holding his special stone Z'armor in one hand and taking my hand in the other, he paused for a moment to feel me, his brow tense in concentration. I felt a bolt of lighting shoot through my body, tingling my toes and making my hairs stand on end. After a few quiet moments, he lifted his eyes to mine to say the thing that would change my life: "You jump your energy too fast." Now, I had no idea what that meant at the time. But it was true.

Up until that point in my life, I was overexcited all the time. Someone would come to me something they wanted my help with and I was far too quick to see its brilliance and potential. I would rush to please everyone and jump to say yes to whatever anyone wanted from me from me without first pausing to assess if I actually had the capacity to give it to them from a full heart, not just a full and excited mind. I would never pause to examine how I felt, where my own boundaries were, and if I actually had the resources and time to give them what they needed. This was how I got myself into a life where I was constantly giving too much, leaking and losing my energy in unhealthy ways by trying to please and serve everyone all the time. And it was because I was excited, and I wanted to love everyone and be loved by everyone, which really stemmed from my own low self-esteem. I needed others to approve of me to feel okay in myself, so I would say or do whatever I thought they wanted to hear. I said yes without considering my own needs and boundaries. I "jumped my energy" and opened myself to doing things that I wasn't actually committed to following through on. I gave too much, too soon, when I really would have been much better off to pause and assess what I truly could give with a full heart and not empty my own cup in the process.

I'm sharing this because in order to achieve a dream of say, going to India for six months, or Thailand for two months, or Guatemala for a week, you *must* learn to focus your energy on the clear object of your desire. Without this clear focus, you'll spray your energy everywhere. Instead of achieving *your* dream, you could end up feeling empty and drained, having given away too much to other people's desires and dreams, serving *their* reality, but leaving you with not enough left in your tank for *yours*.

Fart Laser

Consider a laser. A powerful laser can slice through concrete and take off your fingers with the ease and delight of cutting warm butter. A laser is *energy* that has been *focused*. Without this focus, it's just a diffused cloud of energy, like a fart. While a fart can cut through silence and tranquility, it certainly cannot cut through concrete. So you have energy, you are energy, it comes and goes through your eyes, your voice, the way you move your body (or don't), and the actions you choose to take.

When these aspects of your energy are just randomly responding to the external world without any specific intention or attention, your energy is like the fart cloud. Unspecific, hanging there, a little smelly, comforting to some, and disturbing to others. So do you want to know where the real power lies? The real power is when you take that diffused fart cloud and focus it to start cutting through concrete. How? By aligning your energy - by bringing your thoughts, words, and actions into congruence and alignment with each other.

But Wait, What Is Energy?

Before we get into aligning and focusing our energy, let's explore more deeply what energy is. What could M sense and see in a person? What is this stuff you must align and bring into balance in order to manifest your heart's desire?

To put it plainly, energy is a subtle, creative force that runs though all things. It's an all-pervasive, infinite, boundless substance. It is the very force and fiber of existence, incomprehensible in its mystery and the ultimate source of all things[3]. It's contained in physical matter, sound vibrations, as well as in light, plus other subtle forms that our physical senses can't yet register (unless you train them to do so using practices like qi

---

[3] *This definition was influenced by "Creating Circles and Ceremonies" by Oberon Zell-Ravenheart and Morning Glory Zell-Ravenheart, a magical book about learning to work with energy and manifestation. Highly recommended.*

gong, pranayama breathwork, yoga, reiki, and meditation). Sometimes it's non-physical, like an invisible swirling cosmic soup of pure potential. Other times, through our intention, awareness, and the natural, cyclic creative powers of nature, this invisible potential gets channeled and becomes dense and physical, like threads that weave together to form what we perceive as our physical reality.

This book is energy that has taken on a physical form. The words on this page are energy. You're receiving energy as you read these words. It is non-physical - like the vibration of the words as they hit your brain - but at the same time it's also physical, as the words take up space on the page or screen. The energy is both things at once. It's like how light exists as a paradox with contrasting qualities.

Have you heard how light acts as both a wave and a particle? I bet this really frustrates some scientists who really just want to label things clearly. Energy is like this - both simple and complex - a paradox grinning at itself. And this can be hard to understand with the mind alone. In fact, it is best felt and understood through direct experience.

I think that's why M would never explain things. He would not play into the demands of my mind to understand, which is a kind of need for control. In order to really discover your energy, what it is and how to use it, you must let go of your mind's need for control, and learn to surrender into the direct experience of your energy and how it wants to lead you.

There is one thing M would have me hold in my mind, like a mental posture. I didn't understand it then, but now that I've lived my life and gained more perspective, I've also gained more of an understanding of this simple phrase he instructed me to hold in my mind. He would tell me to think "*I do not understand, but I accept.*" It was all about letting go of control and the need to understand. As we did the work to clean my very confused, messy, unbalanced, toxic, fast-running energy, I didn't understand what was going on. But I made the choice to trust and accept, and that's why I progressed forwards on my healing journey. I could progress only as much as I learned to surrender to the process.

So energy is an infinite, all-encompassing, and limitless creative force that runs through all things, has an intelligence of it's own, and contains the full potential of all creation. It can be anything, just like stem cells. Vastly potential, extraordinarily flexible, and it has certain qualities. Understanding these unique qualities and how to balance them is key to working with your energy.

The Qualities of Energy

Energy is like water. It flows like a river. It purifies, receives, and brings new life, but it must move in order to be healthy. If you have a blockage in one of your seven chakras, or "energy centers" in the body, then you will exhibit unhealthy symptoms.

For example, if you have a blockage in your throat chakra, which relates to communication, you might find you have a hard time speaking your truth to others. If you have a blockage in your stomach chakra, then you might find that you have trouble digesting food, or the events of the world around you. We don't just digest and process food, we have to digest the things that happen to us.

So, for example, if you don't properly process and digest the passing of a loved one and all the associated thoughts and feelings that come with it, you may find yourself becoming sick in body and/or mind. It's just like how you would get sick if an undigested piece of food stayed inside of you for years without being processed and released. If you have a blockage in your root chakra, you will probably be afraid of the future, worried about money and your survival, and feel unsafe. If your heart chakra is blocked, you might find that you can't fully give and receive love to yourself or others.

It's like a river that becomes blocked and turns into a stagnant body of water, which then builds up an overgrowth of toxins and algae. The water needs to flow and move in order to become healthy again. Clean, flowing water facilitates healthy life. Without it, there's a barren landscape where nothing grows. Energy is the same. Where there is blocked energy, things are lifeless, dull, and sometimes stinky. But when the energy comes back, when the flow returns, so too does new life. So energy has the qualities of water: flowing, purifying, cleaning, and life-giving. When consciously purified and directed, it can bring new life to what was previously a dry and dead landscape, literally or figuratively.

Energy has other qualities. It's like air. Think of the breath of life, the breath of God. Without breath, the body dies. Air is required for creating and sustaining life. It also has a quality of movement and space. Moving air ushers in new things. "The winds of change are blowing," they say, and it's a good adage. It speaks to the quality of air to bring forth new things, like change and inspiration. Imagine blowing a burst of air into a dusty corner. How that force, that fresh energy, clears away what is old and stagnant, just like spring cleaning where we air things out to welcome the new season and clear out the stagnant energy of winter. Imagine a seed being carried on the wind, delivering the potential for new life to the soil. It's infinitely unlimited and guided by the invisible hands of the divine creative force that knows all, is connected to all, and guides the unfolding of life itself. That's energy.

While energy can move like wind and water, it also has the quality of slowing down, becoming still, dense, and taking on physical form. In this way, energy is like the earth. Rich, grounded, stable, and full of potential to grow new things. You and I are energy that has slowed down and become dense in order to hold a physical form.

Sometimes I look at the birds in my garden and I see them as a density of energy. Hummingbirds are so magical in this regard, perhaps because they are perched right at the threshold of non-physical energy. Just dense enough to hold the shape of a hummingbird, while also still holding onto that magical quality of the unseen realm that defies logic. I think that's why so many people equate hummingbirds with a loved one who passed away. It's like their energy is visiting them using the hummingbird as a vehicle. I've heard it said that a human soul is the weight of a hummingbird. When a person dies, it has been recorded that in that moment when life departs, the body loses a tiny amount of weight. The equivalent of the weight of a hummingbird.

Finally, energy is like fire. Perhaps fire is the easiest to understand in terms of energy. What are the qualities of fire? It has heat, of course, like our fart laser. When a body dies, it loses heat. In this way, a person's energy is like their inner fire. Aside from heat, the special quality of fire is its light and the ability to illuminate the darkness. Energy is a kind of illumination. Have you ever noticed someone who has good energy seems to be glowing with a kind of inner light? Aside from heat and light, fire has the quality of igniting and catalyzing action. The spark that lights the fire is an impulse that seemingly comes from nothing and turns into something. Recognizing and tapping into your energy as an inner fire is an extraordinary power that can ignite you into action and drive you forward, especially in the face of fear and adversity.

But a word of caution. Too much fire can destroy. Too much fire looks like rageful anger, an unchecked forest fire that can wipe out miles of habitat and life because it was not tempered. And yet even in its destructive qualities, there is creation. Sometimes the best thing for the growth of the forest is a good fire that clears away the old trees and plants. From the scorched earth new plants will grow like a phoenix rising from the ashes. For this reason, the energy of fire - and disturbance itself - are integral to healthy growth and the renewal of life.

So when considering these qualities, healthy energy comes down to balance. Not too much, and not too little. I am of the belief that the journey we go on is a process of learning to discover and master our energy, to balance these forces within us, so we can be our true selves at our most optimal and harmonious state. That's what M was trying to teach me. To understand energy is to no longer let it control us like a puppet. Think of a man who cannot control his anger. As soon as the anger begins to rise he cannot control what he says or does, or who he hurts. Once he calms down and comes to his senses, he may feel shame for what he said or did. He was not in control of his fire. He was not a master of his energy. His energy was the master of him.

Balancing Our Energy

What this hot-tempered person might need to balance and restore himself would be to bring in the energy of water to counter his fire. Water is emotion, it is a clearing out. He might need to look at the reasons behind why he's so angry, and perhaps let some tears out. Tears are good for processing and cleaning away old pains and traumas. Imagine a dirty floor. You bring in the water to wash away what no longer serves (like puppy pee). In this way, we can become clean again, no matter how dirty things got because of what happened in the past. As long as we're *willing* to do the work to get honest about what's really going on inside instead of hiding or avoiding our feelings, and let some emotions flow, we can achieve balance.

However, too much water can drown you. Too much water looks like too much emotion. Emotion that turns into drama for the sake of drama itself is a kind of self-indulgence, and also a way to manipulate others. I am a person of intense emotional sensitivity who used to drown myself in drama. *A lot* of it. I understand now that my work is not to flounder around in the emotions, self-pity, and drama, but rather to summon the courage to get crystal-clear honest with myself to discover why those emotions are really there, what message they really have to bear, and to help them move along.

In order to move them, I need to face them. I need to look at my feelings and ask myself, what they are trying to help me see? What do I need to get honest about? Often times my work is to find the sadness underneath the anger, and let it flow out. Feel and deal, instead of suppress and repress. Remember, whatever you suppress and repress just pushes back, and has power over you. And we can only heal what we acknowledge. Only when we face our feelings, and find the cares and desires underneath them, is healing, balance, inner peace, and acceptance possible.

My emotions are like my energy sensors that are there to help me understand where I am out of balance. When I listen to them, I can adjust my course, much like captaining a ship. Allowing myself to feel my feelings helps me recognize where I've gone off balance so I can make adjustments to bring my ship back on course.

Aside from too much water, I also used to be a person of too much wind. That's what M meant when he said "I jump my energy too fast." I was moving too much, thinking too much, talking, walking, and eating too fast, and always excited about new ideas without thinking clearly or following through. I was blowing around like a leaf in the wind. My life was like this too. As a child, I grew up all over the world. Thanks to my diplomat parents, I was fortunate to grow up in India, Paris, and Singapore. When I was stateside, we lived in Maryland and Chicago. Once I grew up and became more independent, I hoisted my own sail and the current of life took me to Washington DC, New Orleans, New York, Los Angeles, and Boston.

I had a lot of wind (farts included). In fact, all I ever knew was movement, and often very frantic movement. I was like a plant that was constantly being ripped by shallow roots from the earth, unable to grow anywhere for too long. In this way, my energy was ungrounded and out of balance. I think this is a big part of my excitement to now be living and rooting myself in Guatemala. It feels so good to finally balance all that wind with some lush earth into which I am putting down some extremely satisfying and nourishing roots.

So, your energy has many different qualities and it can be out of balance, as mine was. Too much fire destroys with its angry, vindictive heat. Too much water overwhelms and drowns. Too much wind enlivens the raging forest fire or blows the seeds away before they have the chance to take root and grow. What about too much earth? Too much earth energy is heavy, lazy, and stagnant. It's not moving. It's not breathing. It holds on and doesn't let go. Imagine soil that is dry and hard. The earthworm can't push through, and neither can the seeds of new life. People who are too grounded might be afraid of change, afraid of taking chances, or afraid of taking a risk - even if it's the thing calling to their heart. Too much earth energy might mean roots fixed stubbornly in place, resistant to change, resistant to motion and flow. This kind of control is the opposite of surrender. To that person, I would advise that they let themselves do something wild. Like a good dance with the wind. I mean it, *literally*. Next time there's a storm, go outside and dance with the wind and rain (and shout Disney songs?). It might be very good for your energy.

So coming back to the question, *what is energy*? Whatever this mysterious creative force is, we each have our own energy signature. Just like we each have our own physical body, we also have our own energetic body. It can change depending on the foods we eat and activities we engage in, just like our physical bodies. And I think that's what M could see in a person. He could see their energy body and understand certain qualities they held or the ways they were suffering. That's how he knew if people needed more movement, or less, more space, more time in nature, different kinds of foods, or more emotional release. He could see where they were lacking, deficient, or out of balance. His strange and illogical methods were all about opening, cleaning, and balancing a person's energy.

What Balance Feels Like

When your energy is in balance, you will flow naturally with the raw forces of life that want to prosper you. Balanced energy feels light and right, like the eagle in her power who soars gracefully and effortlessly over the mountain range. She isn't *trying* to be a powerful eagle, she's just being herself, fully, easefully, without trying. Your energy is like this too.

When your energy is balanced, you can tap into that supreme creative flow, so infinitely ripe with potential for life. When your energy is healthy and flowing you will feel peaceful, safe, and healthy. You will exhibit a skillful balance of endurance, energy, enthusiasm, grace, and dignity. You will feel the emotions of life, but you will handle them with care and process them in a healthy and appropriate way. When all chakras are fully activated and spinning without blockage, you will feel love and a sense of unity and connection to all that is. You won't try to control anything or anyone, because you will have a deep sense of trust in life. You will see that nothing is good or bad, it's just the way the energy is moving and coming into being with its own wisdom and timing.

How many times in life does something awful happen, like the death of the person you love, or the death of the relationship with the person you thought you would marry? And the intensity of the pain seems like a good reason to drink or commit suicide. Yet when enough time passes, we gain wisdom and perspective. Sometimes we may even look back and see that this event was actually an important catalyst for our healing and growth, if we let go and allow it to be. All along, the pain was our teacher. This is how energy works. It flows and it changes. Guided by divine grace, it weaves together to form new things. In moments of human suffering we may not be able to see that our heartaches are actually seeds. If only we would breath with them, flow with them, not try to control them, or make them wrong. Instead, ask your pain "What message do you have for me?"

So energy. Energy. ENERGY! That was a lot of energy. It's subtle. It's creative. It's vastly potential and ready to respond to your intentions and desires. If only you could learn to dance with it. To surrender, lean in, and follow where it wants to flow. And yet your job is not passive. You have a role to play, just like we need to tend and care for plants in the garden. Imagine a climbing vine. You give it a trellis on which to grow, and in doing so you're providing structure to influence its growth. Your intentions and awareness are like this. *Where attention goes, energy flows.*

The metaphysical science experiments they talk about in the movie "What the Bleep Do We Know?" demonstrated that the observation of the scientists conducting the experiment had an impact on the results - their intentions and expectations impacted the outcome of how the atoms danced. You and your energy are exactly the same way. So one way you can dance with your energy is by setting clear intentions, which we'll explore more deeply later in this chapter.

You Can Do It

Let me assure you - no matter where you are, no matter how old you are, no matter what pains you have suffered, no matter how traumatic your past or how painful your present may be, no matter what you feel is holding you back - just know that healing, growth, and a new life are possible for you. But it depends on you making the commitment to cleaning your energy, to the purification of your water. And this will require work.

Imagine a very dark and neglected pool of water that's overgrown with algae and gross stuff. You could look at that pool with great sadness and say "Oh, when I was young I could swim there and I was happy," and then just give up, give into the feelings of powerlessness, and go watch TV. Or, you could roll up your sleeves and decide to clean that mess up. But you'd have to get dirty in the process, right? You have to get into that muck and grab fistfuls of the gross stuff and hold down the feeling of wanting to throw up as you move it out little by little. The task might feel overwhelming, like it's too big of a job, that you don't know how or just can't do it.

That's why it's great to ask for help in this process. Seek an expert. Hire a coach. Find a meetup group dedicated to healing and personal growth. Enroll in a 12-step system of recovery or new program of healing. No matter what you choose to do, the most important thing is that you *yourself* are resolved to clean out this pond. You must be committed to purifying the water. Others can help, but no one can do it for you. And no one can want it for you *more* than you want it for yourself. And no matter how daunting or confusing the task may be, when your resolve to do the work is clear, the answer of how to do it will be shown to you. When you have committed to the journey, the path to it and through it will be be revealed. When the student is ready and willing to grow, the teacher will appear.

How to Start Directing Your Energy

When I decided I was going to make my pilgrimage to India for six months, the first thing I did was I wrote it down. I declared it to the Universe with my written word. Then, inside my mind, the conversation was all about going to India. Sure, there was a lot of debate amongst the voices within me around how it would happen and how *dare* I think of doing such a thing. There was a kind of war. But the overarching subject of debate was my inner resolve that I was going to India.

Next, I started talking about it with people I trusted. I used my words to convey my intention of going on this trip. I spoke as if it was real, even though I still had no idea how it could possibly happen. And finally, I started taking action aligned with the thought "I'm going to India for six months by myself on my twenty-ninth birthday." I said no to producing the next season of Quiet Desperation, "because I'll be in India then," I said. Even though I was barely able to afford my monthly expenses, I started thinking, speaking, and acting as if it was real. By doing this, I was bringing my energy into focus, like a laser.

You can do this too, and it's not so complicated to do. It's simple to do, but it's also simple *not* to do effectively. Especially when we've been used to doing things unconsciously, just reacting and responding to the world around us without intentionally using our desire and energy to influence the weaving of our reality.

We're already doing it, just most of us don't realize it. That's because most of us are not making active choices about what we want to call in. Most people are passive participants in this process, like trying to paint while asleep. What could be possible if we woke up and started consciously directing our energy?

A Visualization Exercise

When I was facing the fears and doubts about the first trip to Thailand for the opening of Labracadabra, one of the most simple and helpful things I did was to create a vision board on Pinterest. You can see it here: bit.ly/ThailandVisionBoard. I compiled photos of Thailand and the kinds of things I would do there, like yoga or spinning fire on the beach. I included images that gave me a sense of place and feeling. I was very *specific*.

Every day, I pulled up that screen, drank in those images, and added more. I drew in the energy of Thailand using my eyes. And I didn't just look. I closed my eyes and really *felt* into the pictures I had just absorbed. What would it feel like to have my toes in the sand? How hot would the fire be and what would it sound like as I swung those fireballs around my body? What would the fragrance of orchids and other tropical flowers smell like dancing in my nose? How would I look wearing those colorful hippie clothes? With eyes closed, I used the power of my imagination to put myself in the scene and really felt into it.

In my videos online, I often share about the beautiful little handmade beaded hummingbirds and how they represent people who will one day visit me in Guatemala. If you feel the call to come join me for one of these group retreats I'll be offering, I encourage you to close your eyes and imagine what it would feel like to hold that hummingbird in your hand. What will the energy we exchange through our eyes feel like the moment I present it to you? How excited would you feel to receive it from me in person? Put yourself in that moment. Feel it fully. Use your imagination to experience the details of that moment. And that, my friends, is a very important step towards calling it into your reality.

Your Words Have Power

It's vitally important for you to become extremely intentional about what you're consuming through your eyes and ears. I can't stress this enough. At this point, it's a good idea to stop or limit watching TV, especially the mainstream news. That content is intentionally designed and engineered to keep your energy down, outwardly focused, to make you feel not enough, fearful, engaged in unnecessary drama, and unaware of your true desires, values, and priorities. Along the theme of becoming hyper sensitive about what kind of energy you're feeding yourself, I also encourage you to become super aware of your language. This is a key part in the process of becoming intentional about how you use your energy and focusing your laser.

Realize that the words you choose are like symbols, like little energetic shoeboxes that hold a vibrational charge that impacts the form that the energy takes as it travels the mysterious journey of manifestation from non-physical into physical matter. So keeping in mind that the first step to change is conscious awareness, I encourage you to start mindfully observing your patterns of language. What kind of words are you using? Do you speak in a way that is kind, compassionate, and encouraging towards yourself and others? Or listening to the words coming from your mouth, do you notice words that are disempowering, self-limiting, angry, blaming, shaming, fault-finding, argumentative, or self-defeating?

A big part of this process is bringing your attention to your language and making a conscious effort to observe the pattern that you've been running. It's just like noticing a computer program. But this is not the place to judge what you're observing. This is not about making yourself wrong, indulging in self-pity, or punishing yourself. That's not the point of the exercise. The point is to observe and collect the data on yourself, and *all data is good data*.

So at this stage, I encourage you to be like a curious scientist in observation mode. If you see something that you don't like, instead of saying "I suck" and running the same old stories that shame you and put you down, set your intention to suspend your judgment.

Inflate your curiosity, and try this phrase instead: *"Isn't that interesting?"*

The Water Experiments of Dr. Emoto

One of my favorite things to share on the subject of energy, intention, and language is the work of the late Japanese professor Dr. Masuru Emoto. He's famous for the experiments he conducted on water and the fascinating discoveries he made. He took water samples and exposed them to different types of energy using words, images, and sounds. In one experiment, he would speak to a water sample with great love and affection, saying things like "I love you. You can do it. We can do it together. You're beautiful. I believe in you." The other less fortunate water sample received a very different kind of energy. To this poor cup of water he directed a much lower vibration. He said things like, "I hate you. You make me sick. I'm going to kill you." *Ouch.*

What happened next is where the real magic and mystery lies. He would freeze the water samples and photograph them under a microscope, wherein he made the most phenomenal discoveries. The water samples that received the loving vibrations froze into the most beautiful configurations. It was like visual poetry looking at these perfectly formed snowflakes, as if the Goddess herself had drawn them on her best day. The shapes were so elegant, graceful, and artistic that they looked like art on the walls of the Louvre in Paris or some famous cathedral. They were just that breathtaking and beautiful. But the other sample?

The other sample looked like Satan's vomit. It was disfigured, deformed, and misshapen. There was no beauty in its form. The water samples exposed to the negative vibrations created snowflakes that were ugly and disturbing with holes and broken edges. There was nothing elegant about them. In fact, these images were so striking in their disturbance that the truth was clear: The energy of the words, thoughts, sounds, and images we choose to expose ourselves to have a powerful impact on us, especially considering that the human body is made of more than 80 percent water.

If we speak to ourselves using words that are disempowering, or if we choose to share time and space with people who transmit words to us that are angry, disheartening, deflating, or any other form of discouragement, the shape of our potentially beautiful snowflake will become something less than what it could be if we had chosen to feed ourselves a higher vibration.

Furthermore, it wasn't just a question of the beauty of the snowflakes. His research demonstrated that plants who received the "structured" water exposed to the loving vibrations grew better, faster, and didn't need chemicals to keep the bugs away. They had a natural resistance. They had more life and vitality. And the poor plants fed Satan's vomit water? As you can imagine, they didn't do so well. They were inherently weaker and more prone to attack from bugs and disease. If we were trying to farm these plants, they would need a lot of outside input, like chemical fertilizers and pesticides, just to survive.

You can watch a video about Dr. Emoto's water experiments here: bit.ly/HiddenMessagesinWater and read his book "The Hidden Messages of Water" here: https://amzn.to/2T2DR6J.

Understanding the power and impact of our words on our energy means we must take responsibility for the kinds of words and energetic inputs we're feeding ourselves. Positive affirmations can be one tool to assist you in this process. For me, something I did in my darkest times was an exercise that is very simple. In spite of its simplicity, it actually had a powerful impact on lifting my energy out of the pit of despair that I would so often find myself wading around in.

Simply, I would stand in front of the mirror. 1 would look myself squarely in the eyes and just say: "*Yes*." Then again, "*Yes*." I started out softly, then got louder. Faster. Brighter. "*YES*!" Even though everything around me felt like a "*No*," I would say "*Yes*" to myself. I would increase the pace, increase the volume, turn up the energy and shout "*YES*!!" Next thing I knew I was jumping up and down in front of the bathroom mirror, looking absolutely ridiculous with my arms outstretched above my head, shouting *"YES! YES!! YES!!!"* and finally adding, *"CONGRATULATIONS!"*

I would congratulate myself because in that moment of high energy (which I raised using my voice and eye contact with myself in the mirror, and then adding my body movements, increasing the pace, volume, and amplification as I went), I pretended as if it was real. That I had made it to India. That I had paid my rent. That I had achieved what seemed impossible. I raised my energy and then I directed it with conscious awareness toward the desired outcome I wanted to manifest, and that's why I have the life I do today.

I dare you to let yourself look silly and give it a try. You have nothing to lose (except your pride), and everything to gain.

Try This at Home, Kids

Here's another exercise you can play with. All you'll need is a candle and your imagination. Find a quiet space where you won't be disturbed, and take a moment to arrive and settle. When you're ready, light the candle. Next, take a moment to observe and recognize whatever is going on in your mind. Is it busy in there? Are there fist fights going on? Are there imaginary conversations playing out? Are you thinking about what happened yesterday, or maybe what you'll cook for dinner tonight? No judgment, just observe what's going on. Nod your hat to whatever is going on in there and then tell it to not go anywhere, and that you'll be right back.

Now, turn your attention to your breath. Where are you breathing from? Are you taking shallow breaths in your upper chest? Find your breath and then direct it down, down, down into your belly (you might have to loosen your belt for this one) and start breathing from this place. Take a few deep belly breaths and notice what that feels like.

Next, shift your attention to your body. How is she or he doing? With your outer eyes closed, use your mind's inner eye to look around. Are you holding tension anywhere? When I do this practice of scanning my body looking for tension, I will typically see that my shoulders are tight (maybe the outcome of my career as a professional photographer, or perhaps a deeper reflection of my need to carry the whole world there?). As I bring in my awareness with the intention to release the tension, they will drop an inch or so. Follow this process and scan your whole body, searching for tension. Make sure to look in your face, around your eyes and mouth, hands, and even your scalp too. You'll be amazed how much tension you're holding in your body when you look for it. And when you find it, release. Breathe, and let it melt away.

Now that you've come back to your body and your breath, bring the object of you desire into your mind. What do you want? It doesn't matter how big or small it is, like Yoda lifting the spacecraft out of the bog, or simply manifesting himself a cup of coffee. For me, initially it was to go to India for six months. Whatever it is for you, bring that successful outcome into your mind. Gently open your eyes and let them settle on the candle. Watch the way the flame dances.

Now, bring into your awareness the phenomenon of a moth being drawn to this flame. It's like there's an irresistible magnetic force that draws in the moth. It's beyond logic or definition - the moth just cannot resist nor deny this pull towards the flame. Next, (and this is where your homework begins) imagine that the flame is inside of you, from the base of your spine to the tip of your crown, and everything you need to achieve your goal is like that moth being irresistibly drawn to this flame inside of you. *Trust that it's coming to you.*

Feel the same magnetic pull acting on the moth is also acting on your desires; their manifestation is being irresistibly drawn to you. No matter what it is you desire, get yourself into the feeling place of already having it, and trust that those feelings are racing to you by the same undeniable force that the moth races to the flame. Imagine the feeling of your toes in the sand in Thailand, or rolling the beaded wings of a handmade hummingbird across your fingers while smiling in knowing that you made it to Guatemala. Whatever it is you want, use your imagination to put yourself in the scene. Lean into the feeling of having it. Hear the sounds of the busy marketplace, or whatever other images, places, and feelings you curated on your vision board. The finances you need, the people you need, whatever resources, opportunities, or support you need is now moving towards the flame inside of you, just like the moth. *Feel this.*

Even if that little critical voice inside is going "Um, WTF are you doing? This is *ridiculous.*" Hand that voice an imaginary cookie and tell it to sit down. Keep your focus on that flame and drawing in what you need. Trust that it's coming, even if just for this meditation. Suspend your doubting beliefs. Rest from perfectionism. Be childlike, and just pretend for a moment that it's real, and *it's happening.*

Do this for however long you can maintain it - even just a few minutes if you can. More important than trying to sustain it for a massive amount of time, stop the exercise. Go about your life, but then come back and *do it again.* Make this visualization exercise a new habit. Make it part of your daily routine, perhaps in the evening as you're laying bed. This is just like the farmer analogy. A farmer doesn't go out one time to cultivate his or her crops, do the work and go, "There! I'm done. Gimme a harvest now." No, they have to keep coming back to the land. They need to be patient and keep watering, weeding, observing, and responding. When they see a plant they don't want growing, they take it out. And they do it again and again, day in and out, because that's how you grow something that feeds you. Energy and manifestation work in the same way.

When you look around at your life, what you'll see is what you've been growing over the past seasons. You have this because in the days, weeks, months, and years prior you planted and nurtured certain seeds with your thoughts, words, and actions. Sometimes we will not like what we see, and that's because we've been using our energy unconsciously, like painting while asleep. Imagine a garden that no one tends to - things get overgrown. We don't know what's going on in there. It's a *mess*! Sometimes our lives can get messy in the same way that a neglected or poorly-tended garden can, because we haven't taken the time to tend to it with wakeful, conscious, intentional awareness. We haven't made the focused effort to consciously direct the water of our clear intentions and desires. We haven't stopped to take the time to remove the plants we don't want, or to even assess what's growing there in the first place.

So my friend, your mind is a garden and your thoughts are the seeds. You can grow flowers, or you can grow weeds.[4]

---

4 *My dear friend and herbalist, Maria Fernandez, pointed out that what we call "weeds" can actually be highly beneficial plants. For example, dandelion, often considered a weed in Western culture, is a highly medicinal plant with all sorts of great health benefits (https://bit.ly/DandelionBenefits). So I'd like to clarify that I used this terminology to mean a specifically unwanted plant, while also understanding at the same time that all plants have value. In no way do I mean any disrespect to my plant allies. I love you all. Thank you for your medicine.*

HOMEWORK:

ENERGY EXERCISES

Let's start consciously directing our energy. By now, I hope you've become clear on what you want, whether it feels big or small. There's no right or wrong answer when it comes to the call of your heart. Remember, the smallest nudge or desire can lead you into a fantastic adventure. And as with any exercise, the more you practice, the better results you'll get. Here's what I advise:

✽   Go to www.pinterest.com and create a Dream/Vision board. Give it a name that inspires you. Search the internet for images that resonate at the frequency of your desire and "pin" them to your board. Get creative and search for different images that embody the fullness and complexity of your desire and the thoughts, feelings, images, and experiences associated with having it. If you don't know how to do this, Google it, watch some videos on Youtube, or just play around with Pinterest until it accidentally works. You're not allowed to use "But I don't know how!" as an excuse. Spend a few minutes looking at your Pinterest board every day. Put yourself in the images. Lean into the feelings and sensations of being there. Go ahead, close your eyes. You're allowed to dream again.

✽   Do the moth-flame meditation before bed. Make it a regular practice. Do it often, at least once a week, if not more.

✽   Do the exercise where you say "*YES*" to yourself in front of the mirror. Put on some music if you're afraid of being heard. Dare to get loud. Move your body. When things heat up, add a "*Congratulations!*" Pretend as if it's real and congratulate yourself for making it happen.

Chapter 6: Planning Your Adventure

When I was a kid, my dad and my cousin Scott were my travel role models. Unearthed in boxes of old family treasures I would find old and tattered postcards my dad wrote to his mother back in the seventies from places like Machu Picchu in Peru. At family gatherings, Scott would show me old photos from the eighties of him with wild hair and regale me with tales of what it was like to go traveling down the river in Thailand or Costa Rica.

I remember listening with eager ears about the wild slugs, bowel-excavating illnesses, and totally epic adventures he encountered there. They spoke to me of the life-changing experiences they had out on the open road exploring Europe, Asia, and South America. As a kid, I was enthralled by the exciting tales they wove with themselves cast as the main characters, and I just *knew* one day I would embark on my own adventure.

Travel Doesn't Have to be Complicated

When most people think of travel, I think they imagine it to be a complicated, extensively pre-planned, and expensive endeavor. According to what I imagine to be the typical American belief system, "travel" equates with big rolling suitcases and carefully detailed itineraries of activities and sightseeing that one must engage in to achieve the "correct" experience. But it turns out, what we've been led to believe about traveling isn't true. It doesn't need to be such a structured, controlled, nor expensive endeavor.

In other countries, it's common for young people to go backpacking. While youths in America are following a system of graduating high school and immediately feeding like cattle into expensive colleges, youths in other parts of the world are taking what's known as a "gap year." This is the time after high school when they take whatever savings they earned working their summer jobs or whatever, put the bare minimum possessions in a bag, and head off to explore the world. These young humans go traveling to places like Asia, Europe, Australia, and the Americas.

They make discoveries and gain experience out in the field of real life, mixing and mingling with other humans and cultures. When they return to their homelands, they come back with far more perspective, wisdom, and a sense of self than they had when they left. *Then* they pursue their studies and professional careers.

I wish more young Americans did this. I think it's very unfortunate the way our culture places so many demands on eighteen-year-olds fresh out of high school. We put so much pressure on these kids to know exactly what they want to study and do with their lives before they even know who they are.

Why I Love Travel

I love traveling because it gives me that priceless life wisdom and perspective that money can't buy. You must earn it through direct experience, and going out into the world offers me that direct experience. Traveling lets me step away from the culture and society I know and affords me the opportunity to experience something completely different. Sure, it comes with challenges and contrasts, but that's valuable for growth.

I think that's why so many people have such a profound experience in India. Because everything, and I mean *everything*, is done differently there. The mind is constantly going "*WTF*?!" And that's valuable because it forces us to question what we blindly assume to be true, and what we take for granted. It forces us to take a look at what we believe about life and how it should be lived. It forces us to stop taking things for granted and to really understand our privileges. It forces us to start questioning things, and that's a very healthy inquiry.

When we get the chance to try on new ideas and ways of living, and challenge our existing beliefs, consequently we end up stretching the shape of our mind into something much different than it was back in Indiana. And that, my friends, is an invaluable gift on the journey towards becoming who we truly are and understand how we're meant to shine our light in the world.

How to Start Planning Your Adventure

So, where do we start? In the "Hearing the Call of Your Heart" step of the Adventure Path, you took the time to make the brave and honest inquiry to connect with your heart's desire. For me, once upon a time that was to venture to India. Other times it was Thailand, Indonesia, Egypt, and most recently, Guatemala. Once you know where you want to go, then you pick a date by which you'll leave, come hell or high water. I like to use my birthday on November 4, which also coincides perfectly with the arrival of winter in the US. So you've got a destination, a date, what next?

Now is the time to start searching and feeding yourself new information online to get some ideas of the logistics involved. This process can also assist you in inspiring your visualization exercises, to which you'll continue to actively and intentionally direct your energy (and keep adding new pins to your board as you make new discoveries that inspire you).

How to Find Cheap Flights

The basic place to start is to start looking at flights (and *congratulations*, when you get to this step it's more real than ever before. You're *doing it!*). I like to use a combination of Google Flights, Skyscanner, the Hopper app, and other websites I find through searching around. I put in my desired dates and I see what's available. I cross check the other sites to see if I can find something cheaper. There are other ways of finding cheap flights, but that's not my area of expertise. However there's nothing to stop you from learning. If you want to be a detective about it, do some Googling and Youtubing around "Travel Hacking." And look at you! You're taking new action and changing as a person already! *Good for you.*

But hey, if looking at the price of flights sends a lightning bolt of fear and nausea up and down your spine, just know that's also okay. If that voice starts screaming at you that it's too expensive, you can't possibly afford it, that you don't have the time, etc. - it's okay. Just sit with what comes up. Do the aspecting exercise again, as many times as you need. Commit to being the captain of your ship. No matter what debilitating factors rear their ugly heads at you during this stage, just know that it's okay. You're going to get through this, if you want it badly enough. Here's a video of how excited and terrified I was the moment when I was buying my ticket to India: bit.ly/BuyingMyTicket. Just know that if you're experiencing the combination of excitement and terror, and especially if you feel like throwing up, that's a good sign you're moving in the direction of exciting new possibilities for your life.

Keep going.

Another thing on this subject is something called an "Around the World Ticket." Some airlines have special deals where you can get a great price on a kind of ticket that lets you visit many places over period of time, like a year. Typically you just have to keep moving in one direction around the globe. If this interests you, Google it and see what enticing opportunities and information you can find.

How to Sign Up for Frequent Flyer Programs

It's a very good idea - before you buy your ticket - to sign up for a frequent flyer program. I didn't do this until years later and I don't know why. It would've been great to earn all those miles and be able to cash them in for a free flight. But that's okay, I'm not trying to do this perfectly, I'm just trying to learn as I go. I really like flying United, so I went on their site and signed up for a free account. Super easy. There are also other methods to do this with credit cards that give you points you can use towards flights. But again, not my area of expertise. However, with the power of Google and Youtube at your fingertips, you can learn this too. Save your frequent flyer info on Google Drive, or any place that's easy to refer back to when you're ready to buy your flight.

How to Save Money for Your Trip

If you have the money to buy the flight, great! But if you're like I was - financially unprepared to launch - then you'll have to start saving for your dream. Some people seem to be very uncertain about this, probably because saving for adventure travel is an entirely new concept to them. Have you ever heard of the phenomenon of "saving up to buy a car?" Well, it works in the exact same way.

If you ask me, for longer trips of six months to a year, I recommend saving up $5-10K. That will take you a long way. For shorter trips, aim for somewhere around $3K, which can vary depending on a lot of variables like how far away you want to go, how many different places you want to visit on one trip, how much time you want to spend there, where you want to stay, if you choose to volunteer, the kind of activities and experiences you might want to invest in, etc.

Going into this, I had *no experience* with saving money. It was an entirely new skill and philosophy I needed to learn how to integrate into my life in order to achieve my heart's desire. Previously, I just had one bank account that I operated out of, and this was a highly inefficient way to manage my money. One of the best things I learned in this process of becoming the person who *could* travel the world was how to start saving money for my dream. So to start, I opened a free online savings account with Ally Bank (www.allybank.com). Any time I earned any money whatsoever, I developed the habit of sending thirty percent into my Adventure Fund, and then another portion into an Emergency Fund, and also a Tax Fund I had opened.

Separating my money and intentionally putting it aside for important things was super helpful because by not seeing it in my main account meant I wouldn't automatically spend it. I would give myself very little operating cash in my main account while my other saving accounts quietly grew behind the online curtain. I couldn't see them unless I went out of my way to check. This was hugely important for me because, for the first time in my life, I was actually able to work and put aside money toward my dream. This was also important because it gave my life and my work new meaning. It's very satisfying to work for something you believe in, compared to just working to pay the bills.

Now, some people might say "But I can't afford to save money with my current income." To that I say, then *go find some new income.* We live in an incredible age of internet connectivity where anything is possible for those who are *willing* to put in the work and show up. You could start driving for Lyft or Uber, start teaching English online to kids in China, you could do tasks for elderly people through Task Rabbit app, put your talents up on fiverr.com, teach guitar lessons, or so many other ways to create value for other humans who are willing to pay for what you can do or teach them. You can also start selling your stuff on Ebay, which Gary Vaynerchuck talks about here: http://bit.ly/GaryVMakeMoneyonEbay. This Youtuber also breaks it down even further for beginners: https://bit.ly/EbayforBeginners. I also really like the work of Gillian Perkins and Sunny Lenarduzzi who teach on the subject of making money online. They are two powerful, entrepreneurial women who offer some great in their videos on Youtube.

There are so many ideas. You just need to start leaning into them. When we stop making excuses and saying it's impossible, and instead pull up our big kid pants and start looking for the way, it *will* appear. So I say: *Stop complaining* and *start seeking.* Get on that search bar and invest the time to educate yourself and find the answers that resonate for where you're at and what skills you have to offer the world.

How to Get Visas and a Passport

Next thing, or perhaps the first thing before actually buying your flight, is you'll want to check out the visa situation for the country you want to visit. The visa is like your permission slip that gets you into the country. Americans are historically pretty lucky because many countries will allow you to get what's called a "visa on arrival," which means you don't have to do anything in advance. You just have to show up and they'll let you in. Lucky you! Typically a VOA is for stays less than thirty days. You'll have to do some research for the country you want to visit. When I wanted to go to India for six months, I could not get a visa on arrival for this amount of time. So I had to do a little Googlin' to find the local embassy or consulate and actually go in person to fill out a visa application. I had to pay something like $40 for the privilege. Keep in mind, there *will* be a buffer of time required for this process, so make sure you figure this out in advance and set the machinery into motion with your action (Hey, *look*! We're aligning our energy! Shoot that fart laser, baby!).

Next, do you have a passport? If not, get all Googly-moogly again and find out what you need to do to get one. For my American friends, it's super easy. Just go to your nearest post office and ask for a passport application. Fill it out and get that baby sent off. If you already have a passport, check two things: (a) When does it expire? Some countries won't let you in if you don't have at least two to six months remaining validity on your passport, if not more. So be aware of when your passport expires and get it renewed, if necessary. (b) Make sure you have enough blank pages for new stamps. Now, if your passport is so full that you can't hold any more immigration stamps, then you probably don't need this book. All the same, it's something to keep in mind.

How to Find Places to Stay

Next, how do you find a place to stay? I get this question a lot, especially when people see where I end up in my videos, like this cute little house in Thailand (http://bit.ly/CuteHouseThailand). Now, if you're coming to meet me for the group retreat in Guatemala or other magical places around the world, I will arrange all of that for you. But if you're doing it on your own, then what I'll tell you is that you just need a starting point. Often when I'm going to a new place, I'll look online at websites like booking.com, agoda.com, or airbnb.com to see available rooms and lodging options at my destination. Sometimes when I'm already familiar with a country or city I'll just show up with an idea about the part of town where I want to stay and I'll find something I like once I get there. However, I don't recommend this technique for first-time travelers who are newly out of their element and don't have a feel for the place yet. Better take care of yourself by figuring out where you'll sleep in advance so you know where to go once you arrive at the airport (plus they'll ask you for an address where you're staying when you're filling out the arrival forms at immigration, so it's good to have an address on hand). Again, there are about a billion apps and websites out there to help you with this step. *Seek and ye shall find.*

Keep in mind that there are many different options for where you can stay. In the past - before I knew how to travel - I would just get an expensive hotel room because I didn't know any better. Now I know other options include private rooms in low budget hotels, shared dorm rooms (which can get suuuuuuper wicked cheap depending on where you're going), and you can also rent a room in someone's home via Airbnb (or the whole home).

Speaking of homes, some of the sweetest times of my life were when I rented a small house for myself in places like Thailand (bit.ly/AtHomeInThailand) and Guatemala (bit.ly/MyHouseInGuatemala). In those places, the monthly cost of renting my own little house was about $350. I found those houses once I was on the ground and was able to look around in person, and in the meantime I stayed in a temporary place like a hotel or guesthouse I found online. For that place in Thailand, I used a real estate agent on the island (who I found through the local FB groups) who showed me different properties until I found the one I liked. I didn't have to pay the agent's fee, the property did. *Win!*

The good thing about staying in an Airbnb or renting a whole house is, not only will you get more of a local experience, not to mention that it's less expensive than a hotel, but often times you can use the kitchen. That means you can cook for yourself to keep your expenses lower while also ensuring the cleanliness of your food. This is far better than if you had to eat out every meal, especially if you plan to stay longer than a few days.

In addition to hotels, dorms, and private homes, there are also places where you can stay for free in exchange for your time and labor, like on a farm or meditation retreat center. You can learn about experiences like that through websites like www.workaway.info. Through the power of Google at your fingertips, you can follow the breadcrumbs yourself to find things I don't even know about, based around *your* unique interests, skills, and talents. If you have carpentry skills, or some useful trade like that, and are willing to work in exchange for room and board, you can go far. Some of my friends also use a website like www.trustedhousesitters.com to find opportunities to pet sit in exotic locations around the world and *BAM!* You've got free accommodation in fantastic locations all around the world petting otherwise lonely kitties. Isn't that nice? You see, once we get beyond the wall of fear and voices that say we can't do it, we find there's a whole field of possibilities where all the ways you *can* do it grow like the most beautiful flowers just waiting for you to sniff them out. *Get sniffin' Scooby!*

How to Get Wifi on Your Phone

Before you leave for your trip, I strongly advise that you get an unlocked cell phone. It's unfortunate that so many people confine themselves within the limitations of a cell phone contract that marries their phone to a single carrier for an extended period of time. I don't do that anymore. Instead, I buy an unlocked and refurbished cell phone off Ebay, which means I don't have a contract and I'm not married to any carrier.

What that means is that when I arrive in a foreign country, the first thing I do is to get a local SIM card at the airport. That gives me a local phone number and internet on my device. *Huzzah*! When I arrived in Thailand, I got a new SIM at the airport in Bangkok and I was pleasantly surprised to discover that I now had faster internet on my phone than I did back in the States. Yay!

As mentioned, you can easily find unlocked cell phones online. Personally, I'm in love with my Google Pixel and bought it refurbished and unlocked for a whopping $300. Ah, the price of freedom.

Some people have a phone plan that includes international talk and text. That's great, if you're willing to pay for it. Google Fi also has a plan that works anywhere in the world.

I like having my own unlocked phone and switch out the SIM card when I arrive in a new country. I personally feel this is the most affordable way to do it. There's a caveat, though. When I leave the US, I don't get to keep my old number. Some people may not be willing or able to let go of their old phone number. It was hard at first, but now I don't mind. I kind of like being difficult for people to find, like a ghost moving through the ether. Totally my style. *BOO!*

Speaking of getting local SIM cards, it's typically pretty easy to get a tourist SIM card at the airport. However, sometimes life happens and you can't connect because your phone isn't unlocked or for whatever reason you can't get online when you first land. I remember having trouble with this when I first arrived in India, and it was a real pain in the butt. That's why I recommend you write the address of where you're going somewhere you can access it without the internet, like a fancy technologically advanced thing known as a piece of paper.

Additionally, just in case your internet doesn't work when you first arrive, I recommend that you download a Google map of where you're going, like the neighborhood around your hotel/ guesthouse. That way you can still access it offline. You can also save a list of places you want to visit in Google maps. That's a very handy and easily-accessible reference to put together in advance, rather than trying to figure it out when you're on the ground. These are the kinds of ways you can do your future self a favor to make their life easier.

Next, if you don't already have it, I recommend you download WhatsApp. This is a widely used messaging app that is a great way to stay in touch with the people you love when you're flying free in the world. Most people you meet will ask for your WhatsApp number in order to stay connected with you, so it's a good thing to use and be prepared to share. It's tied to your regular phone number and allows you to send text messages and media content to other people on the app. So if you can't get your SIM card to work at first, you can still find and connect to a wifi network and message your family and friends to let them know you're safe.

What Makes a Good Travel Bag?

One of the next things to consider is your travel bag. Many years ago, before I started traveling like this, I would travel with two big rolling suitcases full of stuff. While it's great to have stuff, it's not so great to have so much stuff that you feel limited in your mobility. So for the sake of freedom and adventure, I advise you look into getting yourself a traveling backpack. By that I mean something like this: https://amzn.to/3bbqZlt

Typically, I'll have one big bag on my back and then have a smaller backpack that I carry on my front, so I end up looking like a funny double turtle. Double turtle your way to your dream, *baby!* Additionally, sometimes I'll keep an even smaller backpack that contains my most valuable items, like my passport and money. In India, I would use this bag of valuables as my pillow on the train as an extra precaution. I don't let that bag out of my sight. If it's small enough, it can pack into one of the other bags when you're on the move.

Honestly, I cannot begin to tell you the divine sense of liberation I felt when I reduced the number of things I brought with me to that which would fit in a bag on my back. Or rather, fit into a double-turtle situation. That simplicity is so liberating physically, mentally, and emotionally, because traveling is not just about what you choose to bring with you - but more importantly - what you choose to leave behind.

Everyone is different. Maybe you want to go somewhere for only two weeks, then maybe you don't need a backpack like this.

But if you're like me and want to go on an adventure for many months that will take you across who knows what kind of terrain, then you might want to think about investing in a backpack and the unbridled sense of possibility and freedom that goes along with it.

How to Pack for Your Adventure

Now let's talk about what to bring, and what to leave behind. Here's the best piece of advice I can give you: Simplify (and while you're at it, Listen to "Minimum" by Charlie Cunningham on the Leaving America with Erica soundtrack on Spotify here: http://bit.ly/LAWEmusic). You don't need a whole wardrobe, just a few basics. Get a sense of the climate of the place where you're going and be sure to dress for the weather and the local culture. Keep in mind, the way you dress in America, or your home country, may not be the best way to dress in other countries. A good rule of thumb - especially for women - is to cover your shoulders and leave the booty shorts at home. If you wear booty shorts or show cleavage, just know that you're inviting a lot of eye energy and the characters and their agendas attached to those energy lines.

It's good a practice not to expose too much skin when you're in a foreign land. I like to keep a scarf or other cloth wrap with me to cover my shoulders or head when required. This keeps me both respectful to local cultures *and* shielded from sun and unwanted eye energy. This is also important to know and keep in mind if I plan to enter holy places. We want to make sure we are dressed respectfully to the divine as we enter those places of worship.

Even if you plan to go to a country where there's a warmer climate, I recommend you plan for unexpected cold weather. I'm *so* glad I invested in a high quality, lightweight down sleeping bag, like this: https://amzn.to/3bsoeMc. I had no idea just how handy this would come be until I was camping out under the stars in the Thar desert of Rajasthan in India on that fateful camel trek (which you'll read about in Chapter 10). While the sun scorched the land during the day, during the night the temperatures plunged near freezing. As I laid horizontal on that cold sand, I was unbelievably grateful to have my warm down sleeping bag. In that moment I was also grateful to have my lightweight down feather vest, like this: https://amzn.to/35WkuBs. So even when I'm traveling to a hot place, I still make sure to bring a good quality lightweight down sleeping bag, vest, and jacket (like this: https://amzn.to/2AwfnMN) that stuff compactly in the bottom of my bag. Because when those things come in handy, oh boy, *do they come in handy.*

I also recommend bringing an eye cover to help you sleep amidst the unending illumination of planes, trains, and buses. A neck pillow can also be a real treasure in this regard. Lastly, if you find yourself staying in dorm rooms with other travelers, or any other situation where you find yourself plagued by other people's snoring and beeping phones, you'll thank your angels if you have some ear plugs to protect your ability to sleep.

I had a moment of enlightenment splashing around in a river in India when I was super grateful to have water shoes with me, like Crocs (Video: bit.ly/TravelShoesIndia). So when it comes to footwear, leave the sexy heels at home. Instead, I recommend a pair of comfortable sneakers or walking shoes, some good flip flops, and depending on where you're going, a pair of water shoes.

From my own experience, I also recommend packing a small pair of scissors and some kind of twine. You never know when you might need to cut something, or tie something together. These things often come in handy on an adventure.

Keep in mind that it's better to bring less, not more. When I arrived in India I had *waaaay* too much stuff with me and actually ended up feeling really overwhelmed. I had to go through my bags and send a bunch of things home, which cost me around $40. So save yourself the expense and the headache by making sure you have empty space in your bag, because when you're out there you're inevitably going to find cool new treasures you'll want to take home.

Here's the moral of the story: be willing let go of the old so you have space for the new.

Ninja Moves

Next, a super ninja move is to email yourself a copy of your passport and visa, especially if you get a visa sticker or stamp in advance. If something goes wrong and you lose your documents because, for example, monkeys in India are thieves, you'll still have a copy easily accessible in case you need it. If your life was a movie, this could be the key move that saves your butt in the climax scene when the T-rex is chasing you.

Another great move is to download music in advance. You may rely on streaming services at home, but you might not be able to do that where you're going. So if you're subscribed to Spotify, download your favorite playlists, buy songs on iTunes, or if you're a clever wizard then use your wizard powers to download the music of your heart's desire to your favorite device. In those moments where you find yourself missing the familiar things of home, a good dose of music medicine could be exactly what you need to lift your spirit. Downloading audio books in advance is also a great gift to yourself on the road, especially when it comes to long trains, flights, or bus rides.

Self-Care on The Road

When you arrive in the new country, I highly encourage that you find a way to treat yourself. Acknowledge that you've just done something incredibly challenging and amazing and you deserve a treat. In most places you go, especially Asia, you can find super cheap massages and spa treatments. For example, in Bali I was able to get an unforgettable four-hour spa treatment for about $60 (Video: bit.ly/BaliSelfLove). It was a great way to reward myself and show my body and mind some much needed love and relaxation after having gone through such an intense journey to get there. *Do it baby,* you've earned it!

If you're coming to meet me in Guatemala for one of my group retreats, I'll show you my favorite spa in Antigua, built in a remains of an old convent. We'll spend some time getting totally refreshed and rejuvenated. *Hurray!*

Speaking of self-care, honestly this is one of the most important new skills I had to learn on my path towards a more peaceful and happy life. I used to practice a strict regime of self-denial, and it took a serious toll on me. So I highly encourage you to think of ways you can give yourself a special treat on the road. That could be a spa treatment, a nice meal, quiet time with the phone off, fresh flowers in your room, or a cookie. Whatever it is for you, make sure it's something that makes your heart smile. It will go a long way to support you to feel good as you move through the challenges on the road. And in life, frankly. As M would say, "*Love yourself.*"

Don't Waste Your Money on This

Some airlines have a really sneaky way of getting more money out of you at the check-in counter. It used to be that you could take whatever you wanted with you, but in recent years things have become more controlled. When you buy your flight, be aware of whether a check-in bag is included in the ticket price, and if not, then educate yourself on how much extra they will be. If they do charge extra for check-in bags, then you might be better off by paying for your bag online in advance rather than waiting to be professionally mugged at the check-in counter.

For example, once when I was in Iceland the flight ticket was super cheap (you wily beast, WOW Air), but what happened was when I got to the airport they made me pay something like $50 just to check *one bag*! I nearly exploded and punched them. I was so mad. The lady behind the counter, who I imagine endures all kinds of bullshit and abuse due to this outrageous policy, explained that it was only $25 per bag if I had checked-in online in advance. So that's important to keep in mind, and I *highly* suggest you check-in online within 24 or 48 hours of your flight to ensure you don't punch the nice lady behind the counter and get thrown out of the airport by security during the check-in process.

Using Money in Foreign Countries

Now, money. What do we do about money in a foreign country? Well, what do you do with money in your own country? If you need cash, you go to an ATM, right? It's the same thing in foreign countries. I don't bother doing things with travelers checks or any of that nonsense anymore when I can just as easily use my debit card at a local ATM for a small fee. And my bank actually refunds ATM fees, so *BAM. Winning*. I'll typically bring cash with me as well from my stripping money (*Joking*! I didn't end up stripping, although I wanted my dream so bad I might have done it if I couldn't find another way) and I'll change money when I get there.

Though there are two things I advise when it comes to bringing cash money with you, and that is: *Don't change cash at the airport*. The airport is specifically designed to screw you in fees in this regard. Better to wait until you find a more competitive rate wherever you're going where there are more money changers, like dueling pianos vying for your dollars. Next, if you're going to bring cash, bring $100 or $50 bills because you'll get a better exchange rate than just fives or twenties or all the nickels you collected because you wanted this badly enough. I recently went to change some cash at the bank in Panajachel only to discover they would *only* change $50 and $100 bills. *D'oh!*

Also, when you arrive, you won't understand the money at first. That's normal and to be expected, and it's okay to be confused for some time. And that's why I encourage you not to rush. Take some time, look at prices on menus and in local shops. Make some small purchases - like a bottle of water or a cute trinket you like. Be patient and observant as you get a feel for what money is worth here. It will be different than at home, and typically in places like Asia and South America you'll discover that your money goes much further. It's just a question of getting used to *how* much further.

When one of my friends came to meet me in Thailand, he got scammed straight out of the airport at Koh Samui. He didn't know the local prices yet and needed to get to his hotel. A kind Thai man offered him a ride to his hotel for 1000B. My friend did the math and it didn't seem so much, something like $30. To him this seemed fair, especially since he had to get to the other side of the island. So he paid the fare. But, as it turns out, that taxi ride should have cost 300B. So, due to his naiveté, he was conned. It's not a big deal, but it's an example of what can happen when you don't know the local prices when you first arrive, or if you're comparing things relative to the price of the US dollar. So do yourself a favor and ask around and get a feel for things before you jump into big purchases. Trust your gut and be willing to walk away from someone who might be trying to take advantage of you, even - and especially - if they seem overly friendly. A lot of people will be friendly because they want something from you. *Oh, life!*

How to Negotiate Prices

In many places in the world, especially in the markets of South America or Asia, it's possible to negotiate the price of things you want to buy. I don't mean like in a shop like 7-11, where prices are marked and fixed, but rather in markets where you're dealing with locals and locally-made goods. Negotiating prices can be a kind of a game, and it can be fun. The seller typically starts out at a very high tourist price because they know there's a good chance you'll pay it. At this point, you either don't know any better and it seems like a good price relative to the US dollar, so you pay it. Or you can dance with them. You can think of it like acting too.

What I like to do is not let on how much I like or want the thing, so when they tell me the price I kind of shrug and say, "Ahhhhh, welllllll, I don't want to pay that much. I would pay you X for it." Now, X is specifically lower that what I am *really* willing to pay, which is Y. But if you tell them Y, then you won't get Y, because that's how the game works. Here, let me illustrate it for you. In this example I'm going to use the US dollar for the sake of clarity. However, when you're in other countries you'll negotiate in the local currency.

[Cut to scene]:

I'm standing in the old marketplace of Cairo in Egypt. These cobblestone streets have stood for hundreds if not thousands of years, and I can feel the richness of genuine antiquity all around me. As I stroll through the market, colored lanterns splash ruby and saffire light across my eyes full of wonder. The smell of exotic incense fills my nostrils with mystery and delight while a friendly black cat slinks by under my feet. Everywhere I am greeted by eager eyes and welcoming invitations to come look inside the array of curious and fantastic shops that line the cobblestone path.

After meeting the kind eyes of an old shopkeeper who greets me, I enter his shop and feel like I'm stepping into another world. Inside I'm awestruck by an endless expanse of beautiful statues and paintings of Egyptian gods and goddesses. The artwork is phenomenal and the air feels rich with time and hidden power. I find a statue of a goddess with gracefully outstretched wings, and I quickly fall in love with her beauty and elegance. I would be willing to pay $20 for this statue, and I know that's a fair price because I did my research by talking to people beforehand and comparing prices at other shops. Seeing the statue in my hands, the shopkeeper approaches me with a warm smile and gentle demeanor.

Shopkeeper: Hello Madam! You like this statue? Isis is very powerful, very good for a powerful woman like you.

Me: Yes, Isis is amazing. It's very nice statue, I guess (*masking my excitement with a cleverly timed shrug*). But I'm not sure I like it so much. What is the price?

Shopkeeper: I have a very special price just for you, my friend. $40. Very good price for a very beautiful lady like you.

Me: Ahhhh....>pause<.....I see. (*I put the statue down*) Hmmmm...I don't really want to pay this price. It's okay, maybe another time.

Shopkeeper: Madam! (*picking up the statue and placing it back in my hands*) Tell me, how much you want to pay?

Me: >adding a sigh and a pause< I really want to pay only $15.

Shopkeeper: (*playing the game*) Oh Madam, this price is too low. You give me $25, ok?

Me: (*Putting the statue down*) Oh, I don't know. I can do $20.

Shopkeeper: $25, Madam.

Me: Okay, thank you very much. Maybe another time (*and I turn to leave*).

Shopkeeper: Okay Madam! *Wait!* $20 for you. Special price, just for you. *(smiling)*

Me: Thank you, my friend (*handing him the money*).

So it's a game, and you win when you have courage to stand your ground, be patient, be kind, be fair, and just have fun with it. Don't let on how badly you want the thing and be willing to walk away if you're not getting a good price. Sometimes you might have to interact with a few shops to get a sense of what the best price is. That's okay, be patient. Don't jump your energy in the heat of desire for the thing. Also, you can always come back to the shop, so it's okay to walk away if necessary to check the price with other vendors.

Just one thing, please don't screw local people out of a few bucks. While it can be fun to get the lowest possible price, also realize that something like $3 goes a long way for local people. So play the game, but don't be heartless about it. $3 may not be that much to you, but that could be the price of the rice they buy to feed their family for a week. So you have the right to bargain with locals - but remember - you come from privilege and they probably don't. So play the game, but please don't be stingy with a single local mother trying to feed her children.

What to Eat and Drink

One of the most common questions I get is about what to eat and drink on the road. And to that I answer: Food and water, silly! But seriously, wherever you go there will be clean drinking water available in the form of bottled water. And it's important that you're aware of the water you're drinking and don't drink from the tap or unverifiable sources. In fact, one practice to start doing while you're still home is practice *not* gargling or rinsing your mouth out in the shower. That's because if you unconsciously do this when you're in a place like India or Thailand, you can get a nasty stomach bug.

Similarly, to avoid getting sick when it comes to food, especially in a place like India, you want to make sure you eat foods that are cooked and still hot when you eat them. Definitely avoid salads, because while those crispy greens are packed with healthy goodness, the water they were washed with may not be. So better to avoid salads. Keep in mind that things like lettuce and strawberries are hard to wash and because they're low to the ground, they collect more stuff, so they're more likely to be contaminated with something you don't want.

It's also good to pay attention to where the other gringos or farangs eat (that means white or foreign people, and each place will have their own term of endearment for us) and follow their lead. Many times you'll find restaurants owned by gringos who live there, and that also means they generally have a higher standard of hygiene than any random local place. If you really want a salad, that's your best bet. So while street food is delightful in so many ways, it can be like playing Russian roulette with your guts. Click - click - KAPROW!

First Aid + Health

Next, it's important to be prepared for getting injured on the road. If it's a big injury, you can go to the doctor. Yes, in most places there are local hospitals, doctors, and clinics. But for small things, like getting scratched while playing with goats or scraping your knee while trekking to a magical waterfall, it's good to have your own first aid kit on hand.

Personally, at times I've kept the basics, like bandaids and antibiotic ointment. But after my experiences in India, I also make sure to also travel with turmeric, which is one of nature's best remedies for cuts, infections, bug bites, inflammation, and a variety of other ailments. It's a bright yellow root that grinds into a powder that will stain your fingers and clothes. It's great and I love it. When I see someone with turmeric stained fingers, I see that as a sign of intelligence. Put it this way: I've got ninety-nine problems and turmeric can solve most of them.

Now, let's say you do get sick on the road. It's okay, it happens. In fact, some would say it's even an integral part of the adventure. If and when you do get sick you can go to a local clinic and get the medicine you need at a pharmacy. This part may actually make you upset though, because you'll get to see how cheap healthcare can be in other countries when compared to a place like America. My same friend who came to visit me in Thailand got injured on a motorbike and had to go to the hospital for a treatment on his leg. He recounted to me how scared he was of the bill going into the hospital, sure this procedure would cost him thousands of dollars. In the end? About $200 US.

Travel Insurance

If you're concerned about the risks of getting sick, injured, or robbed on the road, you can also opt to get travelers' insurance. In years past, especially when I was riding a motorbike, I used a company called World Nomads. You can learn more about them online at www.worldnomads.com. Personally, I don't get insurance anymore, especially since I'm not riding motorbikes in Guatemala. This choice is neither good nor bad, it's just mine. I encourage you to make the choice for yourself along the lines of what satisfies your boundaries and needs to feel safe.

When I was first learning to ride motorbike, part of the process was to get online and make sure I had an insurance policy activated *before* I got on the bike. So if you're planning to ride a motorbike, or if suddenly you decide you want to learn to ride a motorbike, activating some insurance is a wise move.

Travel Safety

One of the most common questions I get is about safety. People seem to have this impression that other places are really dangerous, or rather more dangerous than the United States. Friends, let me break it to you: North America is super dangerous too. Or at least it *can* be. If you hang out in dubious parts of town, you'll be more likely to run into trouble. If you act stupid, run with the wrong people, and don't listen to your gut, you're much more likely to find trouble. If you get drunk and lose your senses, it doesn't matter where in the world you are - trouble will find you.

So while yes, other parts of the world can come with some new dangers, the rules are the same. Make good choices. Listen to your gut. Be willing to say no to someone or leave a situation that doesn't feel right. If you get a sense you shouldn't walk down a certain street or get in a certain taxi, don't do it. Avoid walking around alone at night. Don't get drunk or high on the train or you might wake up and find you have no bags. Don't accept candy from strangers. Do be careful about trusting people you just met. Guard your heart, your body, and your wallet. But also make sure you're not *too* suspicious of others, because while you may successfully keep out a threat, you may also successfully keep out genuine kindness and connection.

So here I encourage my friends to practice the fine art of discernment. That's the subtle art of listening to your gut feeling, aka that inner sense of what feels right for you, right now, from moment to moment. Be careful about judging people and situations too much with the eyes (as we'll learn later in the "Jaisalmer Camel Scandal" story in Chapter 10). If you practice the fine art of listening to your gut, or your intuition as I've been referring to it, you'll be fine no matter where you go.

Here's the deal: it's not so much about where you go, but rather the energy you bring with you. You are at the center of your

102

experience. So walk tall, walk confidently, walk with love... especially if you're approaching a group of dogs on the street. The last thing you want to do is run away afraid or they might respond to your fearful energy by chasing you.

One super practical thing I can offer is to bring your own padlock. In guesthouses in Thailand, India, and other places they will give you a lock to put on your door, but the reality is that you don't know who has a copy of the key. So I like the Islamic proverb that says *"Pray to God, but tie up your camels."* To me that means pray for guidance and protection as you walk the path, give love to everybody, but still make sure you take care of the practical things you can do to protect yourself.

Your wellbeing is *your* responsibility. So lock you motorbike, lock your room, say no when something doesn't feel right, and stay sober in vulnerable situations. Tie up your camels and pray to the God of your understanding. Ask for protection and guidance, and follow those nudges when you receive them, even - and *especially* - if you don't understand them. Do this, and you'll be fine no matter where you are in the world.

Getting Vaccinations, OUCH!

Depending on where you go, you may also want to look into getting vaccinations. I got a few vaccinations before I went to India, but I met plenty of travelers on the road who don't bother. Today, I don't bother. Again, it's a personal preference. Do your research and do what feels right for you. Here's the moment I got shot up before going to India: bit.ly/GettingShotsforIndia. *Who's a big girl? :)*

How to Avoid Getting Conned

When you're brand spankin' new in a place, you're most likely to get ripped off, like my friend in Thailand. That's because you're not yet familiar with how much things should cost or even the value of the local currency relative to the local economy. That's why I advise asking some questions in advance like "How much should a ride from the airport cost?" When you know what to expect, and someone tries to tell you a much bigger number, you can laugh out loud as you tell them no and go find a more honest tuk tuk driver. If you don't know anyone yet where you're going, these kinds of questions are best directed to local Facebook groups. These groups are a free, public, invaluable resources - which we'll cover in the next section.

Scams that take advantage of tourists' privilege, goodwill, and naiveté are prevalent. Especially in places like India. When someone tries to scam you, they will typically try to use you goodwill and emotions against you. "My baby needs milk," the poor young woman will say, waving an empty milk bottle in your face. Then, out of understandable pity for the baby and a desire to help, you follow the woman to a local shop intending to buy milk. But it turns out she doesn't want *that* milk, she wants the big expensive container of powered milk. "Oh okay," you think, "the baby is hungry and I want to help." So you buy the expensive milk and the mama is happy, and you get to feel good because you did something that you thought was really good. You make the purchase, hand over the expensive milk, and everyone says goodbye full of good feelings and smiles. You walk away with a happy ego because *you did the good thing*.

Or so you thought. Meanwhile, as you turn the corner, the woman goes back to the shop where she and the shopkeeper were in cahoots the whole time. She returns the big expensive dry milk and the shopkeeper gives her the money. They both take a cut, and you're the fool.

Famous last words: *"But I was only trying to help!"*

So better yet, if someone comes to you with a sob story about how hungry they are, it's only natural to want to help. Relative to these humans, you have *so* much privilege, and it's a good thing to want to use your privilege to alleviate the suffering of others. Just don't be a chump about it. Make sure the money goes to where they say it will go. If that means sitting down with the person, buying them lunch, and literally watching them eat - do it. But you might end up watching them squirm because they actually wanted to get the money from you so they could take their family to the new Shahrukh Khan movie.

One of the best pieces of advice I can give you in this regard is don't take out more money with you than you're willing to lose. Keep your money safe, and sometimes that means *safe from yourself* in a moment of emotional impulsivity. It's good to keep a buffer of time and space between you and your money because in the process of going to retrieve it, you have some extra time to assess if this is something, or someone, you really want to spend your money on (as we'll see in the camel story in Chapter 10).

Sometimes a local business, like a travel agency or affiliate, might try to scam you. They overcharge you or don't give you the original bus ticket as promised, and by the time you figure it out you're far away in the connecting city and finding yourself having to buy *another* ticket. So it's a good idea to have a clear idea of who you're paying for what. Make sure all tickets are included and clearly marked. Ask questions if you're unsure. With businesses, get a receipt with the name of the company and phone number clearly outlined, just in case you need to submit a claim to the local Tourist Police.

Local Resources to Help You Find Your Way

When doing research about the country you want to visit, one great piece of advice is to join Facebook groups relevant to that place. For example, the island I visited in Thailand had an infamous Facebook group called the "Koh Phangan Conscious

Community" (https://www.facebook.com/groups/KohPhanganCC/). Chaing Mai, one of my favorite cities in Northern Thailand, has a group specifically for women called "Chiang Mai Nomad Girls" who meet up regularly for lunch (www.facebook.com/groups/ChiangMaiNomadGirls). Locally in Guatemala, there's a women's group in Antigua called "Girlfriends in Antigua" (https://www.facebook.com/groups/GirlfriendsinAntigua/). For Lake Atitlan, there are a number of groups like "San Marcos Atitlan Community" (https://www.facebook.com/groups/100536950112887/) and "Lake Atitlan Spiritual Community" (https://www.facebook.com/groups/524460981000811/) - just to name a few.

These Facebook groups are a great way to connect with fellow travelers, ask questions, get answers and advice, find places to stay, interesting workshops to attend, and so on. You can even ask to meet up with someone for coffee if you just want to make a new friend and get advice in person. It's all right there waiting for you to ignite your desire and take action. Wherever you want to go, I bet there's a Facebook group for travelers there. *Find it!*

How to Get Around

I mentioned a "tuk tuk" before and some of you were probably like, "Whoa there, what manner of martian spacecraft is she referring to now?" Nay friends, a "tuk tuk" is a marvelous invention designed to get you where you need to go for super cheap. It's an elaborate scooter someone drives you around in, like a motorized rickshaw with a covered caboose for you to sit in. Most importantly, it's a fun and inexpensive way to get around town. In Guatemala, I love the way the tuk tuks are pimped out. Each one has its own theme, like Batman or Jesus. It's great!

That said, wherever you go, there *will* be a way to get around. When I was on the island in Thailand there weren't tuk tuks, so I had to face my fears and learn how to ride a scooter. While it was terrifying at the time, figuring it out and learning to ride a scooter around the island was one of the most empowering and fun things I've ever accomplished - not to mention it totally boosted my self-esteem in ways I never would have imagined from my first terrified moments getting on the bike. With that new and empowering skill, I then went on to do some amazing motorbike explorations around northern Thailand driving through the mountains like a total badass. I felt so alive in a way that I will cherish forever, like a fine wine called *"A Life Well Lived,"* which I will happily sip on my deathbed.

A scooter rental is typically a few bucks a day, or if you stay in a place long enough you can do monthly for a cheaper price, which should come out to less than $100 a month. It can get much cheaper depending on where you are and the piece of shit you're willing to ride. When it comes to motorbikes, and I can't stress this enough: use common sense, strong discernment, helmets, and travel insurance.

In bigger cities, they have car services like Uber. In Asia, they also have the equivalent app called Grab. So this is again why it's *so* important to have an unlocked cell phone and a local SIM card that gives you wifi on the go. I really appreciated having that, especially in Egypt (that was before I met up with my group, as I arrived solo a few days early). Being able to get from place to place after dark when I wasn't familiar with the neighborhood and didn't feel safe to walk around alone was invaluable, like when I was in Cairo. I just called an Uber to pick me up and went back to my AirBnB, *voila!*

In those cities, there are also taxis available, but taxis can be scams, especially if they tell you the meter is broken. Sometimes in India they'll take you for a ride to go visit their friend's shop where they get a commission. Taxi drivers can be all kinds of sweet-talking con artists. So if you're going to take a taxi, it's cool, just be clear on where you want to go, and before you launch make sure the meter is running. Don't listen to any sweet talking stories, unless you're feeling bored and would enjoy being taken for a ride.

How to Learn Foreign Languages

One of the most satisfying things you can do on the road is learn a few words and phrases of the local language. I like to carry a small notebook where I write down notes on words I learn by talking to people. Sometimes I'll create a voice memo on my phone if I need help remembering the correct pronunciation. Google Translate is also an invaluable language translation app. This is especially helpful to have if you find yourself needing to text a local person on Whatsapp, like the sweet Mayan lady from whom you rent your dream cottage in the mountains.

When I deploy some basic words in Thai, Balinese, Arabic, or Spanish, I am able to connect with locals in a much more profound way than if I stay merely in the realm of my English language. It's like building a bridge that allows for new friendships and connections to be formed. Not to mention you'll also have more success bargaining and getting a better deal for that unbelievably cool blanket at the Chiang Mai weekend market if you can say the number you want to pay in Thai.

Some examples of things I make sure to learn and record in my little notebook are how to say "hello," "good morning," "excuse me," "please," "thank you," "my name is," "may I have," and then numbers one through ten, and tens through a hundred. This is a great way to stretch your brain in a really satisfying way that can open the door to magical new experiences and connections with others. You don't need to learn it perfectly, nor all at once, just know that a little effort goes a long way and the more you practice, the better you'll get.

What to Do Once You're There

Going back to the idea of attending workshops, this brings us to the pretty important question of *"What do I do once I'm there?"* Great question. Let me ask you, what do you *want* to do? What is your desire? Do you want to learn another language or how to cook? Would you like to live and work on a permaculture farm, or maybe volunteer at a school to help teach kids English? Would you like to learn how to feel and move your life-force qi energy from a Shaolin monk on the beach at sunrise (I recommend Shi Heng Zuan Laoshi, if you can find him: bit.ly/Laoshi)? Do you want to help animals? Make art? Volunteer with horses in Spain or work on a vineyard in Italy? Do you want to learn yoga or get Reiki certified? Do you want to learn to paint, to sing, or dance? What are you curious about or interested in? What have you always wanted to do, but perhaps never let yourself do? What *calls* to you right now? What makes your antennas perk up with excitement and curiosity?

Connecting with your natural curiosity is one of the most important parts of finding your path. However, you don't need to have all the answers upfront. All you need are a few breadcrumbs of what makes your heart look up and say "Yes, I'm interested," even - and *especially* - when it doesn't make sense to your rational thinking mind.

One of the best parts of being out there on the road by yourself is that you get to decide for yourself. You don't have to check with anyone else or see what they want to do. You get to do what *you* want to do, possibly for the first time in your life. So it's a good practice to ask yourself, "What interests me? What would be so cool to experience? What do I want to learn? What would make me really come *alive?*" These kinds of questions can greatly inform the trajectory your path takes, the teachers you'll meet, and the experiences you'll have along the way.

That said, if you don't know, *that's also okay*. When I went to India for six months, I was very confused and had very little idea of what I would do there. I just wanted to get there because it felt important at that stage of my journey. So I just picked a starting point, a beautiful lakeside city called Udaipur, and just figured it out as I went. In fact, sometimes it's even better that you *don't* know what you want, because often times it turns out we don't know what we want. Or what we think we want isn't actually what we *really* want. That's okay. Knowing the complete picture what you want is not necessary for this stage of the journey. Personally, I had to go on a journey to learn what I want. And that's a big part of why my life is so fulfilling today, because I went on that journey to sift through the contrasts of life until I came into alignment with what feels right for me.

So I'd say, ask yourself the questions outlined above. Listen to the answers, come up with a plan if it pleases you, but know then that the most important part of having a plan is the willingness to throw it away and respond to what's happening in the moment. To go with the flow of where your heart is calling you in the moment. When friends interested in traveling to a place like India tell me all the things they plan to do, I just smile and say to them, "You may have a plan for India, but India also *has a plan for you*."

I am of the belief that our Creator is a better writer and guide than we are, so sometimes the best course of action is just to surrender into the flow of energy, into invisible hands of *your* concept of God or Higher Power, and say: "*Lead* me. *Show* me where you want me to go and what you want me to learn." Then follow the breadcrumbs as they are presented to you, without attachment to the outcome. That's ultimately one of the best lessons of my journey, and something I had to learn the hard way.

The Hardest Part of Traveling

So there you go, there are the basics of traveling. Often I tell people: the hardest part of traveling is just *getting there*. Once you're there, you'll go through the motions of life just like you do at home. You're hungry, you find something to eat. You wander around. You run errands to meet your immediate needs, like "I need shampoo, where can I buy shampoo?" In the natural flow of life, you'll meet people and make new friends. If you're like me, you might flex your courage and learn how to ride a motorbike and find yourself exploring wide open sunny roads on some tropical island where palm trees sway overhead. As you experience the taste of real freedom, your heart warms from the inside while the bright sun of an endless summer warms you from the outside (Video: bit.ly/RidingAMotorbikeInThailand).

Once you're there, life will unfold with the same ease of a flower blossoming. You won't need to force it to happen, nor know how it will happen, only *trust* that it will happen. In fact, it's better that you don't know in advance and leave it up to the Universe to show you the way, step by step and day by day.

But wait, we're still back at home and there's still work to be done to manifest this amazing new reality....

Chapter 7 - Receiving the Way

The mind loves knowing how things will work out in the future, and it becomes an annoying, whiny, fearful scoundrel when it doesn't know how things will happen. The ego desperately *needs* to know in order to feel safe. This is one of the most challenging parts of this process, waking up early in the morning to the sound of your mind loudly banging on your door like an asshole neighbor, and all he wants to know is *how, how, how* and hates you because you're doing a thing that doesn't give him a clear answer. At least, that's how it was for me.

There I was, sitting alone in my little studio apartment in Malden above the Haitian hair salon and the drunk guy who lived downstairs. I had just scrawled out the words *"I am going to India for six months by myself on my twenty-ninth birthday,"* and feeling absolutely overwhelmed by the daunting question of *how* it could possibly happen.

Even though I didn't have the How, what I did have was more important - it was the What and the Why. The What was clear: I was going to India by November 4, 2014. No debate, I was doing it and I would give my blood if I had to. The Why was also in line. I had to do this because I believed there was more to life than just working to pay my bills, and I could not live with myself if I did not fulfill that promise I had made to myself while I still had time. It felt painfully evident to me that time was running out before I became a mother and no longer had the freedom to travel. It felt like the walls were closing in. I was Princess Leia, and it was time to take action and get out of this dump.

But *how*?

You Must Understand This

It's important to understand that you will need to grow and change as a person in order to accomplish your heart's desire. You will need to trust in this process, even, and *especially,* if you do not fully understand it. When you throw the switch of creation with your decision to heed the call of your heart, the energy will move and pieces on the board will begin shift. Some unexpected new pieces that you didn't know existed will be introduced on the board and - if you're "lucky" like me - you'll be wise enough to recognize them and start playing them.

If I can get you to do one thing, just accept that you don't know what you don't know - and that's actually okay. You could freak out about it, which is a perfectly valid choice and certainly one I've entertained with tea and cookies on many a tearful occasion. However, there's a better way. Try saying this aloud, if you dare: "*I choose to stay in the mystery.*" Instead of being afraid of not knowing how it will happen, I encourage you to *get curious* about how it will work out. This involves a level of trust that it *will* work out (as it always tends to do). Trust is a choice, not to mention an act of rebellion against a fear-based way of thinking that tends to catastrophize the future.

Yes, the unknowable future can be a frightening place full of monsters waiting to bite your ankles as you walk by, but so too in the darkness of the unknown just waiting for your discovery are all sorts of new delights and pleasures that you cannot fathom from where you are now. So I invite you to choose to trust that it will work out, get curious about what good things are waiting for you on the path ahead, and in what synchronistic and perfectly timed ways they will find their way to you. Go ahead, step into your curiosity, while trusting that everything is working out in your favor, even if it temporarily sucks. If you're afraid, just know that's okay - just keep moving through the fear, and don't let it stop you.

Personally, I was full of fear and doubts, yet resolved to find a way. I'll never forget that morning I came into my photography studio and started writing in my journal. I wrote out all my thoughts, feelings, anxieties, and expectations, and eventually, I started trying to figure out the answer to a particular question that had been weighing heavily on me: "*How much will this trip cost?*"

How much would I have to earn, save, or find some way to gather? I started breaking it down, figuring the cost of the flight, imagining daily rations for room and food, extra expenses for things I might want to do along the way, expenses for trains and buses - the list went on. I also had to factor in money to pay my bills while I was gone and include a cushion to come back to. I gulped. With wide eyes I looked at the number at the bottom of the page. It was $10,000. Shit. *Really?* Damn it.

I had never seen 10K in my possession before, and back then it seemed like a fortune. How would I do this? An all too familiar lizard of self-doubt crawled up my shoulder and hissed in my ear, "It's impossible, *you fool*," licking his little purple tongue against my ear lobe. *"Scat!"* I said, shooing him away with one hand as I turned back to the pages of my faithful journal and the outrageous number I saw staring back at me.

But again, I was resolved. I *must* do this. I *must* figure out a way. I flexed my courage and started the wheels of my mind in motion. But *how?* The answer didn't come in that moment (*this ain't no instant-noodle process, friends*) but rather the answer arrived through a series of moments - thoughts, conversations, and epiphanies - strung together like Christmas lights that illuminated my path.

Somehow, I arrived at the curious notion that I would try to crowdfund my trip. But there was a problem: I didn't have a crowd. Sure, I had gained a nominal number of fans and friends in my career as an actress and photographer, but my circle was limited and it felt like something was missing.

Why I Started Making Videos Online

Around that time, Brad had been talking to me about this new platform called Patreon. It was a new concept (yet fundamentally "patronage" is very old concept, all the way back to Michelangelo) where people who create creative content give their fans the chance to become patrons of their work. In exchange for a financial contribution every time that creator put out a piece of work, fans would receive insider access, exclusive content, and even gifts. Most importantly, patrons would gain the chance to feel closer to the creator and know they're supporting this person to do their art. *"This could be it!!!"* I thought with multiple exclamation points in my heart.

As great as this idea seemed, the most obvious problem was that I didn't have a crowd. Nor did I have any content. And that's when the idea was born to start a YouTube channel and start making videos online. I decided I would make videos to discover who was my crowd. Who would want to see me go on this adventure, so much so that they might even be willing to financially support me to do it? The idea felt crazy, yet plausible. In fact, I had always felt a kind of tug inside of me to make videos online, but I didn't know what they would be about so I never got started. My rational thinking mind didn't understand, so I didn't take action. "Confused people do nothing," I like to say.

So I had the idea, but I put it off because I didn't know the "right" way to do it. There were times when I felt the desire to press record rise in me, but the part of my mind that doesn't like me doing new and unfamiliar things ran up front with its arms flailing madly and started shouting "No! No!! *NO!!! You're not ready! You don't have your makeup on! You can't do this! Don't do it!"* And so I didn't hit record.

Yet this desire grew inside me like an inflating balloon, and one day the pressure became so great that I needed to let the air out. I'll never forget that moment, sitting in my car. I had just gotten back from a preliminary interview for jury duty and I was sitting in the parking lot just outside Foundry24, about to open the door and get out. That's when I felt that desire to press record rise again. But this time, something *else* came with it. It was my *courage* who ran up the spiral staircase of my spine into my brain and said "Now! Now! NOW! *DO IT NOW!*"

The guy in charge of the self-deprecation department must've been out getting coffee or something, because for this moment the window of opportunity was open. I could feel it. So even though I didn't feel ready, I didn't feel like my hair was right, nor was my makeup, nor was my face in general, and I had no idea what I would say, I pulled out my phone. As my heart raced as if trying to escape from my chest, I pressed record and made my first vlog. It was called "Just Do Something." You can watch it here: <u>bit.ly/ JustDoSomethingVlog</u>

I imagined the finances coming together would be through crowdfunding my trip, so I started making daily videos as honest, vulnerable, and authentic as I could, because I wanted to find the people who loved me *for me*. After watching Brené Brown's phenomenal TED Talk about the Power of Vulnerability (Video: <u>bit.ly/TEDpowerofvulnerability</u>), I understood that if I wanted to reach people's hearts, then I would need to courageously open mine. And I did. I showed my love, my studio, my life, my truth, my fears, and my hardships. I shared my big epiphany (Video: <u>bit.ly/MyEpiphanyVlog</u>) and that self-realization happens in the doing (Video: <u>bit.ly/SelfRealizationHappens</u>).

Every day, I put out a 1-minute video blog on Youtube, and by the time I got to India I had over 250 vlogs of my life in North America shared on my channel. The only thing I wasn't honest about up front was my plan to go to India and to ask people for money to help me do it. I wanted to give my new audience a chance to get to know me first. I wanted to give them something of real value before I asked for support.

I Didn't Expect This to Happen

Then came the episode in our acting studio when asking people for money became something that felt really icky, and I didn't want to do it anymore. You see, one way that I was affording my photography studio in that old factory building is that I split the $900 rent with two other artists. One was my best friend and fellow photographer Morgan (who, by the way, would later come to visit me in India and meet M for a life-changing journey of healing and disruption of old patterns) and an acting teacher named Rich, with whom we started hosting acting classes along the Meisner method. In fact, at that time I liked to say "I can't afford to pay for acting classes so instead I started my own acting studio!"

We advertised the classes on Facebook through Hollywood East Actors Group, and for a time, it went well. But then something shifted. The constant promotion started feeling yucky. I didn't like asking my fellow actors for money for these classes and the whole process started making me feel really uncomfortable. So I pulled away. It came to the point where the last thing on earth I wanted to do was start asking my viewers for money because I wasn't convinced I was giving them real value yet. I didn't want to ask to receive without first *giving* them something of real meaning in their lives.

And yet, the strangest thing happened. People started telling me that my videos were helping them. They said that watching my videos were helping them get through their day, that they enjoyed watching them, and sincerely thanked me for sharing my journey with them. So even though I gave up on the idea of crowdfunding my travels to India, I continued to make daily videos and post them on YouTube and Facebook. The feeling of helping others, just by sharing my story, was enough.

The Arrival of the Unexpected Gift

While I didn't want to ask people for money, I did hold onto that idea that I might have to if I couldn't find another way. But that's when something else unexpected began to happen. Brad had a startup company that offered a new and unique kind of social events photography that used iPad technology they programmed themselves to instantly deliver a photo taken at an event to the delightfully surprised party attendee standing in front of them. Suddenly, business was taking off in a whole new way and - *luckily for me* - one of the partners who had been the main photographer on the team became exceptionally drunk and disagreeable and was asked to leave.

What that meant for me was suddenly, as if out of nothing, new jobs started flowing in. I had already done the work to build up myself to be a reliable professional photographer who could take the jobs, and I did. I took one job, then the next, and the next, and soon enough, that 10K didn't seem so impossible after all.

I had my financial goal clearly defined in my mind as I boosted my own personal marketing on Facebook to let others know that I was available for hire. I went *all in* to get my work out there, scheduling posts to go out every day. So even while I was busy brushing my teeth, people were seeing my work online and messaging me to book a photoshoot. It was a *miracle*!

Letting Go of the Old

While I was saving money and making my calculations, one of the biggest things I realized was holding me back from reaching my financial goal was my rent payment on my little studio apartment in Malden, MA. With a heavy heart, I realized I would have to let it go. *But where would I live? Where would I go?* I didn't have the answer. With hands visibly shaking in fear, I made the call to my landlord and gave him my 30-day notice. As I made that terrifying call, my mind screamed at me that I was insane and that I was going to die for this horrible mistake. Yet something in me trusted that it would work out. Besides, I couldn't live there anymore alone. I couldn't bear it after Brad had packed up his things and left. You see, Brad was crashing at his office in the factory before we started dating. After falling in love and getting our hooks into each other, he moved in with me. We were happy for a time and even had plans to get married. But as time went on, the mountain cracked and things between us began to fall apart.

Getting honest with Brad about my plans to go to India was possibly one of the most difficult and heart-wrenching things I've ever had to do. I had known for weeks that this is what I needed to do, but I avoided telling him for the same reason I often avoided those uncomfortable, honest conversations - I didn't want to hurt him. In fact, that was one of my primary codependent characteristics during these time. I valued the other person's emotional experience over my own, and I constantly tried to manage their emotions at the expense of my truth. I would not speak my truth because I was afraid of how it might affect the other person. I didn't want them to get angry, sad, or hurt, so I didn't say how I was really feeling. I stuffed my truth down where it couldn't hurt anyone except me, like drinking poison. But India was happening. I was thinking, believing, and acting like it was so, and that meant I had to speak it out loud to the people I loved.

Getting Honest with Others Can be Painful

I'll never forget that day. Brad knew something was wrong for weeks. In a weird funk of all the unsaid things we didn't want to admit, we decided to take a walk together to the forest. It was winter at this time, and the ground was covered in snow. The air was freezing, just like my courage had been these past days. As we walked up the hill, I blew my breath into my hands to warm up my fingers and courage. I couldn't deny any longer the truth I had to speak.

We stood together at the top of that icy hill, saying nothing, feeling the immense tension of all the things that had been left unsaid between us. Finally, I ended that pregnant silence by painfully slicing its belly open to deliver the words that would break Brad's heart: "*I'm going to India.*" I might as well have pulled out a dagger and stabbed him in the chest. He took the blade with the strength of a noble warrior, and after collecting whatever pieces of himself that had gotten dislodged, he asked two questions. "*When?*" I explained I was going for six months, for my birthday. Everything about him sunk. "What does that mean *for us?*" he asked. I paused to look out at the city skyline, then answered honestly: "*I don't know.*"

That was by far the most difficult part of this process. More than facing the terrifying uncertainty of the unknown, more than fist-fighting the demons inside of me every day, what hurt the most was hurting the person I had to love. In this process, I had to make the almost unbearable choice to gravely disappoint the person I loved by speaking my truth. A truth that was not what they wanted to hear. In fact, one of the hardest things to do is to speak your truth that you know will make someone angry, disappointed, or hurt because it's not what they want from you.

If they hear those things and become upset, don't backpedal and take away what was just said. No, at that moment, on that frigid hill overlooking Boston, just having stabbed my boyfriend with the knife of my truth, I had to stand there and take it. I had to watch him bleed. I had to watch him turn away from me and start walking slowly down the hill alone, saying nothing, while I cried inside and out. I had to stand there and feel my immense sadness and remorse, cursing this thing inside of me that wanted me to do this crazy thing instead of staying put and making everyone else happy. It takes an enormous strength that I cannot describe to speak your truth and then face the emotional consequences. This is an example of why it can be so hard to listen to your heart, because doing what it asks can cause a lot of suffering in the immediate moment, both to yourself and others. And yet it was a necessary pain, because I knew that what I had wasn't right for me and what was calling to me was too important, even though at that moment I did not understand what it was or why. The only thing I understood then was that *I must go*.

What Kind of People are Around You?

I was lucky that Brad was a strong man. He had integrity and did not try to manipulate me away from my truth using guilt or shame. Fast forward several years and relationships to Alex from London, the Indian martial arts teacher I was dating on Koh Phangan in Thailand. He was a big part of the reason I was working so hard to get back to the island after I met him on one of my earlier trips. After the initial high and rush of the new relationship energy faded with him, I could feel something wasn't right. I struggled to put it into words. I didn't want to rock the ship with my truth. But three weeks before I was to arrive on the island, I was sitting by the river in Exeter, NH, and had him on video call where I finally let out what had been clawing at me from the inside. "I don't want to move in with you," I admitted. "I feel like I need to get my own little house on the island."

This was not what he wanted to hear from me, and he did not respond well. In fact, if I were to give his response a grade based on its emotional maturity, it would have been a C-. Unlike Brad, Alex twisted and contorted in anger, entitlement, and dismay. The look on his face was like an offended conman who was realizing his trick was getting away. That's when he started pulling out the shame and guilt cards, laying them down one by one, telling me how this truth of mine was immensely inconvenient to him, laying on a thick layer of *"shame on you"* for saying this to him. It felt so vile and uncomfortable.

I wanted him to love me after all, so in my codependent nature, I immediately started backpedaling. "I'm not saying I'm making any decisions right now, I just wanted to tell you how I feel," I said. Understanding how I felt was never important to him. Getting what he wanted from me was important to him. Unfortunately, at that point, I was so insecure in myself and eager to be loved by him that I would gladly sacrifice my truth to please him. I would hang it to dry, offering its hide to him in a desperate attempt to win his affection, all while betraying the most sacred thing inside of me.

I share these stories because it's important to understand that not everyone is going to be excited about you connecting with your heart's desire. If you're anything like me, the people closest to you will be fully invested in you staying exactly the same. Any move you make to step out of the role they've pinned you in, like an unfortunate butterfly, will make them upset. Imagine a bug collector who suddenly realizes his favorite butterfly is trying to escape. Some people will call you selfish. That's okay. Maybe you're being selfish for the first time in your life in a way that actually matters. More than anything, this process of getting honest with yourself and others will tell you a lot about the kind of people around you.

The Story of the Crabs

When crabs are together in a trap, the strangest phenomenon will occur. As they're scuttling around the confines of their prison, inevitably one crab will have a hunch to start swimming up. As this "lucky" crab starts the ascent towards the light at the surface, the strangest thing will happen. The other crabs, looking up and seeing their friend beginning to rise, will actually try to *bring them down*. They will literally reach up and try to grab him or her and bring them back to the bottom of the cage. In some cases, this effort becomes so violent they will even dismember and kill this poor crab. But the craziest thing of all is that humans are the same.

When you start swimming up toward your freedom, sometimes the other crabs around you won't like it and they may even try to bring you down. They will use sharp claws of judgment, guilt, and shame. They will tell you you're selfish or crazy. They will do their best to *make you feel bad* for wanting what you want because it's not what they want. It will hurt. Let me tell you, *it will hurt*. And this is where you'll need to summon your strength and all the courage you can call in to hold fast and not retreat. When the hammers of shame, guilt, and doubt are coming down on you, hold fast, even if you crumple. Don't let them break your spine. Don't backpedal. Don't betray your truth. Imagine your spine is made of steel, or Adamantium like Wolverine's claws, and that you will not break. You must not break. And even if you do break, it's okay. Summon your strength and get back up.

So needless to say, this will be an uncomfortable process of undoing the poison and alchemizing the lead of your current life into the gold of your future life. As you step forward, thinking, speaking, and acting on your truth, the people around you may not like it. They may try to scare you, discourage you, and stop you. They may try to break off your claws to keep you down. *Crazy*, right? And that's why this process is pretty amazing, because it tells you a lot about the people around you. Do the people around you want you to follow your heart and be happy? Do they believe in you and lift you up? Or do the people around you want you to confirm their own fear and misery? Do they want you to agree with them that nothing is possible, that you should stay where it's safe and comfortable with them at the bottom of the cage, and the very act of standing up for yourself and your freedom is enough for them to attack you? *WTF* is *that*?

Now granted, most people are running the program of fear in their minds. It's not their fault. It's just the operating system that was installed in them since birth. Most humans will never stop to even notice that they're running a program, let alone make the effort to update or change it. Most people are afraid of the unknown for themselves and for you, especially when they love you. To that I say, don't let people who love you stop you from reaching your dreams. You can thank them for their love and concern, and go about your planning, visioning, and dreaming. And if someone reveals themselves to be unqualified to handle your truth because they try to smash you over the head with fear, shame, or guilt when you speak of it, then stop speaking to them about it. Don't try to convince them; just stop putting your energy there. They have identified themselves as unsafe to handle your baby, so don't give them your baby.

Trust That Help is on the Way

That said, this is the part about receiving, and not letting fear, shame, guilt, or any of those lower vibrations stop you from receiving the manifestation of your desire (and we'll get more into the things that can block you in the next chapter). While things will come up to try to stop you, other things will arrive to help you forward. But you have to stay open to what the tide of energy brings you. Don't shy away from what comes up. Sometimes it will be a new person who walks into your life out of nowhere to offer you the chance to do a thing. Sometimes the opportunity will come from someone you already know, someone who was sitting next to you the whole time who you never suspected would have the solution you needed.

If you stay attached to an expectation of how it will happen, and it doesn't happen that way, *you will suffer*. If you stay attached to a relationship after it stops being good for you, you will suffer. If you stay attached to the old ways of doing things and hold a commitment to repeating these patterns, you will suffer. If you want to suffer, stay firmly attached to what is - to your beliefs, to the structure of your life, to people, places, and things that feel familiar and safe. The tighter your mind holds onto these things, the more it will hurt when it comes time to let them go in order to proceed forward with your heart's desire. So if you want to suffer less, *let go*. Let go of everything you assumed to be true, get on your knees, and ask your Higher Power to lead you.

I had to let go of a lot of things. For one, I had to say goodbye my apartment without knowing where I would live. I had to give away most of my clothes and possessions, and I ended up moving into my photography/acting studio. I illegally crashed there for several months, sleeping on an air mattress on the floor in order to save on the rent money.

I had to change the way I related to money, cut back on my expenses, and teach myself new ways to bring in business. I stopped buying new clothes and other things I wanted. I stopped eating out as much as I could (which, btw, is hard when you live in an old factory with no kitchen). I stopped buying drinks at the bar with friends. If I had had a subscription to Netflix, I would have cancelled it. That's because everything was now going toward my dream. I was focused, like a fart laser, on what I wanted.

When people ask me how I can afford to travel, I say it's like anything else. If you can work hard and save up to buy a car, you can save up to travel. It just requires that you get clear on what you want, work hard, make the necessary sacrifices, and stay focused on your goal on a day to day basis.

So relax, and as the spirit of this book said to me while I was in meditation, "*Trust that it's coming.*" Trust, get curious, and keep your mind and eyes open. I like to pray, "*God, show me the way. Send me signs and give me the eyes to see them.*" And that's because you're swimming through a vast ocean of endless possibilities, but you can only receive them if your net is open. So let go of your mind's old hooks of wanting to control how things will happen and open the net of your intuition. Cast off the barnacles of your expectations and old beliefs and ask the Higher Power of your own understanding to show you the way. And I bet a million bucks that if you are not in a committed relationship to your own poverty and misfortune, and are *willing* to receive something new, *it will be shown to you*. And when it's shown to you, often in unexpected ways, act on it. When the window is open, feel the uncomfortable feelings, but then jump through. Say yes, hit record, do the scary thing, but get going. *Take action.* Your freedom is on the other side.

Just to clarify – because I can already hear the comment in my mind – I'm not telling you to abandon your kids to the wolves to go chase your dream. What I am advising you to realize is that you have within you the capacity to live the life of your dreams. But only if you're willing to speak your truth, keep an open mind, and make some hard choices that may hurt in the moment, but will have a big impact on your future. Take care of your responsibilities and know that where there is a clear desire, a willingness to grow, patience, an open mind, trust, and determined heart, *there will always be a way.*

HOMEWORK:

 SACRED FIRE RITUAL

Another exercise I credit to my amazing coach Reva Wild (@WildErosAwakening) is an exercise designed to consciously, meaningfully, and powerfully direct your energy towards manifesting your desire. You will need thoughtful preparation, dedicated time, and an undisturbed space to harness the limitless creative energies of the Universe. We will be using fire in this exercise, and you can think of the fire as the "Ear of God" where your prayers will be heard. I also encourage you to *rest from judgment and perfectionism* and just look at this as an opportunity to deeply connect with yourself, your own concept of divinity, and the forces that shape your reality.

You will need:

🔥 Fire - This can be a candle, fireplace, or fire pit.

🔥 A bowl of water - This is a safety precaution to ensure you don't accidentally set anything on fire. If you're using a fireplace or fire pit, this may not be necessary.

🔥 Sage or other purifying and cleansing herbs of your choice.

🔥 A list of things to release - Things that are holding you back, your fears, your limiting beliefs, things you want to let go of that are in your way of having what you want, whether they be physical, mental, emotional, or spiritual "Obstacles to Flight."

🔥 A list of things your dreams and desires - What you want to bring in, what you want to call into your experience. This could be a specific trip you want to take, the feelings you want to have, a new and fulfilling relationship, financial abundance, etc. *What do you want?* Big or small, write it out as specifically as you can.

🔥 A single item, or multiple items, that are meaningful to you. This could be a sacred cross, a special crystal, a hawk's feather given to you by your best friend, your grandfather's watch he gave to you before he passed away, whatever. Some item or items that call to you which are deeply meaningful and special for you that help you remember who you are.

How to prepare:

✦ Decide in advance when you will hold this sacred time and space. Put it on your calendar and clear the time and space to be fully available to yourself and this process of working with your energy. If necessary, get out of the house and treat yourself to a special getaway location for the weekend, like a lake house in a beautiful place in nature. If possible, do it during a full moon when the energy is strongest. If you can't synchronize your activity with the moon, don't worry about it - it's better that you do it "imperfectly" than not at all. Remember, there are no wrong answers here.

✦ Spend some quiet time journaling about what you want to release and what you want to call in. Again, there are no right or wrong answers here, it just depends on you and what you deeply desire. Try to be as specific as possible. Ideally, give yourself some silence and meditation as you contemplate and reflect on your values, desires, and priorities. While you're at it, pour yourself a cup of cacao to further open your heart.

✦ Write out your lists on separate pieces of paper. You are going to work with them independently of each other.

✦ On the day of your sacred ceremony, take good care of yourself. Rest well. Eat well. Meditate. Go for a walk in nature. Clean your body by taking a refreshing shower, a relaxing bath, or go for a swim in a natural body of water. Treat yourself, and this moment of your life, as special and important.

✦ Clean your space. Put on some beautiful music. Burn some sweet incense. Burn the sage to clear the energy, just like you would wipe down the counter before you start cooking. Act is if you are welcoming and receiving God into this space - so *make it nice.*

✦ Plan to dress up nicely, in a way that helps you feel beautiful and respectful to the divine, just like you would to go church, a wedding, or other special events. Do make sure you feel comfortable too. Let's call it: "sacred-casual."

✦ Set up your space to your liking with your sacred item(s) around you.

How to Burn:

〜 When it's time to begin, take a moment to fully arrive. Ground yourself with a few deep belly breaths. Mindfully scan your body for tension and let it go. Relax, and become present to this moment. This is your time, and *you have arrived.*

〜 Light your sacred fire with the intention of communing with yourself and the forces of the divine that shape your life.

〜 Call upon the specific energies you want to help you with this work. You can call on God, Jesus Christ, Mother Mary, Mary Magdalene, your spirit guides, or any archangels you feel connected with. I also recommend calling in and honoring the elements of nature, out of which all things are born and made manifest. You can say something like:

"I call upon and honor the spirit of the sacred earth that grows, grounds, and prospers me. I call upon and honor the spirit of the sacred wind that clears away that which is old and stagnant, ushers in new ideas, creativity, inspiration, and the seeds of positive change. I call upon the spirit of

the sacred fire that burns away what no longer serves me, transforms the old into the new, and catalyzes new growth through action. I call upon the spirit of the sacred waters which purify my heart, cleanse my mind, and deliver me new blessings."

You can call upon anyone you like and want to help you, for example, your grandfather or grandmother, ancestors, the spirit of the land, the sun and moon, the earth angels, your plant allies, Isis, Hathor, Osiris, or any other Egyptian deities, Buddha, etc. It's completely up to you what teachers and energies you want to connect with, feel called to work with, are resonant with, and are comfortable working with. You could even call on the spirit of Charlie Chaplin, if that feels right for you. :)

Additionally, something powerful to say is:

"All spirits, all souls, all ascended masters, all beings here, be for the purpose of growth, love, collaboration, connection, and the possibility of the benefit of all beings - for myself, for humanity, and the earth."

Don't worry about saying these exact words. What's most important is that you speak with *feeling and intention*.

➤ When you feel ready, read aloud the list of things you want to release. Don't rush. Take your time to really feel into the words you are speaking.

➤ Put the paper into the fire and watch it burn, trusting that, symbolically, these things are being burned, released, and alchemized into the healing medicine that you need.

➤ Take a moment to close your eyes and feel this release. This is a good moment to shake it off, sing, dance, move, or do anything to help move the energy in a way that feels like it honors and embodies that action of release. You can also use this time to sit quietly and listen for any messages that come in. Whatever feels good for you, do that.

⌇ Next, repeat the process with your list of dreams and desires, with the intention that this burn transforms them into the smoke that goes to the heavens as a prayer for those things to come back down to you made manifest.

⌇ Again, you can dance, shake, sing - whatever feels good for you to move the energy. Then go and sit in a relaxed state of listening and receiving. Make yourself available to receive any messages, guidance, insights, or anything else that wants to emerge into your awareness.

⌇ When it feels complete, close the ceremony by thanking all the elements, energies, and spiritual allies that came to your aid - all of your guides seen and unseen. Offer them your gratitude and invite them to stay if they will, and go if they must. *"Your energy here is honored and appreciated,"* you can say. Close the ceremony by blowing out the candle, or if you're working with a fire in a fireplace that you don't want to immediately put out, you can invite the fire to let go of its ceremonial properties.

⌇ For added spiritual benefit, now is a good time to roast some marshmallows, or give yourself some other treat, as you bask in the faith of the good things coming.

Chapter 8: How We Self-Sabotage Our Dreams

It turns out that it's not the bad guy on the outside we really need to worry about, but rather it's the foe within our own mind who is accountable for holding us back. Both success and failure are an inside job. But what does that really mean? How do we sabotage ourselves, hold ourselves back, and otherwise kill our own energy?

I could write a whole book on the depths of this darkness. Stick your ladle in that soup and you'll find addiction, betrayal, and sadness. You'll find abuse, neglect, and dishonesty. There's suffering of all shapes and flavors, and the craziest part of all is that it's the stuff *I did to myself*. I need to talk about myself, because it would be cowardly to try to point the finger outward now.

What's the difference between selfish self-centeredness and following the call of your heart? What a question. I admit, at times I have been selfish and cruel, and I have used others to make myself feel better. As I flailed around in the darkness there were casualties, and that's something I deeply regret. There was Brad, of course, whose beating heart I ripped out of his chest while he was just trying to love me. But there were others too, like Cailey, who was my dear friend, and who to this day still doesn't talk to me. I think I know why.

The Poison Within

Under the surface, I was full of poison. I was full of fear, pain, and a secret shame that I was somehow bad, unlovable, and guilty of an unforgivable sin, and as such, unworthy of love. In the face of this deeply rooted pain, fear, and shame, I compensated. I compensated for the discomfort inside by drinking alcohol to make myself feel better. I ran away from my uncomfortable reality by smoking weed so I didn't have to feel or look at things I didn't want to face. I conveniently avoided things that made me feel uncomfortable or didn't help me get what I wanted. I "forgot" things all the time. I forgot what I said I would do, and then felt justified to not to it, as if it was someone else's job to remind me. As if it was someone else's job to hold me accountable to my own integrity. I lied. I lied about how I was really feeling for so long. I let my unexamined feelings rot under the surface, so that by the time I did try to express myself honestly, it came out like a messy explosion of toxic fumes and emotional shrapnel.

But the thing is that *I was doing it to myself*. The problem wasn't just that I was numbing myself with weed, alcohol, or some exciting new romance. Those were just the symptoms of the real problem. The real problem, or primary addiction, was to keep my focused away from myself and down in a low vibration. On a weird subconscious level, I was choosing to do this to myself. I was choosing the pattern of abuse. Even though it hurt, and outwardly I was complaining, something inside kept me coming back for more.

Why might a person be addicted to abusing themselves? Why might they choose people who also abuse them, like accomplices to a crime?

What I Was Most Afraid of

I really like Marianne Williamson's quote about fear: "Our deepest fear is not that we are inadequate. Our deepest fear is that we are powerful beyond measure. It is our light, not our darkness that most frightens us. We ask ourselves, who am I to be brilliant, gorgeous, talented, fabulous? Actually, who are you not to be? You are a child of God. Your playing small does not serve the world. There is nothing enlightened about shrinking so that other people won't feel insecure around you. We are all meant to shine, as children do. We were born to make manifest the glory of God that is within us. It's not just in some of us; it's in everyone. And as we let our own light shine, we unconsciously give other people permission to do the same. As we are liberated from our own fear, our presence automatically liberates others."

So in truth, it's not the darkness we really fear. What's far more terrifying is the possibility of stepping up and out into the light of our true potential. For me, the darkness is actually quite familiar and comforting, even though it hurts. I know myself well in the sadness, the confusion, the drama, the heartache, the back-and-forth tug of war between shame and guilt, and the manipulation I endure because, well, *it feels familiar.* It's what I learned to do. I never learned any other way. And actually, I get something out of playing this game. Even though I complain as I play the game, I do it because it does something for me. But *what?*

Staying in my darkness lets me stay small. It lets me stay hidden away from the potential who I could be. While this noble eagle within me wants to fly free as its birthright, there's also another side of me, powerful and heavy, like a giant serpent that silently slithers below the surface of my conscious mind. And this part of my subconscious mind wants to keep me down. In fact, staying in that lower vibration feels safe in a way, because it means I don't have to do anything. If I resign into my depression, anxiety, shame, and fear, then I absolve myself of any responsibility to show up and be seen. And that feels like a *relief.* So in a way, I hid in my darkness and dimmed my light, doing things that would keep me in that low place, because it felt safer to hide than to be present in the high sensation of my highest and brightest potential.

I'm not proud of a lot of the things I've done. I'm not proud of the people I hurt. I'm not proud of the times I smoked weed or drank alcohol when my intuition was telling me not to. I was a coward not to listen because all I could think about was taking the easy route, the one that would give me instant relief from whatever pain or discomfort I was feeling. I'm not proud of the way I procrastinated or didn't show up when it was important. When things got intense, I drank or drugged to avoid or numb my feelings, giving myself a momentary relief from the pressure, but ultimately sacrificed my integrity and caused even more pain to myself and others. Then I used that pain as a convenient excuse to continue to hide away from the world and my dreams. It was a vicious cycle of abuse that I was addicted to, because it *let me play small*. Even though it hurt, it also felt familiar, safe, and it satisfied me in a way my conscious mind would never admit - in spite of the destructive consequences of my choices.

Finding Peace in my Discomfort

The thing about changing your life is that it's actually a process of changing your vibration - or level of frequency - and that is often very uncomfortable. Take, for example, the ride to Lake Atitlan in Guatemala, from where I currently write these words, perched on a volcanic rock protruding from the side of the mountain in Hummingbird Valley.

In order to arrive at this magical Valley of Hummingbirds, you must first pass through a massive mountain range. I didn't understand why I saw so many helicopters at the airport when I arrived in Guatemala City, but I do now. It's because driving through the mountains *sucks*. As you change altitude - or level of frequency let's call it - you can get really nauseated. Personally, I get so physically uncomfortable that I feel like I could throw up.

It wasn't until I was in Egypt that I had a revelation and the truth became clear. In fact, I also often felt physically nauseated going through the transformation on that sacred pilgrimage to Egypt. While we were not climbing mountains on the outside, I certainly felt like I was on the inside. As we ventured into the King's Chamber and the even more powerful Queen's Chamber of the Great Pyramid in Giza, as we came into audience with Isis, Hathor, Thoth, and Sekhmet, I started feeling really uncomfortable inside. I was getting triggered. Intense feelings were coming up and old patterns were rising to the surface. I got to see the ways I used to keep myself down. Once the excitement of arriving in Egypt faded, I found myself following old patterns. I started feeling bad about myself, comparing myself unfairly to the other women in the group, feeling less than them and not enough, indulging in self-pity, and then following an all too familiar pattern that lead me straight into a lonely pit of depression. I can't tell you how awful it feels to be on a luxury boat floating down the Nile River while feeling as worthless as a sad lookin' piece of poo on the floor.

Ouch.

As Mercury went Retrograde in Scorpio, I had a revelation. These feelings I was having were actually how I had trained myself to respond at the doorway of stepping into a higher vibration, which was what this sacred pilgrimage was calling me to do. In order to keep myself from passing through the mountain range into a higher vibration, I was subconsciously finding a way to sabotage my own passing. I was unconsciously blocking my own ascent, because it felt easier and more comfortable to stay on lower ground. I was both the crab trying to swim toward the light, and the other one, cutting off my claws.

One of my primary self-destructive patterns I used on this trip, and in life, was to compare myself to others. Using a comparative ranking system based on external standards, I kept myself low, and subsequently I learned to base my sense of self-esteem and self-worth on something or someone outside of myself. This strategy stemmed from my childhood when I felt like my older sister was better than me in every way, not to mention that I grew up in a culture that engrained in me the idea that you have to get straight

A's and be a good girl or boy all the time in order to have value as a person. Unchecked, this pattern extended into my adulthood, and I played out the same old pattern of self-limiting beliefs from the past using standards set by the external world to feel bad about myself. I engaged thoughts that lead me to feel like I had no worth or value as a person because I wasn't as talented, beautiful, successful, or abundant as I perceived others to be. Then, I would withdraw and isolate myself in my cave of sadness and then do nothing, not show up, content to curl up into a little ball of self-pity and *"I don't know, I don't care, and nothing matters anyway."* It's like getting off with your own tears. You say it sucks and you don't like it, but you do it all the same - because it does something for you.

How to Stop the Madness

So how do we stop the madness? How do we stop hurting ourselves and holding ourselves back from achieving our dream, whether that be to go travel, or whatever else you know in your heart you *must* do?

The first step towards change is to recognize that we're doing it to ourselves in the first place - that you are the one *responsible* for holding yourself back. To admit that yes, you have a problem, and you are at the source. Now, this is not about playing the judgment game to paint yourself with guilt and shame, and then to inhale the toxic fumes of self-pity. That's an old pattern, and frankly, it doesn't get us very far. The real healing work is about finally and fully recognizing that you are the creator of your reality, and that *your patterns are the source of your experience.*

Real and lasting change begins the moment you recognize this and decide to take responsibility for your experience - for your inputs and outputs. If you got yourself into this mess, you can get yourself out. In fact, that was the big realization I had in one of my darkest moments after that devastating failure of control when the group trip with M fell apart in India. My ego was shattered. I stopped trusting M and I became very sick in body and mind. There I was, standing alone in my hotel room in New Delhi. I was sick, emotionally defeated, and just disgusted with myself and my situation. I was so sick that I had just vomited and pissed myself at the same time, which is perhaps one of the most humbling and disheartening experiences a person can have.

As I was standing in that vile hotel room, staring at the floor and just feeling a level of misery that words cannot describe, I had an epiphany. *I did this*. It was all me. My thoughts and choices got me into this situation. That's when I understood the truth: that meant my thoughts and choices could also get me out. That single moment was possibly one of the most profound moments of my story because for the first time I really understood that *I was responsible for my life*. While the series of disappointing events that played out were not exactly my fault, I became empowered the moment I realized that I was indeed responsible for what had happened to me, and even more so, for what I chose to think and do next.

In order to change your patterns, raise your vibration, take your power back, and reclaim your life, you *must* accept that you are at the center of the pond. Everything you experience ripples out from the vibration you hold at the center. Now, I know some people will want to disagree with me at this point. They'll say, "The accident was an accident." Or, "The sickness was out of my control." And so on. What I hope to guide you into seeing is that yes, in a weird way, maybe you did call it in. But I'm not saying what happened is your *fault*. It's another one of those weird paradoxes, I know. What I'm saying is that while it's *not* your *fault*, it *is* your *responsibility* of how you respond. You are not to blame for what happened to you, but you are responsible for what you do with it, and what you make it mean. There's this great quote from Buddha on the wall of the outdoor shower at Karuna Atitlan. It says, "Every experience, no matter how bad it seems, holds within it a blessing of some kind. The goal is to find it."

Nobody intentionally wants to get sick, hurt, to experience the tragic death of their child, or any of the other ways we suffer as humans. All I'm saying is that the suffering can be our teacher and our guide if we let it. If we surrender into it and ask to be shown the deeper lesson. What happens when something about the way we are living, believing, and speaking is out of alignment with the truth of our greatest and highest good? What if our soul, conspiring with the mysterious forces of the Universe that know neither "right" nor "wrong," is trying to get our attention and guide us towards another path?

Perhaps there were signs and signals our bodies and intuition were trying to send us before, but we weren't listening. Sometimes, and very understandably, we don't want to listen to or see the misalignment in our energy. Sometimes the mind isn't ready to accept what the intuition knows and is trying to communicate. Often times we would rather avoid facing the truth, shut our eyes, and stick our fingers in our ears like a little child and go *"nah, nah, nah I can't hear you!"* and pretend everything is okay. But what happens then? Your soul will find another way to get your attention, just like any teacher. And it will get louder until you wake up.

Sometimes that will take the form of a fall and cracking your head on a rock and getting a concussion. Sometimes it will show up as cancer in your guts. Sometimes someone close to you will die. These are all the ways the unseen forces of life coalesce in an effort to get your attention and send you a message to help you change your course. If you don't want to believe this notion, that's okay. It's your right to decide what you believe.

What I'm saying is that you can choose to see these events as meaningless suffering, or you can choose to receive your suffering as a wake up call, as a catalyst to start making some changes in your life, and forge a new path. The pitfall of suffering is to use it for self-loathing or self-pity, which is a kind of self-indulgence. It's a way to use whatever unfortunate, painful thing that happened as a way to get cheap energy by playing the victim. However, if properly grieved and processed in healthy and appropriate ways, suffering can be a valuable tool for learning, self-empowerment, and healing. Like Luke said in the foreword, "If suffering is a teacher, healing is the lesson."

If you really want to heal yourself, take your power back, and change your life, then I invite you to try on this notion that you are indeed the center of your reality. While it can suck to look at what you have and not like what you see, it could also be for you as it was for me in that vile hotel room in New Delhi that smelled like shit and vomit. Suddenly, amidst all the misery, I was empowered because I realized that I had done it to myself. If I had done it, then I could also undo it - by changing my thoughts, my beliefs, my words, my actions, and my choices. In order to change my situation, I had to change at the source. I had to change *me*.

Addicted to the Keeping Ourselves Down

Now let's cross lines with addiction. Addiction is something that lets us play small, that keeps us running in the same deeply engrained lines with little chance of escape. It's something we do that hurts us, and often others, and makes our lives unmanageable. It's a kind of insanity that keeps us doing the same destructive behavior over and over again while expecting a different result.

Addiction is the difference between letting yourself smoke one cigarette while you're grieving the loss of your pet, versus chain smoking all day because you feel angry. It's the difference between taking a nap when you feel tired, versus sleeping all day when you're feeling depressed. It's the difference between smoking weed to isolate yourself, instead of facing an uncomfortable conversation you know you need to have with someone and then sharing a joint with them at the end of it as an act of communion. It's the difference between enjoying a piece of chocolate cake, versus pounding a whole chocolate cake to numb your feelings. The thing itself is not the problem, but rather it's how we use it to hide or avoid our feelings.

When most people think of addiction, we think of drugs and alcohol. They're obvious, they're right in our faces, and we can see the inputs and outputs quite clearly. But what Seulki helped me understand (and you can watch a free video lesson about it here: bit.ly/SeulkiEnergyAddictions) is that more than anything, we form addictions to *energy* and ways of getting it. Some people (and maybe you know them?) are addicted to resisting, using anger and fighting, blaming and shaming, or judging and complaining. They just can't seem to stop, and that's because this is how they learned to get energy and a sense of place, power, and identity.

For me, in the past I've struggled with an addiction or tendency to being an energy parasite on others, and the people I was attracted to or chose to stay close to were people whose own energy dynamics reflected, complemented, and enabled me. I was naturally and unconsciously looking for someone to save me, to complete me, to feed me, to nurture me, to provide for me, and essentially to give me their energy, because I felt like I didn't had enough on my own.

This unhealthy pattern had a lot to do with some experiences that happened to me in my developmental years as a new human on the planet, when my parents got divorced when I was a teenager. I love my parents deeply, and looking back, I know my parents did the best they could at the time with what they had going on in their lives. However, the reality for me at the time was that it was a pretty traumatic experience for me as a young person just stepping into the world. I got the short end of the divorce and it felt like I was being left out to the wolves. I felt abandoned and exposed in a big scary world, and this made me feel very unsafe and wounded at the root of my being.

At this time, I was overwhelmed with fear, I had painfully low self-esteem, and because I didn't believe in myself or trust myself, I looked for someone stronger to save me - like a prince charming. What I found instead were highly toxic, codependent relationships that ended up hurting me. And I settled for them because I was full of fear and I didn't love myself. I interpreted the things that happened to me while I was just being initiated into life on this planet to mean that there was something inherently wrong with me, that my sister was better, that I didn't deserve love, support, and nurturing the way she did.

I went forward into my future feeling like I was not enough no matter what I did or chose, and instead of facing and healing the original wound - the root of my problem - I looked for a bandaid: something or someone to make me feel better, to give me that sense of relief from that inner turmoil I was constantly feeling. I just wanted someone, anyone, to love me and make me feel safe. To make me feel okay. And do you know who naturally attracts a parasite? A martyr. Someone who gives too much without strong boundaries to protect themselves, and they give and give until they are steaming with their own anger and resentment over what they feel was taken from them. The martyr may act like a victim of the parasite, when in fact the martyr archetype willingly gives of themselves without adequate boundaries and protections for themselves. They feel they are supposed to give, and often it comes out of a sense of obligation or guilt, because it's what they "should" do. The martyr wants to feel needed, so they give too much in a self-righteous act of self-destruction in order to feel valued and wanted by others.

These dysfunctional energy dynamics are our way to get the love and energy we want and feel we didn't get in childhood. As new humans on the planet, often times we didn't receive the appropriate nurturing and support we needed from our caregivers (who were often doing the best they could and didn't know any better), and so we learned to adopt maladapted coping strategies in order to get our energetic, emotional, and physical needs met.

A vampire doesn't just become a vampire for the sake of it. They end up taking too much from others because they don't feel like they have enough. They don't feel like they *are* enough, they doubt themselves and their own worth, so they lie, manipulate, and take too much from others because that's how they learned to get the energy they needed to survive. It's not that they're bad people, it's just that they're looking for nurturing and safety from the outside. They haven't yet learned how to properly nurture themselves and cultivate energy from an inner source, so they keep their focus on taking energy from others.

I am of the belief that these toxic energy dynamics all stem from an overgrowth of fear and unexamined shame from our pain and traumas of the past, often times from our families and the love and safety we feel we didn't get when we were new humans on the planet. This is why we violate ourselves and each other, and why it's *so* important that we each do our inner work - to heal the original wounds from childhood. We do these toxic dances with our friends, partners, roommates, families, and lovers in an attempt to feel safe - and ultimately we sacrifice our true freedom in the process.

So if we do what we do in order to help ourselves feel safe, and if that's why others do what they're doing, even if we don't understand or agree with their actions, that's why it's *so* important

146

that we treat each other with love and compassion. We must try to see that we are each learning to overcome the dilemmas of our childhoods. And this is why it's so important to not judge, shame, or condemn ourselves and each other, but to recognize that we are all still *learning* how to be human.

We would not shame a child who is learning to walk when they fall. We would help them get back up and give them encouragement to try again, knowing that they're learning and will not get each step perfectly. This mindset implies compassion and forgiveness, and that's the key to a successful learning process. The healing journey is like this - it requires practicing new skills, which we won't always get right, especially when we're doing the work to change old, deeply engrained survival patterns. And that's precisely why we must treat ourselves and each other with compassion and forgiveness when we miss a step and fall. In that way, we can play a supportive role in our own and each other's healing and learning, instead of being another voice that further shames and condemns us for being wrong and bad.

Of all the people I hurt - myself included - I never did it maliciously. It's very rare that someone will hurt someone else knowing what they're doing. Rather, the pain and suffering I caused to myself and others was an unconscious act stemming from my own untended wounds and rampant fears of rejection and abandonment. "Assume no ill will" is a great philosophy to live by, especially when we're assessing the actions of others. Alex wasn't intentionally a vampire, it was just a survival strategy he learned as he faced and endured the challenges and rejections of his early life. I didn't set out to be a parasite either, it was just a strategy I developed because, unconsciously, I felt alone and unsafe with myself, and at a primal level, it felt like my survival was at stake. I hadn't learned yet how to be my own source of nurturing. While outwardly, I came across as an upbeat and confident person, inside

I was scared. I didn't believe I was enough. And so I wanted someone else to take care of me because it made me feel safe, loved, and I didn't trust that I could do it myself. So I did these things that caused hurt to others for innocent reasons: to feel better, to feel safe, and to feel loved.

And yet sometimes, people *will* hurt each other intentionally. Yesterday, to start writing this chapter, I followed Luke and two women on our Karuna "Writing Your Dreams True" writer's retreat up the mountain. We arrived at a little seating area with an altar constructed out of concrete blocks. Luke explained how this was the second altar they built because someone smashed the first one. He recounted how the builder called him in tears to report the offense. True to Luke's style, he breathed deeply and told the builder to build it again, and that each block he replaced was to be a prayer of forgiveness for the perpetrators of the crime because they were hurting on the inside - which is why they destroyed things on the outside. *Hurt people*, *hurt* people. Like Jesus said up on the cross, "Forgive them, Father, they know not what they're doing." And by that I think he means everyone deserves to be handled with compassion, because we are all full of fear, poison, and hurting on the inside, which is ultimately why we hurt each other and ourselves.

Again, that's why compassion is the answer - with ourselves and others. We must remember that everyone is going through their own journey, their own process, and we are all *learning* (some more willingly than others). It's not our job to fix, save, or rescue anyone else from their choices. It's our job to support their learning by holding them with compassion, accountability, and to remember their inherent innocence and worthiness, even if we don't understand or agree with their choices or actions. Love the other learners, accept them in all their imperfect humanness, help them when it is safe and appropriate to do so, but let them make their

148

choices (and yes, endure the consequences) while also remembering to take care of ourselves in healthy ways that fulfill our own needs and protect ourselves with strong boundaries. When we stop enabling the dysfunction of others, playing these games that cause us to leak our precious life-force energy by trying to manage someone else's process, and instead make the choice to come back to ourselves and plug the leaks in our own system, we will then have more energetic nourishment to give where it matters.

So where does true freedom lie? True freedom lies when we lay down our weapons and walk toward the monster with forgiveness, compassion, and love, instead of anger, resentment, shame, blame, judgment, and fear. Instead of running away and avoiding the problem, instead of distracting ourselves from the pain, instead we heal and change the pattern by *facing it*.

How to Face Your Monsters

Krishna and Govinda were in the forest and night was falling. They decided they would take turns keeping watch while the other slept. Govinda took the first watch while Krishna went to sleep. As the night rose around him, so did his fear. Unfamiliar sounds bumped and swished and Govinda's heart raced. Suddenly, out from the bushes appeared a gigantic, ferocious-looking monster. It had long fangs and wild eyes and upon seeing this creature, Govinda fainted. As his body collapsed on the ground, Krishna roused from his slumber. He stood up, yawning and stretching, and saw the monster. "Oh, hello," he said with childlike curiosity.

As the monster roared and took a menacing step toward him, fangs bared, Krishna merely smiled and laughed. Krishna started walking toward the monster as if he was approaching a friend. As he did, the most curious thing began to happen. The monster started shrinking. Shrinking and shrinking as Krishna got closer

149

and closer. With great care and affection, Krishna picked up the monster, who was now the size of a chipmunk, and placed him gently in his pocket. Govinda soon woke up and upon seeing his dear friend said "Krishna! Krishna! I'm so glad you're okay! There was the most horrible monster and I thought we were done for." Looking around and seeing no monster, confusion fell across his face. "Wait a minute, what happened to the monster?" Govinda asked his friend. Krishna happily pulled the little chipmunk-sized monster out of his pocket with a smile, saying "What, *this* monster?"

So you see, the monsters stay big and scary the further away from them we stay. The more we run and hide from them, the more they have power over us. So how do we change? How do we heal? I love Teal Swan's videos on YouTube, and especially the one where she talks about healing and what it really is (Video: bit.ly/WhatisHealing). She states plainly that healing is nothing more than changing a pattern. What's the first step to changing a pattern? The first step is to recognize what the pattern is. As my friends at the Kembali Recovery Center in Bali taught me, "You cannot heal or change anything you do not acknowledge." If you see your patterns are not giving you the outputs that enrich and enliven you, then it's time to make the choice if you're going to allow them to continue, or if you're going to do something to change them.

This was what my time in Bali was all about. You see, I hit a kind of spiritual bottom in Thailand thanks to my ex Alex. I was so "in love" with him that I made him out to be someone he was not. I conferred upon him the abilities of someone else, the hero of my dreams who would ride in and save me from my own confusion, self-doubt, and deep inner sadness. I imagined a vision of us being a power couple and all the great things we would do together as the wind under each others' wings. I held the expectation of us supporting each other into our greatness. We were going to build a business together and take over the world! Or so I thought. What I was actually doing was placing unrealistic expectations on him and the role he would play in my life, and I gave him a lot of power over me - something he did not deserve. Instead of a being powerful man who would give me the sense of safety I desperately sought, the reality of what I got with him was more like an entitled, angry boy in the body of a man who was looking for a mother to take care of him.

What I got was someone who mirrored my own addictions. Someone who was a *reflection* of my own inability and unwillingness to face the repressed and undigested anger and sadness inside me. He was someone with whom I could engage in my own addiction to be the rescuer, aka the martyr, giving him everything I had to try to lift him up and help him fly. Doing this I got to feel good and valued, important and loved by playing this role where I feel needed by him for what I could do for him. A role where I'm going to come in and save you, where I'm going to help you and give you all my energy so you can grow. I was going to help him with his business and all the things, and we were going to support each other - or at least I thought so.

Along this vein, I loaned him money to this day, years later, he still has not paid back and probably never will. Like a victim and a good blood donor, I willingly bled for him, longing for his love and approval, and like a good vampire - an entitled liar and master manipulator - he gladly drank.

There's one thing I'd like to make clear though. I see clearly now that was *not* his victim, as much as I wanted to think of myself in the heartache that followed our breakup. While it's not my *fault* that he lied to me and didn't pay me back when he said he would, now I see that it was my *responsibility* for choosing this kind of partner. It was *my choice* to engage in this dynamic instead of facing myself and my own issues. I willingly played the game, putting the focus on him, and kept playing even when I could feel something wasn't right. I was responsible for my choice to give him money, even though I could feel my body was contracting at the thought and my intuition was screaming at me not to do it. In fact, it was as if I was the one who willingly slit open my own veins and offered him a drink, because I wanted him to love me, even though I could feel it was hurting me.

By ignoring the signals from my intuition, minimizing my own needs and desires, not standing up for myself and what I wanted, needed, and cared about, and ultimately by placing someone else's experience before my own, I was creating the prison that I felt trapped in. Even though he was the one who disappointed and hurt me, *I was the one responsible for allowing it to happen to me.*

Healing What's Outside Starts Inside

I made mistakes in *so* many relationships and caused profound harm to myself and others because of my addictions and lack of self-esteem. Sometimes I was the parasite or vampire, feeding off the energy of the martyr whose own pain and dysfunction perfectly complemented my own. Sometimes I was the rescuer and sometimes I was the one who was being rescued. Most times I gave too much, content to play the martyr role. The martyr is the kind of energy that feeds and nurtures everyone and ends up feeling depleted and unappreciated.

I oscillated between the roles of parasite, vampire, martyr, and victim, sometimes playing them all in the course of one day. I slipped into those toxic roles as easily as I would my favorite pair of shoes, tried and true, and oh the vast distances we covered together. I naturally gravitated towards and partnered up with people who helped me play these games, like energetic puzzle pieces fitting together. I was getting energy, sure, but on the inside I was angry, resentful, fearful, sad, dishonest, selfish, self-seeking, afraid of being rejected or abandoned, doubting myself, trying to please everyone else without regard for the damage I was causing myself, and generally existing at a low vibration. It's no wonder I sought some kind of relief from this inner turmoil.

All along the way, my intuition knew something was off (and we're going to get more into the ways our intuition speaks to us in Chapter 10). It was *trying* to talk to me, but I wasn't listening. In fact, I remember one instance as clear as day. I touched a selenite stone and received the message loud and clear: "Let him go." I was shocked. I didn't understand it. I didn't like it. And I sure as hell didn't want to be responsible for taking action on what I heard, so I ignored it. I put the stone down and pretended I hadn't heard it. Learning to connect with your intuition is a wonderful thing, but I'll offer you a disclaimer: you might not want to hear what it has to say. For me, for example, I didn't want to look at the reality that I was dating a vampire who was feeding off my lack of boundaries. Or that I was a flaming parasite. Or that my victimhood and entitlement were out of control and at the root of so much of my discontent.

In the example of dear Alex, I had felt something was off and felt called to get my own place instead of moving in with him. When I tried to admit how I was really feeling, he responded with a heavy dose of anger, guilt, and shame - as energy vampires are prone to do. In the heat of his anger and disapproval, I retreated. Backpedaling on my truth was not what I wanted to do - especially as I was trying to to stand up for myself. But I was too afraid of being rejected by him, so I caved and did what he wanted. This pattern of not standing up for myself and what I wanted, and instead being coerced into fulfilling the needs and desires of others while minimizing my own, ended up hurting me a lot. But it was also a great learning experience that gave me valuable perspective so I could start to do things differently. Failure can be a great teacher like that.

While it was important for me to have this painful experience, it was also important for me to learn how to get myself out of it and learn a new way. I believe that's why I was led to meet my teacher Seulki Koo (if you haven't already, check out her teachings and offerings at www.seulkikoo.com) on my third day on the island and embarked on two courses with her that would forever change my life and my relationships. The first was "Boundaries and Self-Awareness for Empaths," followed by "Developing Your Intuitive Abilities." In these two life-changing courses, I was able to see myself and my patterns in a whole new way.

I got a whole new perspective and understanding on what M meant with those simple words "I jump my energy too fast." What that really meant was that I was *addicted* to getting my sense of value and self-worth by inappropriately serving others, by giving too much energy and focus to others, and not enough to myself. In spite of my good intentions, everything I was giving was coming from a place of guilt, shame, obligation, and generally compensating for my lack of self-esteem in an attempt to win love and acceptance from others in order to create a false sense of safety. I wasn't taking care of myself, and then I was giving from an empty cup all while expecting others to fill it up for me. By choosing to do this I ended up feeling drained, sad, resentful, unappreciated, and hurt, when - in fact - *I was doing it to myself.*

Signs You're Violating Yourself

I've come to recognize some signs that indicate I'm not standing up for myself, and instead, I'm getting lost in another person in a potentially unhealthy or codependent way.

A big red flag is when I'm not getting enough sleep because I change my routines to accommodate the other person and their routines, and in doing so, I sacrifice appropriately meeting my own needs. Giving things like my time and resources that I don't really mean to give, and finding myself doing it out of feelings of guilt or obligation, is another red flag that I am misaligned with my best and highest interest. Having loose or no clearly defined boundaries with myself and others means I end up saying yes when I really meant to say no, and consequently, I find myself doing things I didn't really mean or want to do, which is no bueno. When I focus all my attention on the other person and their reality, I become unclear of my own goals and priorities, and that certainly doesn't help me achieve them. Obsessively needing and thinking about the other person becomes a huge drain, especially when it leads to trying too hard to get their attention, affection, or approval. Consequently, in these situations of unhealthy, codependent relating, I often end up giving more energetic focus and nourishment to the other person and insufficient nourishment to myself. And I have suffered for it.

This is not freedom, this is a kind of slavery and addiction to the other. No wonder in these kinds of relationships I was sad and tired all the time, and my integrity was in shambles. I was so desperate for a sense of love and belonging, I would give or tell you whatever I thought you wanted so you wouldn't reject me, as I had felt by my parents. That kind of fear runs deep in a person and their unconscious. And I didn't realize I was doing this until things got bad enough and I *had* to wake up, simply because I could not go on living this way.

Seulki laid it out even clearer: she taught me there are four main red flags you're violating yourself and what's good for you. Be careful if you find yourself saying or using these justifications or excuses for your choices. It could be a sign you're not in alignment with yourself, and making other people's reality more important than your own. The first sign is when you do something

155

that doesn't feel good or right for you, but you justify it by saying "I can handle it." You feel a contraction or uncomfortable feeling in your body, but you choose to endure it instead of recognizing your discomfort and speaking up. That's not a good sign, and that's why Seulki's motto is "Never endure anything." It's like when I sent Alex that money - my body tightened up, and something didn't feel right inside me, but I ignored it. Even though it palpably didn't feel right in my body, I was like, "It's okay, I can afford [handle] it." Months later, when I could barely afford my plane ticket home from Bali, you better believe I was regretting that decision not to listen to what felt right for me.

The next red flag that you may be violating yourself is using the relationship as an excuse. Be careful and aware if you find yourself saying "Well, it's my mother so I have to do it," or "It's my husband, so I should say yes." Using your relationship to this person as a justification to do something that doesn't feel right for you - to violate your own boundaries - is no bueno. In the same case of this loan, I did it because he was my boyfriend, and I didn't want to see him suffer because I cared about him. I believed his victim sob story, and we said we would support each other, when in reality that actually meant *I* would support *him*. My intuition said don't do it, but I used this logical red flag as my excuse, and I was deeply hurt for it. If I had listened to my wise inner knowing, I would've saved myself a lot of heartache and grief!

Next, another thing to look out for, according to Seulki, is saying something like "Well, if she's happy, I'm happy." That, my friends, is a flaming sign of codependent behavior, which means you're not standing up for yourself and your reality, but rather caving into someone else's and making someone else's emotional experience more important than your own. That is *not* the path to personal joy and freedom. Basing your choices on what someone else wants is how you get yourself into situations that do not feel right, and sometimes, situations that are unsafe or unhealthy for you, as is evident with my situation with Mr-Not-So-Charming.

The last sign you're violating yourself is saying something like "Well, they need it more than me." Using that kind of statement as an excuse to justify doing or giving something that doesn't feel right is not fair to you and what you need to be happy and whole, and when we're giving from that kind of spirit then we're giving from a place of guilt and obligation, instead of a place of genuine generosity. Again, the loan. >face smack< *Sigh.*

Granted, there will be instances when it's okay to push through our boundaries in order to help other people, especially when it comes to children and people who are not able to take care of themselves. I think it comes down to having strong discernment from situation to situation, knowing yourself and your limits, and ultimately recognizing the distinctions between genuinely helping rather than enabling the dysfunctional behaviors of others.

What are Boundaries?

Treating others with love, acceptance, and compassion - especially people who are hurting you - doesn't mean you have to keep the a dysfunctional person close or condone their behavior. In fact, I think remembering to choose compassion, practice loving detachment, and holding strong boundaries are a winning combination to protect you and your precious life-force energy so you can live the life you truly want.

In my darkest, most toxic, unhealthy, addicted, codependent, and love-starved times, I had zero boundaries. None. Zip. Nada. No one ever talked to me about boundaries and consent, nor modeled them for me. So as a new human, I never learned what they were or how to use them until I took that first class from Seulki. As it turns out, healthy boundaries are *the key* to living in our joy, being true to ourselves, having healthy relationships, manifesting our dreams, meaningfully serving others out of true spirit of generosity, and ultimately, taking responsibility for what's ours and letting go of what's not.

So what are boundaries and how do we use them?

Imagine we are sitting together at a table. You are very thirsty and I just happen to have the most thirst-quenching water to share with you. This water has been loved, its crystals are vibrant, dynamic, and glowing with aliveness. This could possibly be the most satisfying and life-giving drink of your life, and *oh friend*, do I want to serve it to you. In fact, there's nothing my heart wants more than to give you the gift of this water, and in doing so, to give you the gift of life.

Now, if I reach over and just start pouring out the water onto the table, what happens? Well, it makes a *mess!* The water spills across the table, onto the floor, and not to mention onto your lap. Instead of getting the most satisfying drink of your life, now you have to explain why it looks like you peed yourself. Needless to say, you're not happy with me and our exchange, and neither am I. While my good intentions were activated and seated in their designated places in the rocket ship, we failed to achieve lift-off. Actually, the rocket ship exploded and everyone died. *Shit*.

Rewind the scene. We're looking deeply into each other's eyes from across the table, a soft and knowing smile shared between us. You're thirsty and I want to give you that drink. This time, what do I do? I place a chalice on the table. It's made of elegant crystal, and into *this* vessel I pour my gift - the water of life that represents my time and energy I wish to share with you. I pick it up and pass it to you with a big smile on my face and generosity overflowing from my heart. With enormous gratitude, you lift the cup to your lips and receive the most satisfying drink of your life. This time, no explanations of why you look like you peed yourself are required (unless, of course, it's *so* satisfying that perhaps the explanation will be required after all).

So in one instance, I had very good intentions. I wanted to help and contribute to your wellbeing, but I ended up making a mess of things. In another instance, we had a satisfying exchange of the gift I was sent to earth to deliver. What's the difference? The cup, of course. And what is the defining factor of the cup? The container that's created by its walls. The constraints of the cup that hold the water in are its *boundaries*. They keep in what needs to be kept in, and they keep out what doesn't need to be there. *The boundaries of the cup protect the wholeness of the gift.*

Now, what did it look like in my life when I didn't have healthy boundaries? My water was spilling everywhere. I would commit to things with the best of intentions, but without appropriate boundaries to support those words and intentions - and then I wouldn't show up in the way I promised. And because of that lack of alignment and integrity, I disappointed a lot of people. And worst of all, as I made a mess of things, I consequently didn't like myself very much either. Neither did a lot of other people I was close to.

I think back to my times at Labracadabra, so ripe with opportunity and potential. While we had some fun and amazing times there, I look back with both a sweet and sour taste. That's because most of the time I committed to something, in the end I didn't do what I said I would do. I would get excited about projects and things I wanted to help with that I threw my words around without any thought or structure to support them. Because of this, I ended up not showing up for my friends in a way that really disappointed them and led them to lose trust in me. "If Erica says she'll do it, it probably won't happen," was the consensus, which I relay with great pain and regret.

Here's the thing: I wanted to be loved. I wanted to be in service. I wanted to participate and contribute. I wanted to be part of the fun with the group and feel like I was welcome and belonged with the cool kids. But because I was still jumping my energy all over the place (and if you watched my earlier videos, you could probably feel it) I wasn't connected to my truth of what I could actually give from a full cup.

I wasn't taking care of myself, and consequently, I was constantly over extending myself, making empty promises in moments of excitement because I wanted to help, be loved, and to belong in the group. But in reality, I was distracted, my attention was stretched thin, I was unreliable, I was fun to be around, *sure*, but I was all over the place. And because I wasn't clear on my limits, because I didn't have good boundaries with myself and others, I consequently became a person who lacked integrity. As a result of being out of integrity with my word and my intentions, I was not in alignment with my truth and consequently everyone suffered - *especially me.*

That's an example of stinky fart cloud, not at all a laser. Because I wasn't clear, focused, and aligned with myself, my friends couldn't trust me, and neither could I trust myself. I was trying to define myself based on other people's acceptance and approval, when in reality, I didn't know who I was, what I really wanted or honestly could give, and I wasn't yet willing to face myself and give myself the time to figure those things out.

Today, I'm living my amends and practicing what I've learned about boundaries, which feels like a never ending trial-and-error process of learning and refining my understanding of myself, who I am, what I care about, and what I truly want and need to feel happy, whole, and accountable to myself and others. What setting healthy boundaries looks like for me is to feel the feelings of excitement and longing to serve, to have that desire for love, acceptance, and belonging, but then pausing. Now I know I need to take some time to really feel what I'm feeling and where my comfort zone is. I allow myself to feel my feelings, I listen to my intuition, and most importantly, I value what comes up. In the process of learning to value what I feel, I'm also learning to *trust* what I feel, and then to take action on what feels right for me. And sometimes that means saying no.

When it comes to boundaries, learning to say no is one of the most important skills a person must learn - especially when we're dealing with a person who feels entitled to or unconditional yes (like in the case of the aforementioned red flag of using a relationship to violate ourselves). Otherwise, I'm constantly basing my choices and actions on what someone else wants, not what I want and need, and that's *not* the path to personal freedom.

Another one of the most important things I've learned about boundaries is that if I'm doing things to win the approval of others, to try to get them like me, but inside I actually feel uncomfortable and find myself saying yes when I really mean no, then *I'm* the one violating *my own* boundaries. When I don't appropriately communicate what I want and need from myself and others in order to feel safe in a situation, then I'm responsible for violating my own boundaries. Again, they may be the one who causes a breach in my system, but I'm the one allowing it by not speaking up when I feel uncomfortable with something.

In this process of learning to honor and communicate my truth, I've learned that when someone asks something of me, the most important thing is I give myself a sacred pause before jumping to please the other person with an automatic yes. Whether that pause is two minutes, two hours, two days, or two weeks - that time and space gives me the chance to get clarity with myself on what I'm comfortable with, what I want, what feels most aligned with where I'm at, and what I'm ready to give from a full and generous heart.

Once I pause and feel what I feel, value and trust what I feel, *then* I can speak that truth, knowing that it's *my* truth.

When I give myself that space to gain that clarity within myself, I can say yes and give to others out of sincere generosity from a full heart, not out of obligation or an attempt to be loved or to avoid rejection or anger, at the expense of my precious and limited energy resources. When I learn to trust myself and act within my limits, I can take care of myself and also serve others in a way that feels good. And I can also feel good about myself in the process - because I know I'm honoring what feels right for me - which is how I find my highest path in life.

Strong, healthy, appropriate boundaries protect my aliveness, my vitality, and my joie de vivre. When I'm in alignment and operating within the consent of my boundaries, I can feel happy, valued, and full of life. When I'm feeling upset by something that my partner, roommate, friend, or coworker did, then I'm likely leaking energy and not at my full vitality. But those feelings of frustration, anger, sadness, or any flavor of violated, offended, depleted, or unappreciated, indicates I have an unmet need or some kind of violation or transgression within my system. When I feel that misalignment of energy within my system, that means it's time to pull back, assess where my boundaries are, recalibrate my energetic system, then re-enter the situation with a stronger sense of self, and more clearly defined and communicated boundaries to reflect that new clarity.

That's a big part of learning boundaries - the ability to recognize when there's been a violation or breach within my system, and then how to use that system guidance as valuable feedback to create new or stronger layers of protection. When I learn to pull back, reassess, recalibrate, then re-enter the relationship or situation with more clarity, then I can cultivate my sense of aliveness within a container of respect for what I really want and need to be happy and whole.

Learning to Create Healthy Boundaries

When it comes to setting healthy boundaries with myself and others, let's look at the example of Granja Tz'ikin, the permaculture farm right across the road from Karuna Atitlan in Hummingbird Valley. When I found this farm, I immediately fell in love with what they're doing there. Instantly I wanted to be a part of it. I could see the way the water of my gifts could add new life to what they're growing there, and I don't just mean the plants. I could feel my excitement and eagerness to sign onto projects and say I'll do things, but now I know better. Now I know the importance of that sacred pause - that time I take to pull back and sit with myself before I make a commitment. So it was perfect timing that Luke, the founder and captain of Karuna, was doing his annual tradition of going into silence for several days around the New Year, and I decided to join him.

That silence was important for me in several ways (the realization that it was time to write this book came out of that silence, by the way), but most importantly it gave me the container to connect with myself and what was really going on inside. Instead of rushing into making promises to the farm, I slowed down and gave myself the time and space to first examine my motivations behind my intentions to help. You see, there's a shadow side and a light side behind everything. As Seulki once told me, any being that stands in the light of creation will also have a side that is cast in shadow. Everyone has a shadow. And I'm of the belief that it's very important that we examine our shadow side, because there's valuable data in there (and all data is good data).

For me, examining my motivations meant looking into the shadow side of my excitement to serve my gifts and volunteer my time at the farm. When I looked into my shadow, I discovered the need to be loved and accepted. I saw that part of me still didn't feel worthy or good enough to charge money for my services, so I felt more comfortable giving my time for free. I saw a fear based on an old belief that I can't cook or provide adequate nourishment for myself, so I wanted the free food volunteers receive. I saw in the shadow that I was looking for other people to love and nurture me, instead of taking responsibility for loving and nurturing myself. I saw a fear of being alone and the need to help others as a way of feeling included, needed, and wanted, instead of having to sit with myself and my feelings. I saw a fear of missing out on what they were doing and the fun those kids seemed to be having together. I didn't want to be left out, like I had often felt in my childhood. I also saw a pattern of distracting myself with other people's projects instead of putting energy into my own, as if it felt safer to build someone else's dream than to work towards my own. *Whoa.* Prior to doing that self-inquiry, I had no idea all that stuff was there.

Then I examined the other side of my desire, the side that was smiling in the warmth of the light. There I saw shining brightly was my desire for community and belonging. I saw my need to make meaningful contributions in the lives of others. I saw the call to use my specialized skills and experience with those who want, need, and value them. I saw the chance to give of myself where I could make a difference, and even have fun in the process. I saw my love for goats, plants, and the exquisite energy of nature and things growing in the magic of the soil. I saw the simple pleasure I derive when I get to paint stuff, which I could do at the farm. I saw my desire to feel connected to the earth and develop my relationship with her energy. I saw my natural curiosity to learn about the principles of permaculture and how we can come into harmony with nature. I saw my curiosity to explore the magic and medicine of our plant allies. I saw the chance to make a living amends for my failures of integrity at Labracadabra. I saw my desire to eat healthy organic foods grown where I can see them growing and have a relationship with my food. Most of all, I genuinely liked the people there - Neal, Jeremy, Adriana, Maria, Kim, Josh, Matt, and the rest of the farm family, including the cats, dogs, chickens, and goats.

I held my desires and motivations up to the light, inspecting them the way a midwife might inspect a new baby. Because I gave myself that time and space, I got clarity on what I wanted, what I needed, and what I could give from a full heart. I came out of that silence with a commitment to the farm that I would volunteer there two days a week, Tuesday and Thursday. Instead of making an open-ended, undefined promise to help (like I did at Labracadabra), I fashioned a cup made of two days of my week. Two days where I would bring the water of my love and share it with them in whatever ways they needed for the benefit of the life they're growing there. Although since this writing I've pulled back from the farm to favor my own projects, I'm happy to relay that I fulfilled on that original commitment, and in my time there I helped out with the goats and took on the project to redo the entryway, painting the tables and chairs and essentially created a very colorful, fun, and inviting first impression for people walking in, not to mention boosting their exposure and reputation on social media. Doing those things felt really good, because I gave from a full heart in integrity with myself.

So, coming back to us sitting at the table. I want to give you that drink, and you want to receive it. *What's my job?* My job is to design the cup and put it on the table. That cup represents my clarity and honest communication around what I can truly give when my thoughts, words, and actions are aligned with integrity and generosity. It represents what I feel capable and comfortable offering. It's my time, my love, my words, my thoughts - my energy. It's the what, where, and how of my gifts that I can give to you while still maintaining the integrity of my own energy and joy. It's the clarity of what I can give you with a full heart, keeping in consideration all the other things I need to use my energy for.

When I don't give from a full heart, when I try to give from an empty, corrupted, or conflicted cup, I am "over-serving." That means I am out of integrity with myself and others. That means I am giving from a place of guilt, shame, obligation, or fear of losing something I value, or to avoid being rejected, abandoned, or feeling other people's anger or disappointment. And that is a kind of self-sabotage, because if I'm giving to others in an unhealthy and unbalanced way, doing things I don't really want to do out of fear, guilt, obligation, or a need to be loved and accepted, then I am leaking and losing energy in this lower vibration and will not have enough love and energy to take care of myself and give to the seeds of my dreams that I want to grow for myself.

When I'm giving without that clarity of what I can actually give with integrity, I might serve. Or I might not end up showing up, or doing it only half-assed, because I'm actually distracted with other projects and my own personal process, which I didn't realize needed so much of my time and energy because I never stopped to make an assessment of my needs, desires, cares, and limits. When I try to give from that unexamined place, when I don't know what I *really* want, then I am sabotaging myself because I'm setting myself up for confusion, miscommunication, resentment, explosions of anger, manipulation, violation, and entitlement. It does not feel good, nor satisfying, for anyone involved. The best intentions are there, but the boundaries are not.

Boundaries are directly tied to what we care about, and what we need to be happy, healthy, and whole. For example, I need to give myself nourishing food and enough rest in order to feel good. If I don't give myself those things, then it's hard for me to feel good, think straight, and be a clear channel for God's will to play out in my life. Considering this, I need to create and communicate boundaries that support me to fulfill these needs in healthy and appropriate ways.

Boundaries are so powerful, and yet they can be very small, just a few words like "No, I'm not comfortable with lending you any more money," or "I need to leave by 8pm," or "Yes, I can do that for you on Tuesday, but only from 2-4pm," or "No, I can't do that right now. I really need to focus on some other priorities," or "No you can't stay over tonight, but let's spend time together tomorrow," or "I'm not feeling so great, can you do the laundry tonight?" or "I cooked last night and I would really appreciate if you would cook dinner tonight," or "It makes me feel uncomfortable when you don't contribute to the groceries." These are small but vital statements because they help us stand up for ourselves, feel safe, feel good, and respect ourselves and others. They keep us on track to fulfill our needs in order to be happy and healthy, and essentially protect the wholeness of the gift we have to give. Healthy boundaries protect our sleep, our health, our emotional safety, our wallet, our ability to achieve our goals. They are an integral part of valuing ourselves and what we have to offer, instead of just giving it all away because we want to be loved, accepted, and included by any means necessary, even if it means hurting and violating ourselves and others.

Learning to use and communicate healthy and appropriate boundaries *early* means we don't have a big, angry, emotional mess to clean up *later*, when we finally can't take the violation anymore and end up exploding at another person with anger, shame, or blame. Learning and practicing healthy boundaries is how we respect ourselves and live in harmony with others.

Now, for me at least, a lot of my earlier relationships were based on me *not* having healthy boundaries. Alex, for example, was a man who gravitated towards and thrived on dating talented women who couldn't or wouldn't say no to him. Women, like myself back then, with poor boundaries who were eager to help and give him our time, resources, and skills in order to receive that deliciously charming energy from his eyes, words, and body.

Honestly, I would have given him anything to receive his love and energy, and I tried, but so often in his company I found myself giving too much to him and not enough to myself. I ended up feeling drained, tired, sad, needy, and clingy - which was why my intuition was telling me not to move in with him. But I didn't want to listen because I wanted him, I wanted him to love me, and I was all too desperate to fill that hungry void inside of me with what I was expecting to receive from him. I was wanting and needing something from him that he could not give me, and then I resented him when I did not receive it. But *I* was the one who gave him power over me, *I* was the one who chose to make him into the hero who was going to save me, and that was unfair because no one should be your Higher Power except your Higher Power. No human being can fill that role, and if you are expecting them to fulfill that role in your life then you are setting yourself up for disappointment and resentment.

Why did I do it? Because I was addicted. I was addicted to the energy dynamic of using others to get energy and to suppress my own vibration, instead of nurturing my own energy and sense of trust and safety from within. I was addicted to using something or someone outside of myself to make me feel good. I was addicted to that feeling of being wanted by the vampire for what he could get from me because I didn't want myself, so I willingly gave him, and many other lovers, my money, my time, my love and energy, while, like vampires do, he gave me very little in return. *Vampires don't give the blood back.* They give you just enough to keep you alive, so they can keep feeding on you.

I'm grateful for the realization that he was not who I wanted him to be, and the subsequent painful breakup with Alex, because it helped me reach a spiritual bottom - which was the turning point of my story. Because of the depths and despondency I reached thanks to my sacred teacher Alex, I realized that things could not go on like this, no one was going to save me, and something *had* to change. Most importantly, I realized that *I* had to change. In a blubbering, messy moment of absolute dejection, walking barefoot down the street in Asia under the stars, *I surrendered to the truth*. I said "God, I've really messed up. I don't want to live like this. I can't do this anymore. Please, help me. Take my life. I need you." In that moment, I handed the reins of my life over to my Creator. Although it was a messy surrender, it was incredibly powerful. In fact, it was in that humble confession - when I stopped denying and finally got honest with myself and the God of my understanding - when the real healing could begin.

Before we continue, here's a journal prompt around boundaries. Ask yourself, and honestly write the first answer that comes up: "Where in my life do I need stronger boundaries? Who in my life do I need to start having stronger boundaries with? In what way is not having stronger boundaries with this person or situation hurting me? How would having better boundaries with this person or situation help me? How could me having stronger boundaries actually help them too?

Finding the Medicine I Needed in Bali

From there, I left the island, and it was really hard to do because I was very attached to my life in Thailand (Video: <u>bit.ly/</u> <u>PainfulGoodbye</u>). But intuitively, I knew it was time to leave and I had felt the call to Indonesia for several months by then, so I bought a ticket and left for Bali. With a firm resolve to stop blaming others for my problems and finally do my self-work, I followed the breadcrumbs into the loving arms of a twelve-step meeting in a magical place called Ubud, which is Balinese for "medicine." As palm trees swayed outside the open windows of the meeting room, people from all over the world gathered in search of help.

In that first meeting 12-step meeting, my heart cracked open. With tears of courageous vulnerability, I spilled my truth. I expressed the insanity that I had been enduring that had led me into a place of misery and despair. I admitted that I could not go on living like this. Most importantly, in that moment of raw honesty, pain, vulnerability, and courage, *I asked for help*. I asked for as much help as they would be willing to give me, and I don't think I've ever felt like I was surrounded by more loving eyes than I was at that moment.

I proceeded to enroll myself in what I like to call "Spiritual Recovery University." I got a sponsor, a.k.a. a private tutor, who personally guided me through working the 12 steps. I went to every program on the schedule - programs that dealt with addictions related to alcohol, drugs, relationships, sex, and even food. Even though I didn't completely identify with each of these addictions, I fully identified with the insanity that was the underlying problem - the need to use something or someone outside of myself to hide and get relief from the pain I was feeling inside. I went to class every day, willing and eager to learn, like a kid with a bag full of recovery textbooks. Each day, alongside classmates from all over the world, we learned how to surrender our lives over to a Higher Power of our *own* understanding.

In those meetings, we learned how to stop hiding, how to face our pain, and stop drinking, smoking, eating, shopping, co-depending, and romancing the pain away. Instead of running from the monster like Govinda, finally I was supported to approach it with courage, vulnerability, willingness, an open mind, honesty, compassion, and forgiveness. For the first time, thanks to this recovery community and the emotional-spiritual container it provided me, I was able to really face my pain. And truly, my friends, that was where my real healing took place.

I went to over a hundred meetings in my first ninety days, and for my three-month anniversary of my sobriety and spiritual recovery I attended a local roundup convention of all the twelve-step groups from Bali to Australia. I'll never forget getting up on stage and singing the 3rd step prayer in front of a ballroom full of fellow addicts.

The term 'addict,' by the way, is really just a term I use to describe highly sensitive, empathic humans with enormous talent and abilities, but who experienced trauma and never learned healthy ways to process the pain. Without knowing any better, we turned to drugs, alcohol, eating, Netflix, sex, shopping, gambling or whatever other compulsion to dull our sensitivities and feel normal. It's no ones fault. We did the best we could given what we knew, and what we were taught, often by people who were themselves hurting. But the important thing about this group of alcoholics and addicts in that ballroom, and in these life-saving rooms all around the world, was that we had all made the choice to get better. You can see the video from the moment of joy after singing on stage here: bit.ly/MySurrenderSong.

The Way Out

So my friend, you're in the madness. Do you want to get out? Do you want to stop getting in your own way? Do you want to stop sabotaging your own health and happiness? To stop tripping yourself up on the path to reaching your dreams? What do you do? Well, the first step is to admit you've got a problem. And the problem is that you have a sick plant you've been feeding with poisoned water of your own making. So what do we do? We start by recognizing the need to purify the water of ourselves, starting with the patterns of our thoughts, our words, and our actions.

Now, I couldn't do it myself. I tried before, and I failed. As hard as I tried to change, I inevitably ended up slipping back into my old patterns and routines because I didn't have a better system or support in place. That's why I needed those twelve-step meetings in Bali to help me find a new way. I needed help and guidance to find a new way of facing the darkness of my undigested emotions from past traumas, to start feeling my feelings, and to learn how to handle what came up in healthy and appropriate ways. It was like in order to face the big boss, I needed a team by my side. I needed a Spiritual Squad - a transitional team to help me shift from one way of thinking and living into a new way, a better way, a healthier way - the true way.

Finding the people in those rooms was like the climactic scene in the movie where the main character is finally united with their team of allied heroes. In an epic slow-motion scene they walk together toward the monster, united and together, supporting one another where it really matters. That's what those meetings and the people in them were for me. That's the kind of dedicated ally that my sponsor was for me. The people in those rooms saved my life, as they continue to do everyday all around the world in this incredible program of spiritual recovery. Now, I'm can't tell you outright the name of the program. Which is frustrating, I know.

And that's because the anonymity of this totally free, worldwide program is the spiritual foundation of their work. The anonymous nature of these meetings is what allows the groups to create safe containers where anyone can go, for free, without ego, shame, or judgment, to do the work to face their monsters. If you want to find your way into these lifesaving rooms, just do a Google search using your favorite way to relieve your inner pain, like "Alcohol 12 steps," or "Drugs 12 steps," "Codependency 12 steps," "Food 12 steps," "Money 12 steps," "Gambling 12 steps," "Sex and love 12 steps." And the list goes on. Then, show up. Follow the breadcrumbs to find a meeting near you. There's probably one starting soon. They even having virtual meetings online.

I also really like the work of Russell Brand, who's creating some amazing content to bring these principles of spiritual recovery to the people in a really authentic and entertaining way (Video: bit.ly/RussellBrand12Steps) The rabbit hole is there. But it's up to *want* to get better, to be willing to change, step inside, and surrender to where the healing journey takes you.

What is Healing?

Healing is returning to harmony with ourselves and all that is. It's about recognizing our self-defeating patterns and making the choice to change them. Healing is about reclaiming our integrity, the sacred alignment between thought, word, and action. It's an embrace of our intrinsic wholeness. It's the process of the undoing the pain and poison we carry inside since childhood. It's the journey we go on to let the feelings come up and finally look into the shadow of ourselves to see what's there. It's the process we undergo to feel and deal with our anger, face our sadness, and process and diffuse the energy of our resentments so we can finally be free from what happened in the past. We heal when we look at why we are so angry, sad, and ashamed, instead of pulling the carpet over that dark place and continuing to maintain surface appearances of things being alright. It's the process by which we compost the poison within us into the fertilizer that grows new life out of the material of our past. It's the journey to alchemize our pain into *power*.

I can't emphasize enough the importance of this shadow work. It's the kind of uncomfortable work that most people will spend a lifetime avoiding and go to the grave with the poison still in them. And in most cases, the poison is passed on to their children. That's because the shadow is full of darkness and the shameful things we don't want to admit or look at about ourselves, and it's easier and more convenient to avoid it, or to project it onto someone else. But the truth is that the shadow is also intrinsically connected to our light - to deny one is to suppress the other. That's why if we really want to experience the light of peace and joy, we *must* first face and process our darkness.

The key to this healing is to find other committed seekers, like a 12-step group, women's circle, men's circle, or other safe, supportive healing space where honesty, mindfulness, self-inquiry, and vulnerability are the primary values. The key is to find people and systems who support you to do that healing work within yourself, to face the monsters and bring them down to size. When we stop sabotaging ourselves with old resentments, fears, and limiting beliefs, then it's much easier to create the life of our dreams.

And what do you do when you find that group? Do you fight the monster? Cut off its head perhaps? Nay, friends. Fighting, resisting, struggling, shaming, and judging are on the same level of vibration that got us into this mess in the first place. When we approach the monster, the best thing we can do is be like Krishna. Lay down your weapons and approach your monsters with non-judgment, acceptance, compassion, and listening. We approach our pain with a desire to hear what message it has for us. We ask, "What do you need me to hear, dear one? What do you want for me?" Instead of resisting, fighting, making it wrong, and insisting that it shouldn't be here, we open our hearts with compassion and willingness to step into the new terrain of acceptance and forgiveness. When we're no longer afraid of the pain, when we no longer push against it, then these demons lose the power they once had over us. Then the real healing can begin to take place at the root of the wound. Ultimately, this healing work is the journey we go on to face, process, and let go of the hurts of the past, so we can move forward into a happier, healthier future.

HOMEWORK:
RESENTMENT PROCESS

The hardest thing for a person to do is
to take a good honest look at themself.

If you really want to be free, *and are willing to go to any lengths to get it*, then I offer you this simple (but not easy) resentment process. Doing this exercise honestly and openly will help to release you from the bonds of anger and pain from the past. I regularly use this process when I'm feeling angry or hurt, and it's saved my life (and my sanity) and given me new a healthy new perspective on the situation that's bothering me (Video: https:// bit.ly/EricasTrueFreedom).

This process comes from a 12-step program, where, in Step Four "we made a searching and fearless moral inventory of ourselves." The most important part of this process is that you're *willing* to look at yourself and get honest about what you find, and to keep an open mind throughout the process.

Tip: I like to get a separate notebook for this work, and I keep adding to it as new resentments come up.

1. Begin with a prayer to the God/Goddess/Creator/Higher Power/Great Mystery of your own personal understanding. I like to say something like: "God, please guide my thoughts and my pen. Please allow the Holy Spirit to shine within me to find the blocks, barriers, and Obstacles to Flight within me. Bring what I need to know into my conscious mind, so I may be free. Thank you for guiding my healing and direction. Thy will be done."

2. Write the name of the person, institution, place, or thing you feel resentful at.

3. Write the cause - the facts of what happened.

4. Now we consider what areas of our life that this resentment has impacted. Consider these areas: Self-esteem, Personal relations, Sexual relations, Ambitions, and/or Financial. Write down the areas that this resentment has impacted you.

5. Now we ask ourselves, in regards to this resentment, how was I being <u>selfish</u>? Ask yourself, what did I really want? Write the answer as honestly as you can.

6. Now ask yourself and write: Where was I being <u>dishonest</u>? What lie was I telling myself or others? Be honest and dig deep.

7. Next, ask: In what way was I <u>self-seeking</u>? What self-serving action did I take?

8. Finally, let's look at our fears. Ask yourself: What was I afraid of? What <u>fear</u> did I have in this situation? Get honest.

9. For me personally, I like to do another prompt. As I wrote out the last points, I would naturally have revelations and

"ah-ha" moments as I saw my part in what happened. So I like to include a paragraph (or however much space you need) to record any observations, realizations, or epiphanies I had.

10. The final, and possibly most important step, is that you fully and humbly admit to yourself, to the God of your understanding, and then <u>call a trustworthy, non-judgmental, emotionally available friend and share with them</u> what you wrote, and what you discovered. This act of sincere confession is a key step in releasing the poison, and to recognizing and taking responsibility for your actions and behaviors of the past so you can own your part and take responsibility for creating different patterns in the future.

Do this exercise with the person you feel most heated anger towards, and if you *really* want to free yourself, dare to excavate your past. You can create a timeline of your life, from childhood through present, and dig out all the old resentments you've ever felt and do this process on them. Do it on the ones you think you've forgotten, like the bully at school when you were a kid, and even the school itself. Do them all. How badly do you want to be free?

There are other steps involved in a thorough inventory, specifically regarding fear and shame. This work is typically tied to substance addiction recovery, so if you're ready to face yourself, get sober, and do a deep dive into this work and change your life, I recommend you find a 12-step program near you and a trusted sponsor who will, completely *for free*, personally walk you through the full process to achieve the spiritual awakening and personal freedom available to you as the result of these steps.

Chapter 9: Stepping into the Adventure

So, this is it. You've heard your heart's desire and you bravely made the decision to heed the call. You set a date, bought your ticket, took action, removed the obstacles to your flight, and now the day is drawing near. Soon, your adventure will come knocking at your door, and when that moment arrives, your job will be to courageously answer and receive your new guest.

BTW, You Might Freak Out

If you're anything like me, this part may come with a whole other landslide of emotions. In spite of the fact that I wanted it so badly and worked so hard to achieve my dream of traveling in India for six months, right before I left I started seriously doubting everything. "What am I doing? What have I gotten myself into? What am I setting myself up for?" I asked myself one night outside Whole Foods (Video: bit.ly/CrisisofPurpose).

Let me assure you, it's completely normal to have doubts. It's normal to stand on the deck of your ship, still anchored in the safety of your home port and gaze upon the familiar shores with a kind of longing to stay where things feel safe and comfortable. You'll see your friends and family going about their lives, and for me, as much as I was called to leave, right at the critical moment a big part of me wanted to stay. Even though I had worked so hard and made so many sacrifices to arrive at this moment, part of me wanted to ball up my beautiful dream like a wad of tissues and toss the whole plan into the trash and just forget about it. Just go back to "real" life. If you like drama like me, you might find yourself falling to your knees, fists raised to the sky, simultaneously both praising and cursing God for placing this dream in your heart that feels like it's tearing apart your reality. And that's okay. Because this is the step where the focus is *trust*. Trust in the calling of your heart. Trust where you're going even though you may not understand why you *must* go. To trust the urge to step into the unknown and whatever is waiting for you in the uncertainty of the future. To trust that your treasure is out there, waiting for you to find it. Remember, ships are safe in their harbor, but that's not what they were built for.

The ride to the airport is one of the most terrifying parts for me. Part of my brain is totally convinced that we're about to die, like a cow who knows they're being led to slaughter. "We don't know what's out there!" My mind would scream at me like a crazed lunatic as I put my bag into the car, convinced I was leading us into our sure demise. Yes, at this point, when things start getting real, the mind will do anything it can to sabotage the plan. It will find any shred of fear it can to throw at you to incite a riot among the citizens within you to halt this launch into the Great Unknown. And oh, let me tell you, *your mind will play dirty*. It may come at you using the voice of your mother or father, your sister or brother, or even your best friend. This fear may cast itself as the character of someone you know and love, and it will do its damned best to convince you why you should abort your mission. Fear will plead with you to run back to the cool damp nest of safety where your dreams grow mold. But hey, at least we can see the walls and touch all the edges, as if that were a good thing. No, during the ride to the airport, and all the moments immediately preceding it, your stomach may try to escape via your mouth. Don't let it. Hold, soldier, hold the course. You're almost there.

[Cut to scene]:

You're at the airport. You're waiting in line with your passport, you're boarding your plane, your heart is racing but *you're doing it*. Even though you're scared and your mind is telling you the plane might crash or the person sitting next to you might have gas, you continue moving forward, unabashed by the dragons in your

180

path. You take the flight, you watch some movies (maybe *"The Heat"* with Sandra Bullock and Melissa McCarthy?), you eat peanuts and have a small exchange of niceties with the person next to you and *bam*, you've arrived at your destination. *How exciting*!

You have the address of where you're going, great. You'll need that for immigration. They look you up and down, stamp your passport, et voila! You've arrived. You hit the ATM for some local cash, get a new SIM card installed in your phone and walk through the exit.

Arriving is Like, WOW

The moment when the exit doors slide open and I get to take my first steps out of the airport in another country is my favorite. That juicy first impression of the air is so ripe. I like to pause here and feel it to the fullest. I'll never forget the first moment I arrived in Singapore and I emerged out of the air-conditioned bubble of the airport into the intense tropical humidity. I had never experienced anything like it before; the air was so thick with moisture that I felt like I needed to drink it through a straw. I remember the first moment I arrived in Bali, stepping out of the plane after all that heartache and turmoil with Alex in Thailand. The first feeling I had was like arriving into the welcoming embrace of the divine mother herself. It felt loving and forgiving, like she just wanted to take me in and tend to my wounds like a good mother. It was a feeling of relief after so much turmoil and pain.

Sometimes I feel relieved to arrive. Other times, I feel overwhelmed. Sometimes it's a combination of both. I think back to arriving at the airport in Bangkok, emerging with my bags into a whirling swirling hive of activity. People from all over the world merged together like a million rivers intersecting, and there I was both exhausted and excited as I stepped into it. "Just keep breathing," I reminded myself. I took the taxi to the part of town known as Khao San Road, which is a vibrant, debaucherously colorful, and wonderfully entertaining part of town. It's like a Disney World for tourists. Sometimes I know the hotel where I'm going, and sometimes I don't. You can just as easily show up at a place like Khao San Road and find a cheap place when you get there. However, this journey will be tiring and taxing on you, so the more you have set up in advance, the better. I'll never forget swimming through that current and the relief I felt when I arrived at my guesthouse, closed the door, finally dropped my bags, and plopped down on the bed. *Whew, I made it.*

It's Okay to be Confused

Let me be clear: stepping into the new reality can be very disconcerting. With all the new information and stimulus, it's easy for the wires in your brain to become crossed. Suddenly, there are old men with poodles wearing round spectacles, women selling fried grasshoppers, and so many other curiosities, foreign languages, and new flavors swirling all around your being. It can feel very overwhelming, especially at first.

There were times I got really overwhelmed, like this https://bit.ly/AndThenICrashed, this bit.ly/SweatyandDisoriented, and this bit.ly/FreakingOutJaisalmer. Looking back, I wish I had *slowed down.* "Be patient," I wish I would have said to myself. Give yourself time to adjust, and please, *take a nap.* Just take it all in and let your screaming mind know that everything is okay, and that it can have a cookie if it calms down and lets you concentrate on the present moment.

The transition time can be challenging. Especially if you're addicted to running and jumping your energy, like I was. If you're anything like me, when I arrived I was addicted to moving too much and too fast. I had so much wind energy that I couldn't sit still. At that time, I was still deeply entrenched in a belief system that commanded that I had to be doing, producing, and achieving every single moment if I was to "do it right." I'll never forget that little guesthouse I stayed at around Khao San Road. It was $6 per night and it had such character to it (Video: bit.ly/ CheapRoominBangkok). I was to later discover that this guesthouse was almost used in the filming of "The Beach" with Leonardo DiCaprio, but last minute the plan changed and they used another equally charming and decrepit place. There were a few old French hippies who would sit in the lounge at the entryway, drinking coffee and smoking cigarettes. They would always be there as I came and went each morning after my arrival. After several days, I slowed down enough to start chatting with them in my broken French. That's when one of them called me out. He said, "We always see you running. Always running. *Where are you running?*"

Rewind several years prior to the desert city of Jaisalmer in northern India. It was in my first couple of weeks after arriving in India. After my twenty-ninth birthday in Udaipur, I followed my heart's desire to go see some baby camels in the red hot desert. It was my first day, and even though I had a somewhat stressful trip there (bit.ly/StressfulRide), I didn't let myself slow down. As soon as I arrived, I was already up and running, off to explore the city. I wandered to and fro around the base of a fantastic ancient fort that towered over the city. Red bricks everywhere sung to my eyes and it was drier than a pile of autumn leaves in New England.

I found myself wandering down a little street lined with shops carrying the most fantastic creations - colorful pillows and fabrics sparkling with tiny inlaid mirrors, carvings of camels, and all sorts of beautiful handmade pottery. I passed by a shop with a local Rajasthani man sitting outside and he called to me. "Hello my friend! Where are you from?" I paused to talk to him for a moment, and it was very pleasant, but soon my heels were feeling itchy and I pulled back from the conversation. "Why won't you stay and talk to me for a while? Americans are always rushing off somewhere. Why are you running off?" I felt his comment was indignant, unjustified, and excused myself because I really did have to go. I rushed off, turned the corner, and then stopped in my tracks. I didn't actually have any reason to rush off, and I certainly had nowhere to go, I thought to myself as I watched a dog pee on the red brick wall. "Why *am* I always running, as if there was always something better around the corner?" I thought as I watched the pee drip.

Letting Go of Control

My sincerest advice for this stage of stepping into the unknown, and what I wish I had done more of, is to slow down and *trust*. You don't need to have all the answers up front. You don't need to run around, see everything and figure things out. You don't need to understand why you're there. You just need to trust that you are where you're meant to be. You just need to take care of yourself from moment to moment.

Almost every time I arrived, initially I felt exhilarated by the newness and excitement of it all. But it seems almost inevitably and predictably I would sink into a kind of confusion, self-doubt, and questioning about my path and purpose (Video: https://bit.ly/EricasExistentialCrisis). My mind would wrestle me to the ground, rubbing in my face all my choices and try to convince me I made some kind of irreconcilable mistake. But don't let it stay on top of you. Push your mind off and take some deep breaths. Go have a cup of coffee with the hippies downstairs and ask them to tell you stories of their travels and life. Don't try to see all the sights on your first day. Just wander around a few streets near your guest house and find a coffee shop, tea house, or other cute place where colorful lanterns sway overhead and the menu delights you. Sit down, pull out your trusty journal, and write about what you're feeling. Write about the shape of the doorway and the look of the little dog outside and the curious delight of the chicken that followed him. Look up from your phone and see who is there, see who has kind eyes and dare to exchange some words with them. Enjoy your time moving slowly, breathing deeply, and connecting to how you're feeling. Don't distract yourself with your phone. Perhaps after some quiet time settling your energy, you might feel a subtle call to leave the cafe and walk down the street.

Before your eyes emerges a beautiful Buddhist temple sparkling in the sunshine. Golden spires like visual poetry with pigeons flying overhead like fleeting punctuation marks lead you to the next step. Maybe you find yourself entering the temple courtyard (*shoulders covered, please*) and wandering around the quiet space. Perhaps you approach the temple building itself, elegant and exquisite in its craftsmanship, painted in gold with small inlaid mirrors that let you only see pieces of yourself. Enter the temple and find a quiet corner to sit. The marble floor is cool and the walls are decorated with the most fantastic depictions of stories from another world. A world of the Buddha and dharma where mermaids swim through the oceans of the sky and ornately decorated goddesses dance a dance of a thousand years echoing through space and time. Be still, be quiet, and observe. Watch your thoughts and bring yourself back to your breath, to the present moment, and the sensation of your body touching the floor. You might watch people come and go, falling to their knees at the altar, raising incense in hands pressed together at their forehead in prayer. What are they asking for? What might *you* ask for?

Breathe deeply. Watch quietly. Listen fully. Just be who and where you are. Don't run. There's nowhere you need to go. You have arrived. Whatever you're feeling is okay. You're allowed to feel what you feel. This is your time.

The Phenomenon of Homesickness

I think it's important to talk about the phenomenon known as "homesickness." I don't really get this sensation anymore since I exploded my home in Malden, MA, many years ago and have been living with friends and family since then as I continue to pursue this traveling lifestyle. But I do have those moments where everything feels new, different, and overwhelming, when I long to run back to the safety of what feels familiar and comfortable.

I remember arriving in Bali and just feeling *so* out of my element. I remember quite clearly the sensation of standing on the road, motorbikes whipping by in every direction. I didn't know where I was. My phone wasn't working yet, so I had no reference points or ability to search for what I needed. I didn't know where to eat, I didn't know anything anymore, and it felt *very* uncomfortable. Extremely uncomfortable. In fact, I would have scratched off all of my skin in that moment to find peace if I could have. But instead of freaking out, *I sat with it.* I sat with the discomfort without trying to change it. I accepted the situation for what it was. I let myself be present to my feelings and focused on breathing through them. I reminded myself that this was temporary, that I would get through this and I would find my way, and everything would be okay.

I'm glad I grounded myself in that moment because from that more settled space, I remembered the number of the guy that the girl who rented my house in Thailand gave me. I punched it in my phone and next thing I knew he was picking me up on his motorbike. It was such a welcome surprise to end up at the most wonderful local restaurant just down the street that overlooked a luscious green ravine where the most beautiful waterfall I've ever seen in my life tickled my eyes. Soon I was filling my belly with delicious fish, vegetables, and rice, and I felt better. What a beautiful resolution to a moment of discomfort. In other times, when I did not ground myself, instead from that discomfort I would feed into my addiction to that lower vibration by isolating myself in my room, chain smoking cigarettes, lamenting my decision to leave, planting myself in front of Facebook and incessantly scrolling and comparing myself to other people who looked like they were happy and having more fun than me. There are so many ways to make yourself feel bad, and it's a choice. "Up to you," as M would say with his characteristic shrug that says he wants to help you, but only you can help yourself.

Welcoming the New

At this point of the adventure, everything feels new. Sometimes things feel scary in their newness, and it's okay. The most important thing is that you release your need to control what's happening. Release your need to understand, because that's also a form of control. By releasing our attachment to what we want or expect to happen, we create space for life to give us something new. Let go of the shores of everything that feels comfortable and familiar and be willing to be taken by the flow of life. This flow brought you here for some reason, for some learning or enrichment of your soul, but you're not going to get the answers up front.

So first things first, *relax*. Rest. Take a nap. Feed yourself something yummy and nourishing. Write in your journal. Reflect on your feelings. Enjoy the silence. You don't know anyone, and no one knows you. You don't have to do anything. You don't have to be anyone. You've arrived in the open field of possibilities beyond right and wrong, the place beyond everything you assumed to be true. And if you allow yourself to let go and become an empty cup, life will respond by filling you all sorts of new wonders. Go easy on yourself in this time of transition. Breathe deeply, move slowly, and *trust*. Trust that you're exactly where you're meant to be, as you were all along.

Chapter 10 - How to Find Your Joy Once You're There

I'm sitting on the floor of my tiny house in Guatemala in a nest made of my cherished down sleeping bag on a pillow made of camel hide Luke brought back from one of his adventures in the Middle East. Just outside the door in front of me is my little garden where birds with yellow bellies hop along the branches of a Jocote tree. Larger brown birds, like the one I always see perched outside the window near the bathroom, hunt for the fattest, reddest berries in the garden. New berries emerge every morning as part of a cycle of fat and red that delights both me and the birds. We share the feast; I make sure to leave some for them, and they leave some for me. I love this place, my little house in Hummingbird Valley.

In fact, this tiny house in nature was my heart's desire that I envisioned over and over again the summer after I got back from Bali, before I left for Egypt. Even though I was sleeping in the hot attic of a friend's house in Exeter, NH, and had *no* idea where or how I would find a tiny house in the woods, I dared to believe in my heart's new desire and directed my energy there.

I spent that summer living in that hot attic and working hard doing photography to save up for my trip to Egypt. But I didn't know where I would go after Egypt. In the past, this uncertainty would have freaked me out. But now I know better. I know how the unseen can weave itself without the assistance of my worrying mind, and so I decided to trust. I decided to let myself stay in the mystery, and that *more would be revealed*. I chose to trust that when I needed to take the next step, it would appear. Even though it felt hard, I accepted that not knowing how things would work out was okay. I made the choice to let go of my mind's need to control, predict, and understand the unknowable mystery of the future, and I decided to go just with the flow of life.

The Mind is a Great Servant but a Horrible Master

So what's up with these minds of ours? We've talked about the mind a lot so far. I've shown you how it works in many regards, and how difficult it can be when the mind, body, and intuition are out of alignment.

I really wish someone had talked to me about intuition when I was a younger human. I think I would have developed in a healthier way. If I had learned about my intuition sooner, I would have learned to trust myself and my abilities, and see myself with all my human complexities with more compassion and care. Instead, I was part of an educational system that only taught me how to use my mind - rational, thinking, logical - and to view things in terms of right and wrong, black and white, good and bad, yes or no, success or failure.

As a child, I was encouraged to memorize facts and line them up in the "right" way. I was taught how to consume and regurgitate information on-demand, and then I was graded and ranked on how well I could do this, as if this was the best way to gauge a child's intelligence and potential to succeed in the world. I wish instead I had been sent off to Hogwarts where a wise old lady in a funny hat made out of mushrooms taught me how to close my eyes and ask myself what I could feel was true for me in the realm where logic has no jurisdiction. I wish I was taught how to ask my heart what she wanted to learn and explore, then be encouraged in the direction of what called to me naturally, like the kids I met in Sadhana Forest of Auroville in South India.

In this community, nestled deeply into the what could quite possibly be one of the most impressive and inspiring reforestation projects in the world, the children who live there follow what's called the "Unschooling" method. In this method of education, the children themselves are encouraged and supported to connect with what naturally calls to them, where their natural talents and interest lie, and then the parents and community support them to learn and explore that subject (Video: bit.ly/SadhanaKidsArea).

Closer to home, my sister asked her four-year-old daughter Alia what she wanted to learn about. With great excitement Alia exclaimed, "I want to be a corn farmer!" So my sister responded with support and enthusiasm, taking her to the store to look at and learn about the different kinds of corn. They read stories from different cultures about corn. Then the classroom extended to the garden where they worked side by side to plant corn, cucumbers, squash, okra, amaranth, and a cornucopia of nourishing and medicinal plants and herbs that we would later use to brew tea and sit together at the table, asking Alia what she learned, what she liked the best, and what else is calling to her to explore. You should have seen the way that kid lit up, excited to learn and make new discoveries.

We're taught in traditional schools how to use our minds, and that's because our rational, thinking mind is important and necessary for the functioning of a productive society and life. I'm not bashing the mind at all. I love my mind. I need my mind to help me figure out how to budget for my expenses, plan for my trip, put together my grocery list, remember to take my probiotics, track the progress of my goals, or to calculate what time I need to leave for the airport while taking into consideration traffic and all the trees, animals, and people I will need to hug and kiss goodbye before I embark on my adventure. The mind is a wonderful tool to help me stay in integrity with my values and priorities, so I can live a happy, healthy, and meaningful life.

However, an unchecked mind left in charge can make a mess of things. Too much mental control and fear of doing things "wrong" can disconnect us from the subtle call of our heart. An unhealthy mind, always trying to fight to get things "right," can be the finger that pushes down the delicate needle of our inner compass so we can't feel and find our true north anymore.

What is the Intuition?

We've talked about the intuition, but what is it? For me, the intuition is a gentle knowing I feel inside. It's something I hear, like quiet words of wisdom received within, and it's also expressed through a feeling I feel in my body. My mind is different - it speaks to me over a loud speaker, blasting across the surface level of my awareness. Like a road runner, my mind is constantly busy, zipping around non-stop with all of its constant thoughts, judgments, and stories. In contrast, the intuition is like a wise, gentle voice that approaches slowly and silently as if out of nowhere, suddenly arriving to gently whisper something I need to hear, like "Go to India." Or "turn left here," "get in that tuk tuk," "speak to that person," "don't get off the train," or "let him go."

For me, the mind can be a kind of active, pushy, back-and-forth dialogue between disparate factions, while my intuition gives me a clear, short, and direct statement. With messages from the intuition, there's no confusion or discussion - it just *knows*. According to Seulki, your intuition is like your spiritual GPS system, and it's always there in the same way that your eyesight is always there. It's directly connected to the past, present, and future, it knows what's best for you, and is designed to keep you on your spiritual path.

So what blocks or stops us from listening to our intuition? Well, often the messages we receive from our intuition are in direct contrast to the beliefs of the logic-based mind. Sometimes the guidance the intuition has to share is *not* something our minds are ready to hear. The intuition says, "Go to India" and the mind says, *"What?* Hell no! I can't afford to go to India! I have to stay here and work and do what my family wants and I certainly do *not* want to go to India." The intuition doesn't fight or try to justify itself, much to the indignation of the mind, which all it wants to do is fight and justify itself. The intuition merely responds, short and blunt, without explanation, "Go to India."

I can feel it in my body too. When something feels in alignment with my intuition, I feel a kind of expansion within me. When something doesn't feel good to my intuition and higher self, I feel a subtle contraction inside my body. Do you ever have a gut reaction when someone says or asks something, and instantly you can feel a kind of yucky, tight feeling inside? That's it. And that's good to know that I have an inner guidance system in my intuition, which is always pointing me towards my greatest and highest good - towards my own personal true north.

Now, when someone makes a request of me, I pause and check in with myself. Does this request make me feel expanded or contracted in my body? If I feel expanded, I answer yes. If I feel a contraction, I dare to say no, even if it means disappointing them. Disappointing others is also one of the biggest challenges in following the intuition, especially if we really want them to love and approve of us. When we ignore the guidance from our intuition in an attempt to please others, we are not following our inner GPS - and this is how we get lost.

In her class, Seulki likens the intuition to the inner child and the mind to the parent. The child says, "I want to go to the playground," and the role of the mind - just like the role of a good parent - is to serve the needs of the child. The mind's role is to help the child to get safely to the playground, so it says, "Okay, honey, if we're going to go to the playground we should leave at this time, I'll prepare some snacks and now please hold my hand so we can cross the street safely." In this example, the mind and intuition are in harmony. They are working together to serve the inner child.

This is where the magic happens. The kind of magic that puts you in the right place at the right time, to tap into the mysterious coincidences that connect you with the exact people and opportunities you need to change the trajectory of your life. It's what makes the thing that you previously thought to be impossible, suddenly possible. And it's not accessed by trying harder, or using more mental force to figure things out. That's the mind. No, the answers arrive naturally - like water flowing downhill - when we listen to and follow the guidance of our intuition.

The problem, though, is when the mind and intuition are not in harmony. The intuition says, "Go to the park," but the mind responds, "*Hell no!* I can't go to the park. Don't you see I'm busy? I have very important work to do and I can't afford to take the time to go to the stupid park. Shut up and leave me alone." And like that, we block our own destiny and the subtle force of the Universe that is trying to prosper us. By rejecting the innocent needs and desires of our inner child - our intuition - we block our own inner guidance. We cut ourselves off from the receiving the help that just wants to flow to us, if only we would allow it in. If only we could learn to stop resisting - to stop pinching off the flow of abundance - and start opening ourselves to receive the divine guidance and assistance which is our birthright.

Speaking of receiving assistance from the Universe, a big difference between the mind and the intuition is that the intuition is receptive. We receive messages from our intuition that come from another place - a place outside our human mind. A place that is tapped into a greater knowing where the human mind can't reach. In contrast, the mind is more active and penetrative like an archer, shooting a bow and arrow with effort and force. You need to use mental energy to pick up those arrows and shoot them forward, so it's more of an active state that projects and penetrates. Using the mind to think and plan is like using your energy to push a string

194

through a straw. It requires effort. Using the intuition, on the other hand, is like learning to sit still by a river and open a net. You might be surprised by what you catch that way. When we open ourselves to receiving the messages from our intuition, we transcend the realm of logic and effort, the realm where one plus one equals two. Instead, when we are using our intuition, we tap into the wisdom of a power greater than ourselves, where one plus one can equal a million.

I am of the belief that we are taught to use our mind energy and that we must struggle for the things we want. We learn that we must work hard to mentally figure things out, that we must suffer in order to receive, that we must use our best thinking to force life into the configuration that suits our little plans and designs - which is all about control. But really that's not the best way to use your precious energy to find your true path. The best thing I've learned has been how to slow down, stop jumping my energy all over the place trying to win love and approval of others, and finally learn to listen to myself and my inner knowing. How to sit quietly, open the net of my intuition, and receive. And almost more importantly, I have learned to value, trust, and take action on the guidance, suggestions, and directions I receive from this subtle, inner voice of gentle knowing from within.

The Jaisalmer Camel Scandal

In order to really learn a lesson, sometimes we need to fail. The contrast provided by the pain of failure can be a powerful teacher. To that end, I'd like to share a very special story of something that happened to me in India when I did *not* listen to my intuition.

:::insert Bollywood music:::

[Cut to scene]:

The sun was scorching hot over the sands of the Thar Desert of northern India. I had arrived in India a few weeks prior and decided to venture to Rajasthan because my heart wanted to see camels. Once I arrived, I was quick to accept the first invitation to go on a camel trek into the desert. I joined a group with two French travelers and we set off into the sand dunes by camelback, led by a simple and kind man of the desert named Bilal. The journey took us into the great wide wilderness of nothing but desert sand, punctuated by enormous windmills like towering giants spinning their arms in the distance. It was vast, serene, and incredibly beautiful. On the first afternoon of our camel trek, we stopped for lunch under the welcome shade of a few trees in a desert oasis. While we rested, Bilal cooked us a simple lunch of rice and vegetables. He was a kind man and I felt great affection for him as he spoke to us of his life in the desert over the steaming pot on the fire. My heart ached to hear of his family's poverty and rejoiced in the beautiful simplicity of his life in the desert.

The heat was overwhelming, but it was a relief to rest in the shade together while the camels grazed nearby. It was then in that resting space that I pulled out the selenite stone that a psychic woman in Salem, MA, had gifted me before I left on my journey. With a full belly and an empty, relaxed mind, I twirled the stone around my fingers under the shade of the tree. Suddenly, I heard something. But it was not a sound vibration coming from the outside, rather it was a subtle vibration I felt within myself. It was as if an invisible bird landed on my shoulder and whispered something very strange and surprising in my ear. "*All is not what it seems,*" it chirped in words only I could hear. Wait, *what*? What does that mean? I sat up and looked around. There was nothing out of place. The two Frenchies were casually conversing. Bilal was cleaning the cooking pot. The camels were idly grazing. By the looks of it, everything seemed alright.

We mounted the camels and continued on our trek into the dunes, but that little bird followed me. "*All is not what it seems,*" she chirped as I bounced along on the camel's back. I was so confused. Are we not *safe?* We seemed to be safe. I was so confused I actually stood up in the stirrups of the saddle and examined the horizon. Were we about to be attacked by the sand people? *What did that message mean?*

We continued onwards, deeper into the desert, and everything seemed fine. We rode for many hours, mostly silent, seeing very little except the expansive stretch of nothingness in every direction. Finally, we set up camp on the golden sand dunes as the sun was beginning to descend (Video: bit.ly/FirstNightInTheDesert). By the time the moon was glowing overhead, we were happily gathered around the campfire. Bilal cooked us dinner and sang us songs from the desert. He regaled us with desert lore and ghost stories, and my heart was taken for a ride with the way he wove his words together.

Over simple curry and rice, he spoke again of his life in the desert and the extreme poverty his family endured. He told us how he worked for this camel tour company, taking out tourists like us for a meager wage. As the darkness of night rose around us, huddled around the comfort of the fire light, he told us his dream. The dream that would save his family and give his children a better life. His dream was to own a camel. If he had his own camel, he could take tourists out himself and not have to rely on the meager wages from the company he was working for. He explained how he had connections at different hotels and could find the jobs. But he needed his own camel.

I listened quietly and felt the tug on my heart. Here I was, a privileged American with so many luxuries available to me that this simple man of the desert and his family could never have access to. I had all the money I had saved up for my travels sitting in my account and I saw an opportunity where I could do some good in the world. "How much is a camel?" I asked Bilal. His response? About $300.

Now, here's the danger of being led purely by the mind and emotions. I was presented with a logical situation where outwardly *it looked* like I could make an impact on this family. My ego also loved it because I had the chance to look and feel good as the rescuer and savior. I didn't say anything that night around the fire, but the mechanics were set into motion in my mind. The next day we stopped in a village because the French guys wanted beer, and together we drank as we rode through the heat of the day. As my mind became tipsy, I became certain of what I would do: I would buy Bilal a camel and save his family! I would be the hero. I even remember writing a postcard the next morning from the saddle to a friend back home, bragging about my intended good deed. My ego - the part of me that just wants to look good and be right - was having a field day.

It was the final night before we returned to Jaisalmer, and again we were gathered around the fire. This time Bilal was laying it on heavier than usual about how unlucky he was, and I saw my chance. "Bilal, you are not so unlucky after all," I said proudly. He looked at me with hopeful eyes. I continued, "You are not so unlucky, because *I* am going to buy you a camel!" Everyone gasped in surprise. What a glorious moment! Together we rejoiced. This man was going to get his dream! The French men were happy, Bilal was happy, and I was feeling high on being the one to save the day.

Sigh. Can you see where this story is going?

I'll cut to the chase: there was no camel. It was a scam. My mind and emotions were being used against me. I was paying more attention to my mind and the way things looked on the outside than I was to the gentle knowing I was receiving on the inside. In fact, on that final morning as we were making the last sandy stretch back toward the jeep, that same invisible bird came and landed on my shoulder to whisper another message in my ear. It said, *"He is not who you think he is."* What? I looked down at Bilal. He seemed like a very nice man. A simple man of the desert who was just trying to feed his family. What did the message mean?

There were other signs and feelings I ignored. For example, when Bilal was originally talking about the camel, I asked him questions like, "Where would you buy a camel?" He explained that there was a special market where there were lots of camels for sale to choose from. On the night I told him I would buy him a camel, I expressed interest in going with him to see the camel market. Maybe I could help pick out the new camel for his family, I offered. However, the next morning as he was bringing back our grazing camels, he said he had good news. He called the company and they said that he could buy *this* camel, he said happily pointing to one of the animals, Rajah. Coincidentally, Rajah happened to be the kindest and slowest camel of the three animals in our group. How lovely! But wait, didn't you say something about ... "Here, sister! You can ride Rajah. He is *your* camel!" I ignored the feeling that something didn't feel right and happily took a photo with my camel, then climbed aboard for the return voyage. I don't know who was happier, Bilal or my ego.

There were two other things that didn't feel right, which I conveniently ignored. The first one was the moment when I told Bilal I would buy him a camel that night over the fire. In that first moment upon hearing the news, he was very happy. We were all happy. But as that moment faded and the French guys and I happily conversed, I looked over at Bilal and noticed something strange. He had this look on his face that suggested he was thinking a lot, but not in a happy dreamy way but in a more...how to describe it...it was like he wasn't there anymore. With a furrowed brow he was lost in his mind, as if he was trying to figure something out. I saw that look and I noticed that I felt something that I didn't understand - it was a kind of contraction inside me. Something didn't feel right, but again, I ignored it because it didn't serve the storyline I wanted to believe.

The next big thing I remember was that on the final morning of the camel trek, we met his son. He was a young boy of about ten years who met us in a village on our way back to the jeep. He was there to help collect the camels once we disembarked to return the red fort city. Now, I was under the impression I was saving this family's future, giving them hope for a better life, and I fully expected the news of the gift of the camel would be exciting for everyone involved.

When we joined his son I encouraged Bilal to share the good news. However, whatever sentiment Bilal shared with his son did *not* elicit the response I expected. The boy did not look happy or excited at all to hear that their family was receiving a camel. In fact, the boy looked unenthused and looked at me almost smugly after his father spoke to him the foreign words my mind could not understand. "*That's strange,*" I remember thinking. But yet again, I swept that feeling of something not being right about this situation under the carpet. I was emotionally invested in the reality of the camel. I sincerely wanted to help. I wanted to feel good about helping this other person so much that I was not willing to listen to or give value to any feelings or indications within me that would otherwise contradict that story I wanted to believe.

We returned to the red desert city feeling exhausted from the trek but energized by the excitement around Bilal getting his dream. High on life, I went out with the French guys to celebrate. We found ourselves in a charming little cafe ordering chai and cookies when a beautiful woman walked in. I had seen her before as I wandered the streets of Jaisalmer. Something about her stood out to me, and not just the color of her white skin amidst the dark-skinned locals. She was tall, and even though she was a total hippie, something about her was very elegant. The cafe was small with only a few seats, so we invited her to sit with us. We were all cheery and bubbling with joy, and honestly, my ego was eager to share my good deed with whoever would listen. The conversation migrated toward our experience with the camels as easefully as the sun rises, and with pride I told her what a hero I was. She listened quietly as I laid out the series of events and what I planned to do, fully expecting her to congratulate me and tell me what a good person I was. Instead, her response shocked me and sent me into a tailspin of confusion and anxiety. After listening intently she paused, then said, "You know there's no camel, right?"

:::insert the sound of the train of my good intentions screeching to a sudden halt:::

The worst part of being conned is the moment when you don't know what's real anymore. When someone you love lies to you, you want to believe them. When the illusion begins to crack, it makes you feel crazy. Especially if you're as emotionally invested in the lie as I was with the camel. To put it simply, I struggled because I wanted to believe the lie. I struggled deeply and my mind and intuition got into a wrestling match. I defended the existence of the camel. I argued all the logical reasons I thought it was real. In fact, I *needed* the camel to be real because I wanted that story to be true. I wanted to be the rescuer, that Bilal's family would be saved, that they would get a better life, and the generosity of my good deed would be to thank.

I cannot tell you the darkness and confusion I sunk into over this. I didn't know what to believe, and it felt *so* uncomfortable, so I did what I always did. I got stoned and avoided it. I numbed myself out and turned off my phone. The first night after I met the woman who shattered my illusion, I had one telephone conversation with Bilal to discuss how I would get him the money for the camel. You see, I didn't have the cash with me there on the desert trek in the moment of elation, so we had to make arrangements to make the transfer.

I was stoned and confused when he called me, and I didn't know what to do, so I picked up. He laid on the emotions thick, calling me "sister, sister" and using his words to get me into the position he wanted. At this point, I was so confused and accustomed to not standing up for myself, to not speaking my truth when I felt uncomfortable, that I didn't have the courage or tools to admit that this didn't feel right. I didn't have the courage to say no to him, so I agreed to meet him in three days after he returned from his next camel trek.

Like a coward, I turned off my phone. Like a coward, I retreated and pretended that if I ignored the situation, somehow it would just go away. I switched hotels and hid out in my room getting high on desert hash and numbing myself to the confusion and feeling of something not being right that was tormenting me. Days passed. I thought everything had smoothed over by ignoring the problem. I assumed that because he couldn't reach me, he wouldn't come. I assumed everything was okay now, but then I ran into the French guys. "We saw Bilal!" they said. "And he's looking for you." They explained how they ran into him on the streets of the city. He had spent a long and arduous day traveling on buses from his remote desert village to Jaisalmer, to come meet me as we had agreed. *Shit*. What had I done? I had to face this. I couldn't run anymore. What if the camel really *was* real and I was just screwing over this simple man from the desert who was just trying to feed his family? I turned on my phone.

No sooner did I turn on my phone, it began to ring. It was Bilal. "Hello, sister!" he cried on the line, a subtle mixture of desperation and hope in his voice. "Hello, Bilal," I said, defeated. I gave some lame excuse for why he couldn't reach me, and he said it was okay and asked when he could come meet me. I didn't know what else to say. My courage to speak my truth was as limp as a wet noodle. So I said I could meet him in the town square in an hour.

I walked through the city streets feeling confused, lost, humiliated, and ashamed. I was ashamed of the potential hurt I had caused this innocent man if there really was a camel, and I was embarrassed for what a fool I was being if it was a scam. I arrived and waited, watching a group of white and grey pigeons taking flight against the background of the desert fortress that loomed over the scene. Soon enough, Bilal arrived and was happy to see me. I feigned pleasantries and we walked a few steps together to take a seat nearby. In his broken English he asked me what happened and explained how he had come looking for me as we agreed. With downturned eyes and frail courage, I repeated my lifeless excuse. Then he asked me if I brought the money. My skin was crawling. I would have torn out my eyes and hair at that moment to escape if I could. Reaching around in the darkness, I tried to find my words to express how I was feeling. I tried, but he responded with his sob story about his family and their poverty and misfortune, and the level of guilt and shame I felt rose like the water level on the Titanic. As the water level rose, the ship of my integrity and truth sank.

Just then, a man saw us and walked over. He looked like a shopkeeper from near where we were sitting and mumbled something to me that I don't think Bilal could hear or understand. He said something like "You better not listen to this desert man, come to my shop and I will explain." But I was too deep in it, Bilal had wrestled me to the ground with shame and guilt and I couldn't move. So I caved. Instead of standing up for myself and saying no, instead of speaking up when something didn't feel right, instead of bearing the pain of potentially causing hurt and eliciting anger in another, I fell on my own sword of good intentions and handed him the money. But it wasn't all the money. It was amazing how the price of the camel instantly dropped and dropped again the more I squirmed. In the end, I gave him about $80, justifying it by saying there *might* be a camel and I didn't want to hurt him. I justified the violation because it was easier than saying no. The shopkeeper looked on at the scene and just shook his head with disappointment and walked away. I felt so much shame in that moment that I could've built a house out of it and lived inside it forever, feeding off the sour milk of my dark emotions.

After the exchange, we got up and started walking back through the square and down the little streets toward my hotel. During the scandal as I mentioned I switched hotels because the first one was a scam anyway (Video: bit.ly/ScamHotel) and I didn't want Bilal to know where I was staying. Yet here he was following me there. I felt like all the shopkeepers down the line were watching and snickering at me, this naive little chicken, and I felt miserable. But at that moment I did something more powerful than ever. I recognized my discomfort and I valued my experience. I recognized that I did not want this man to follow me home, that I was not okay with this, and was not going to allow it to happen. So I stopped and said no. For the first time, I set a boundary. I said, "No Bilal, I want to walk alone now." He tried to protest, but I insisted. I wished him well and went on my own. It was a small action, but I realize now that it was one of the most powerful healing moments of my story. I finally had enough and I wasn't going to allow myself to be taken anymore.

The Conman Closer to Home

I think now about the parallels between this story and the stories of some of my romantic relationships. I had a habit of dating codependent addicts and alcoholics who would tell me what they thought I wanted to hear so they could get what they wanted from me. With the best intentions they would lie to me, and often it felt like I was back in the desert with Bilal with my good intentions and desire to help them being used against me. I gave so much money to the men I was dating because I wanted to believe their victim story and save them from it. I went into relationships where, without consciously realizing it, I wanted to rescue the other person. Just like I wanted to be the savior of Bilal and his family. And I ended up getting hurt.

While I denied myself basic things like good food and a better place to live, I would eagerly hand over money to men who I wanted to love me. I wanted to feel loved and needed by them, so I gave then what they asked for, even when my intuition was telling me not to. And no surprise, to this day, the majority of those men have never paid me back, and probably never will. But the thing is that *they didn't do it to me*. They didn't steal my money. I'm not the victim here. I willingly handed it over. I willingly handed over the money to Bilal, Alex, Dom, and Raz, because I wanted them to be happy and taken care of. I wanted to alleviate their suffering and feel good about myself. I wanted them to need me and stay close to me. I wanted to feel important to somebody. I wanted to be their answer, and so I sliced myself open and bled the life-force of my time, energy, love, and money for them, and they happily drank.

While I got hurt, it was of my own doing. I actively participated in the dynamic by my own free will. I ignored the signs that something didn't feel right. I chose to follow my hungry eyes and base my decisions on what I was seeing on the outside instead of what I was feeling on the inside. And therein lies my true problem: *I wasn't listening to myself.* I wasn't paying attention to the messages I was receiving from that invisible little bird of my intuition who would land on my shoulder and speak to me. It wasn't the message I wanted to hear, so I ignored it. I shooed that bird away and her inconvenient truth and went further into the labyrinth of lies and deception, only to get to the center feeling violated, resentful, disappointed, angry, depressed, and ashamed. I know that place well, and it's a sad place to be. But just like I realized standing in that hotel room stinking of vomit, if my thoughts and choices led to me to this place, then my thoughts and choices could lead me out.

Healing these patterns of self-deception and abuse, taking your power back, raising your vibration, and setting your life on a whole new course of self-realization and discovery starts realizing what your patterns are and having the willingness to start doing things differently. Even if you don't know how, the important thing is to *seek* the way and be *willing* to be shown. For me, it hurt so much that I became willing to face reality. I finally became willing to stop deceiving myself, to stop believing in the illusion that I so desperately want to be real. I had to stop feeding this storyline in my head that he is "The One" and we'll live happily ever after, and instead start listening to what my intuition was gently whispering to me. *Ugh.*

If you're in a place where you don't want to be, the first step to transforming your life is to slow down, stop distracting yourself with drugs, sex, alcohol, Netflix, work, gambling, or whatever you normally lean into when you get uncomfortable and become willing to actually start listening and get *honest* with yourself.

This will take time and periods of introspection, preferably sitting alone by the ocean, in the forest, by the river, or any other quiet place (ideally in nature) away from the confusing energies and agendas of other people. For me, it's a place where I can really hear myself. I go there and I listen. Then, when I get a message, a feeling, a clear direction from my intuition (i.e. "Let him go"), I value it. I don't sweep that inconvenient truth under the rug. Not anymore. Instead, I pick it up and I put it on the center of my inner altar where I can see it, and I make it important. I ask questions, I meditate, I pray, I listen, I gain clarity and trust what comes up, and then I take action to communicate my truth to others.

At the beginning, learning to speak your truth to others most likely won't be a perfect communication, especially if you haven't had a practice of listening to your intuition, getting clarity on your needs and desires, figuring out where your boundaries are, and then honestly speaking your mind in the face of the fear of what impact it will have on others. In fact, at first it probably will be messy and make some people mad. That's okay. I had a hard time learning boundaries because of this.

Learning to set and receive them was extremely uncomfortable for me because my fear was that it was a kind of denial or rejection of me as a person. If someone said to me "No, please don't do that," it felt like they were reprimanding or rejecting me, and it triggered my old fear of being abandoned and not being enough. But I've come to realize that healthy boundaries are not about rejection, they're about *protection*. Protecting myself and the way I want to be treated by others. While it can hurt to say no to others, especially because I want to love and accept everyone, often times that desire for love and acceptance was what caused me to get violated by other people and myself.

I wish I had the courage to stand up for myself and say no to Bilal and risk hurting his feelings. I wish I had been able to endure the discomfort of making Alex mad instead of backpedaling on my truth when his temper rose. If I had done these things, I would've had to endure some temporary discomfort in the moment, but ultimately I would've protected my heart, my emotions, my energy - and not to mention my wallet. But I wasn't ready then. I had to have those painful experiences in order to know what it feels like to allow myself to be violated.

Those painful experiences are valuable because they gave me a direct experience in my body that I can refer back to if I get myself into a situation like that again. If I know what I don't want to feel, if I start to tense up and sense that inner contraction because something is making me feel uncomfortable, that's good data. When I start to recognize the pattern emerging, I can call it out when I see it coming up again. Then I can consciously choose if I want to keep running this same old program, or if I want to choose something different this time.

In the 12-Step program I learned a great way to change these patterns. First, you must do the inquiry about what's really going on and come into the full awareness of how your behavior (input) is causing the violation (output). Once we come to recognize our self-defeating patterns, we then admit them to ourselves, to another human being we trust, and finally, to the God or Higher Power of our own understanding. It's like an act of sincere confession, fully and honestly owning up to how we messed up. Then, with humility and surrender (preferably down on your knees), we ask the God of our own personal understanding to take it away and replace it with something better. This act of humble honesty and surrender to a power greater than ourselves is one of the most transformational actions we can take on the healing journey.

There are no right or wrong answers here, it just depends on what you want. Do you want to be in relationship with people who respect your truth and boundaries, or do you want to be around people who make you feel uncomfortable? Do you want to be in relationship with people who lie to you, manipulate your choices and behavior (always with the best intentions), and slap you with shame and guilt when you try to say no and stand up for yourself and what you want? Do you want to continue to ignore what doesn't feel right so you can stay faithful to a story that only exists in your mind? A self-defeating, disempowering story that causes you to waste, leak, and kill your precious energy? I hope you can really start to recognize the value of your energy. This special stuff you can direct towards making your soul happy, to go do the thing that would make your heart sing. As M would ask, "Why are you *killing* your energy?"

Everyone will have their own truth. That's the point of this book. It's not up to me to tell you what to do. All I can say is that for me, the little bird was right. Back there in the desert, much to the dismay of my mind and ego, all was not what it seemed. Bilal was not who I thought he was, as much as I wanted him to be that person so I could rescue him and feel good about myself.

Today I'm grateful for these experiences of heartache and suffering because they gave me perspective and helped me recognize my own self-destructive patterns of thinking and behaving. Thanks to this perspective that I earned and learned through my own direct experience, I do things differently today.

I'm not perfect, nor will I ever be, but I've made small but important adjustments to how I do things that have made a big impact on my life. For one, I've learned to slow down. I make a practice of examining my motives behind my actions. I take feedback from others about how my behaviors impact them. I've stopped jumping my energy all over the place. I've learned to practice self-love and self-care instead of placing unrealistic expectations on someone else to take care of me or provide me my sense of safety, value, and self-worth. I listen to myself now, and I value that gentle knowing I receive from within.

When I receive the messages from my intuition, I make them real by daring to speak them and act on them. Even when it's scary and I'm afraid of being rejected, I summon my courage and dare to be honest. Today, I speak my truth and follow my intuition, and that's how I tap into the real magic of what it means to be free, and how I discovered my treasure.

How I Found My Treasure

As I mentioned before, I didn't know where I would go after Egypt. Instead of getting stressed out and rushing into a decision to make myself feel safe, I trusted that it was okay to not know. *I decided to stay in the mystery.* I decided to trust that more would be revealed. The next step on the staircase would be shown when I needed it, and not a moment before.

In the weeks leading up to my exodus to Egypt, I went to Maine to see my dear friend Will of Nature, with whom I have shared much contemplation and conversation around God, trees, and seeking the truth of the soul. In a state of quiet receptivity in the woods up in Maine near Sunday River, I received the hunch that I should get back in touch with my teacher Seulki. It had been almost a year since I had met her in Thailand and embarked on the life-changing journey to learn about boundaries, intuition, and a plethora of other abilities that start emerging once those become aligned. I felt the desire to pick up where we left off. I wanted to do some interviews with her online and generally just reconnect with her.

I reached out and she was happy to hear from me and to relay that she was doing well in Guatemala. I had heard her speak of Guatemala before, but back then it always seemed like a far-off, inaccessible place to me. Suddenly, it felt different listening to her talk about this special place. Her life there sounded so simple and magical as she described the satisfaction of getting fresh eggs from the monks at the Qi Gong temple, or about going for a swim in the beautiful waters of the Lake Atitlan, or how this place was a special vortex of energy where accelerated spiritual growth takes place as a plant naturally raises its eyes in prayer toward the light.

As she spoke, I could feel something waking up inside of me. It was that subtle, expansive voice of gentle knowing that said, "*This feels right.*" So I asked her, "Seulki, how would you feel if I came and visited you in Guatemala?" She responded with the delight of an open heart and welcoming arms spread wide, eager to receive me. That's when I knew. After my pilgrimage to Egypt, I wasn't going to do the logical thing, like explore that side of the world. I was going to follow what felt right, which was to come back to the same side of the world that I had started on. Just like walking the labyrinth and going all the way to the other side, only to follow the path back near the place I entered. I decided to follow an illogical path in order to reach the center.

I decided I was going to Guatemala.

Arriving in Guatemala

I encountered all the same emotions when I arrived in Guatemala. I was delighted by the newness and excitement of it all. I was grateful she showed me around the main street of San Marcos (also known as "Hug Street" because it's the place where you see everyone you know and hugs abound). We continued our lessons about boundaries and the way we violate ourselves by not taking responsibility for our own vibration, and the danger of looking for someone else to make us feel good. I had moments of deep gratitude and connection, but I also had moments of familiar confusion. *"What on earth am I doing here?"* I asked the volcano in front of me.

After a week or so, I became eager to find my own place to live and I started stressing out about it. In a low vibration of worry, doubt, and trying too hard to force a solution, I spent time late into the night on the local Facebook groups when I would have been better served by going to sleep. With a furrowed brow in the darkness of night, I scoured the groups looking for a cute little house. Some place charming and hopefully cheap where I could spread my wings and feel at home. But I hit walls of disappointment. It wasn't working, so in my frustration I pulled a tarot card. A wise tree, The Hierophant, was closely examining something lifted up to the light. He looked patient and discerning. Okay, slow down, be patient, don't try too hard. Trust that the answers will come. Trust that nature has its own timing. Okay, fine. *Sigh.*

Several days later, I was having a marketing coaching session with Seulki. When we were done, the energy in the house just felt so intense that I just needed to get out and go for a walk. I didn't know where I wanted to go, except that I just *must* go. For the first time since arriving at the lake, I got a feeling that I needed to walk in the other direction than I normally walked towards town. "I want to walk toward Tzununa," I announced to Seulki. "Do you know a place where I can get a cup of coffee?" I added intuitively, without thinking. She told me about Granja Tz'ikin, with no explanation of what it was. "Gran-ha Chicken? What?" She told me that it was pronounced with a "ts" sound and how I should walk to the docks and grab a tuk tuk up the hill from there. The tuk tuk driver would know the place. So I left, following that subtle inner nudge down the dirt path overlooking the lake. The dust swirled up around me, like all the unanswered questions and frustrations in my mind. I walked until I found the dock and got into a tuk tuk.

I rode up the bumpy, unpaved road higher and higher up the hill, wondering if perhaps we were lost. Finally, the tuk tuk dropped me off, much to my delight, at the entrance of a cute little permaculture farm nestled in the side of the mountain. I was immediately enchanted by the colorfully painted tree at the entrance and the lovable German shepherd puppy that bounded up to greet me, immediately throwing herself at my feet like a long lost love that finally found itself. That was how I found the farm.

Finding My Bliss

That's about when I met the goats. If there's one thing you should know about me, it's that I love goats. I love how mischievous and funny they are. I like their faces and horns and the way they bleat like they don't care what you think ... and oh, look, they just did a backflip and landed on the wall. Don't try to tell a goat what to do. They will laugh and stand on their heads like a good trickster, and then try to steal your tortillas the moment you're not looking.

The moment I met the goats and started petting Jersey and fondling her weird neck balls, something in my heart went off like fireworks. It was a vibration of love and delight. It was *my bliss*. It's the thing Joseph Campbell identified as the key to personal fulfillment after a lifetime of studying the greatest human stories across all cultures and times. According to Campbell, the ultimate lesson for the hero to find their path and claim their treasure is to find and *follow their bliss* – that high vibrational, expansive feeling that the mind will say is crazy and doesn't make sense but the intuition will quietly and gently lead you towards.

I quickly fell in love with the goats and jumped at the chance to walk with them up the mountain every morning at 8am. There was a private room open at the farm for a few days and I was ready to find my own place. However, in my mind I was attached to the idea of having a house. I wanted my own little house for so many reasons, and this clearly wasn't the house I wanted. It was just a room at a farm. While my mind protested at not getting what it wanted, I recognized the vibration of bliss that the goats sparked in me. Even though I wanted a house, I decided to forgo that idea for the moment because I had found something else that was calling to me, undeniably ringing the bell of my heart loud and clear: my love of goats and this unexpected new opportunity to be near some.

I decided to stay on the farm for a few days and take advantage of the chance to walk with the goats up the mountain every morning. Following a kind and quiet Mayan woman named Rosa, I embarked upon my ultimate career as an apprentice goat herder in the mountains of Guatemala. My heart sang! I loved it so much I could write a whole book about the goats and what they taught me about influence and leadership. Oh, how I enjoyed those mornings with the goats, cresting over the mountain's edge overlooking the spectacular Lake Atitlan and the majestic volcanos who hug her.

After a few days, my time in the private room was coming to an end. It was already booked by someone else. Initially, when I took the room I imagined when my time was up I would leave and go across the lake to San Pedro to stay with a local host family and learn Spanish. But as the days went on, I couldn't deny that I loved being at the farm. I loved the goats and the people who tended them, so much that I didn't want to go. After all, I was practicing and learning Spanish every day with Maria, the sweet Mayan woman who ran the farm kitchen. It became clear to me that I wanted to stay. That's when I asked Jeremy, one of the owners, if he knew any place nearby where I could find a room, so I could keep close to the goats and my new family at the farm. "You should meet Luke," he responded on a hunch. "He's building some kind of artist residency thing. I think you would fit right in."

That's how I discovered Karuna Atitlan, the birthplace of this book. As soon as I saw walked into Karuna and looked around, my heart sang. Colorful Tibetan prayer flags danced in the breeze, hammocks stretched across the outdoor living room, openly inviting me to relax. A beautiful Jocote tree, which I would later come to learn was called the "Hanuman Tree," seemed to smile and wave at me in the sunshine. I could not deny or ignore the fact that everything about the place made my heart sing. Being there just felt so *right*. I felt like I had arrived home. And that's when I saw the little house, and my heart nearly exploded with joy.

The tiny wooden house, separate but still close to the main building of Karuna, was still under construction with no windows and doors. As soon as my eyes fell on the humble wooden structure, my heart stood up, pointed, and said *YES!* I knew this little house was to be mine. I even went up to the workers to introduce myself in my broken Spanish, thanking them for their work to build my home, much to their confusion since they had never seen me before. It was even funnier considering I hadn't even met Luke yet. He was out of town in Antigua and essentially handed me the keys to come in, make some tea, and have a look around before he even met me. From there, the rest just flowed like water downhill. One thing lead to the next without trying or force, and now here I am writing these words from that tiny wooden house as the first artist in residency at Karuna.

I started out lost, confused, and feeling alone. But having gone on a journey to learn how to listen to my heart, heed her call, and connect to the vibration of my bliss, I found the treasure of my heart - a happy, nurturing, supportive home in the mountains of Hummingbird Valley.

The Importance of Pleasure

So you've decided you're ready to listen to your inner guidance, raise your vibration, and follow your bliss. Great! What's next? One of the most important things I learned is that our bliss is connected to our pleasure.

When speaking in terms of "pleasure," I don't just mean sex and orgasms, as our culture would like to reduce and shame this powerful vibration that is directly connected to our vitality, life force, and ability to manifest our desires. No, real pleasure is what raises your vibration. Sure, you may think you're getting pleasure from spending hours playing video games, watching Netflix, or getting drunk after a long day - but is that really pleasure, or is it *relief*? There's an important difference.

Pleasure is what I felt when I first pet the goats and felt my heart vibrating like a hummingbird's wings. Pleasure is the feeling I get when I adorn my body with flowing, silky, and colorful fabrics I wear because I genuinely like the way I look. Pleasure is what uplifts my spirit from within and makes my heart smile. Pleasure is playful. Pleasure is joyful. Pleasure isn't concerned with drama. It's in the present moment and we can feel it in our body, just like that expanded feeling I get when something is in alignment with the spiritual guidance from my intuition. It's what happens inside of me when I stop to appreciate the beauty of the mountain or connect with the hidden voice of the tree. Pleasure is taking time to give affection to a dog or person I love. It's making the time to take myself to the water for a swim, or for a relaxing walk in the forest without my phone.

Pleasure is what I feel when I go out of my way to show myself love and thoughtful care. It's in knowing what I like and actively giving it to myself, instead of waiting for someone else to do it for me (then resenting them if they don't bring me flowers).

Pleasure is all about taking responsibility for making myself feel good in healthy and appropriate ways. It's making a special trip to town to get myself flowers because seeing them in my home brings me joy. It's going out of my way to treat myself to a piece of chocolate cake after facing a difficult challenge, savoring every bite, knowing I've earned a reward. It's the sensation I get when I stop to smell the roses, literally.

Pleasure is what I feel when *I say yes to myself* and slip into a hot saltwater bath dotted with lavender oil, or just take a quiet walk in nature. It's investing the time and energy to cook a special meal with my favorite ingredients. It's taking the time to take a break from work to let myself enjoy a quiet moment sitting in the garden, noticing the way the plants grow.

Pleasure is all about self-care, and it's whatever raises my vibration on a moment-to-moment basis. What it is for you will likely be a different formula than it is for me, and that's okay - and that's why you must become *a detective* of your *own pleasure*. It's contained within whatever yields that sense of deep presence and beauty - whatever brings you back to yourself. It's how we help ourselves feel good in a healthy way. And connecting to what truly gives me pleasure is directly related to learning how to give myself the space I need to slow down, breathe, and connect with the true energy source that is greater than me, greater than all things, humans, and especially our little dramas.

What I Learned In Egypt

When I was in Egypt, I learned a lot about pleasure. Specifically, I learned I wasn't really giving myself any.

In fact, at that time I was following a strict regime of self-denial. I had a deeply engrained habit of giving myself the bare minimum just to get by. My wardrobe consisted of plain white t-shirts and just a few pair of pants. For a time, especially while I was starting my recovery work in Bali, I started dressing this way because at that time I felt it was important part of stripping away the layers of ego and its wanting to look good on the outside to gain approval from others. But when I arrived in Egypt, I found myself immersed in a group of beautiful, magical women who were existing at a very high vibration.

At first, my mind wanted to believe that I was better than them because I wasn't focused on outside appearances as they seemed to be, adorned in all their beautiful clothes and jewelry. But as time went on, I saw this wasn't just about outside appearances. The way they showed up in their beauty and grace, and subsequently the high vibration they held in the essence of their being, was *not* about ego. It was about how they were taking *care* of themselves. How they were showing themselves love. And it was in direct contrast to how I was treating myself.

In fact, I started playing that familiar game of comparing myself to these women and then feeling bad. I started feeling less than them and not enough. But then I realized something: *I was doing this to myself.* I was choosing to dress like a boy and then comparing myself to these beautiful women, radiant in their feminine power and beauty, and using that as a reason to beat myself up. I realized this was the exact same pattern I followed when I compared myself to my sister in my childhood.

I decided that if I wanted the vibration they had (output), I would have to stop playing the same old game I was used to playing (input). Instead of playing out my past patterns, and the results it always got me, I chose to start doing things differently. If I wanted what they had, I would start doing what they were doing. I watched the way they would treat themselves to a massage or spa after a long day sightseeing, and while it felt very scary to me to spend that money on myself, I decided to face my fears and take the risk of showing myself some love and much needed self-care. While my fearful mind kicked and screamed at this new behavior, my body rejoiced at this new level of attention and care. I watched the way these women bought themselves souvenirs and jewelry, so I swallowed my fear and picked up a few special trinkets that made me happy.

In fact, one of the scariest things I did on that trip was to buy myself a beautiful gold Isis ring. I had seen it in the gift shop of our hotel and was instantly mesmerized by its elegance and beauty. I longed for it, and previously I would not have let myself buy it out of fear of running out of money. I had worn nice rings before, but they were always put there by a man, by someone that was not *me.* I had never given myself that kind of gift because I had never considered it to be my job. I always thought it was a man's responsibility to make me feel good. If there wasn't a man to provide the thing I wanted, then I justified my desire away, saying I couldn't afford it and I would be fine without it. But now things were changing - *I* was changing.

I'll never forget the moment in my hotel room in Cairo, holding the cash for the ring in my sweaty hands. I was sitting on the bed, practically shaking, when my roommate walked in. She was a lovely woman from France named Sarah. She was always smiling and I like to think of her as a giggle in human form. She was full of so much aliveness and grace, and in that moment it felt was like an angel was arriving.

I looked up from my darkness as she entered the room. I was obviously distraught, holding the money in my hands. She immediately came and sat next to me, soft and loving, and asked me what was wrong. I expressed how much I wanted that ring, to give myself a special gift to commemorate this important journey to Egypt, but that I was afraid to spend the money on myself. She received me and my fear with warmth and compassion, congratulating me on my courage to give myself something special, something that I really wanted. She reassured me it would be okay and that this was a nice thing to do for myself, adding with a giggle, "Enfin, you're an alchemist now."

Showing Up For Myself in Guatemala

After a series of humbling experiences flexing my courage to learn and practice new and nurturing behaviors to love and care for myself in Egypt, by the time I got to Guatemala I was ready to step into my beauty and power unlike ever before. Instead of making those same old choices that kept me down, literally experiencing my life at a lower vibration, I dared to do things differently.

Even though it was scary and uncomfortable, I spent money on
new clothes, some beautiful silk designs handmade in India. When
I put on these clothes, I felt like a goddess. And I didn't do it to
impress anybody on the outside. I did it because, for the first time,
I really *liked* the way I looked as a woman. I did it for me.

And it wasn't just about clothes and jewelry. I started feeding
myself better too. I remember passing a French restaurant on the
lake that I had heard so many good things about. I was hungry, and
my first impulse was to go in and have lunch. My mind, however,
still entrenched in the old beliefs of fear and not-enoughness, stood
in my way with fists clenched and practically screamed at me.
"You cannot afford this! If you spend this money you will be
empty and alone and you will *DIE!!!* Ugh, *so* much drama. By
this time, I was getting tired of my mind's fearful drama, and
happily, I was coming to know better than to believe everything I
thought. I waved my mind aside with a hand adorned with a golden
Isis ring and decided to follow my body and intuition into the
restaurant.

Much to my delight, I found a table overlooking the water with
tropical yellow flowers hanging overhead. I treated myself to a
delicious fish lunch with a fresh lemonade for less than $20. It was
an extremely satisfying moment, writing in my journal, reflecting
on my journey and just affirming to myself that I am worth taking
care of and I don't need someone else to do it for me. I was finally
learning to take responsibility for my own wellbeing. Through
recognizing my old patterns and choosing to make different (and
initially very scary) choices, I was becoming self-empowered.

I began to adopt these new habits and patterns of self-love and
self-care, treating myself as I would treat someone I love. I began
to see quite clearly how giving myself these nice things and
experiences helped me feel good about myself, and subsequently
raised my energy and my vibration. And that was not something

anyone else could do for me, because it was a feeling that came from inside. The big change in my life started when I began to value myself, my body, my wellbeing, and my experience of life more than I ever had before.

Coming Home to Ourselves

M would always say that things like coffee and drugs were "copy energy." This is not real energy, he would say. Real energy comes from inside. It comes from connecting with the truth within us. These petty control dramas we do amongst each other, as I did with my family, partners, lovers, and myself, were all just a desperate attempt to take energy from a secondary source in an attempt to create a sense of safety. The back-and-forth exchanges with an abusive partner are just like any other addiction; we do it because we get something from it.

The victim plays a role that draws in energy from others, just like a vampire but with a slightly different flavor. The vampire takes energy, while the victim allows it to be taken from them. The self-righteous martyr serves too much to others without setting boundaries to protect or care for themselves, while the parasite accepts being served without mindful reciprocation. And it all comes down to control and safety.

The martyr is trying to control someone else by serving, helping, or trying to save them. They feel safe when they do this, like they won't be abandoned if someone needs them and what they are receiving from them. The victim is trying to control the flow of energy they receive by engaging in way that elicits pity from others, and in its darkest shadow, by victimizing others out of an entitled desire for retribution. The parasite is trying to feel safe and control the energy by leeching off others who are typically playing the martyr role. And the vampire is trying to control the energy by taking it from anyone they can seduce into allowing them to do so.

When we play these games, we get a hit of energy that says we're not alone. It helps us fill that hungry space within us, that bottomless pit we desperately try to fill with something or someone outside of ourselves. But it only gives us temporary relief, not lasting joy. And needless to say, it's not a healthy exchange, and it's contingent on the absence of clear and direct boundaries, with ourselves and others.

Arriving Home in Heaven

I had to travel to the ends of the earth to discover that the old adage is true: there's no place like home. And that home is inside my heart, and so too is the Kingdom of Heaven.

Heaven is not some place we go when we die. If heaven and hell exist, then they are right here, right now, and we create them for ourselves by how we choose to use our minds and our energy. Heaven and hell are of our own making.

If we are taking, allowing to be taken from, giving, or receiving energy from others out of entitlement, guilt, shame, fear, anger, compensation for perceived failures, pity, obligation, control, a need to be loved or rescue others, and consequently enable others, then we fall out of alignment with ourselves and the truth of our hearts. If we are allowing ourselves to be taken from in a way that makes us feel uncomfortable, like I was with Bilal or Alex, outside of what feels good and what feels right for us, then we are losing energy. This is how we fall out of harmony with ourselves and the forces of nature that wish to prosper us, if only we would learn to get out of our own way.

So the question becomes, how do we bring ourselves back into alignment? How do we return to integrity and tap into the real energy source? The same source that grows the plants toward the sun without trying? Indeed, plants don't try, they just grow towards the light. And so can you.

First we recognize our choices and how they impact our energy and our vibration. We take some time to walk quietly through the garden of ourselves and observe what we have been growing there. When we find the undesired plants growing in the garden of our life, it can be easy to feel despondent or overwhelmed. It's easy to throw ourselves to the ground and become upset for the disaster our life has become. But that doesn't help our future garden. In fact, that victim pattern only feeds and pumps the same cycle of drama and lower vibration that got us into this mess in the first place. We must first *observe* without judgment what we're growing. Then, we decide if we want to grow something else. Even when it feels challenging and uncomfortable, we make the choice to start doing things differently.

And with all things the grow, it won't happen in a day. We won't make the decision in a moment of inspiration, toss some seeds on the ground, and expect the flowers of our dreams to burst forth. No. This process of transformation takes time, hard work, and most importantly, *patience.*

We must first do the work to clear the land. Ripping out those plants does not feel good in the moment. I know that pain all too well, especially as I gave away all my favorite clothes and possessions so I could go travel. But remember, *the sacrifices are worth it* because we're making space in our garden for something new to grow (Video: On Letting Go http://bit.ly/ EricaOnLettingGo). So first we get a vision, then we endure some temporary discomfort as we clear out what we don't want so we can make new space for something new to grow. Then we start planting the new seeds with our energy and intentions.

We plant our ideas and we *trust* in the process. But that doesn't mean we're absolved from hard work. No, *not* taking responsibility for doing the necessary work to maintain our desired vision is how the garden got messy in the first place. Our responsibility to our new seeds is that we must come back again and again to give them the water of our love. We must water them day in and out, even when we can't see the results yet, when nothing green and delightful has broken through the surface. We water the seeds of our dreams with our thoughts, words, and actions, and that's how we begin to come into integrity with our true selves and manifesting our desires.

We direct our energy towards what we want, and so too must we take the time to remove the weeds of what we don't want - the patterns of thinking, speaking, behaving, and relating to others (including substances) that hurt us, keep us playing small, and hold us back. When we give energy and attention to what we want, become aware of what isn't working, and then take action to change those self-defeating patterns, we create space for miracles in our life. When we are in that kind of alignment, our life-force - our limitlessly creative energy tapped into the unlimited potential of the Universe - can flow in a natural and healthy way, yielding the prosperity and abundance that is our natural state and our birthright. When we align our energy and direct it towards our true desires aligned with the guidance of our intuition, new life is possible where we thought there was only a barren landscape, a dreary desert of old habits.

Today, the pieces on the board of my life have shifted, and what I thought would always be is no more, and what I have instead are people who love me for who I am. They can receive my truth without flinching. And the crazy thing of all is they *want* my truth. These safe, loving people want me to check-in with myself and see what's there. They want to know how I'm feeling and they encourage me to express myself honestly. They don't get angry or shame me for what comes out. They receive it, they handle it, they hold it, and they love me no matter what. These are people who love me as I am and support me to go after my dreams. And that is the most amazing treasure of all. And it's one I gave to myself by refusing to accept unsafe people in my life, even if that meant I needed to be alone for a while as I did the work to recognize and change my patterns and find my new tribe.

One of the most important lessons I've learned on my path is that once I started doing the healing work inside, the Universe starts to deliver me the complementary people, places, and things on the outside. I could not find my home on the outside until I was led home on the inside. And it turns out, I didn't need someone else to give me the answer, as much as I thought that's where my answers would come from. In fact, I ultimately found my answers by tapping into the truth within me, a truth that was always waiting for me to wake up and seek it. *It was there all along.*

So again, there are no right or wrong answers here, just inputs and outputs. And all data is good data. No matter what happened in the past, it doesn't need to determine the trajectory of your future. That is, unless you want it to. Unless you're committed to your own misery and doing things the same way you've always done it. Unless you're emotionally invested in a storyline that ultimately hurts you, like I was up with Bilal until the point that I decided I had enough and decided to start making different choices. Just know that wherever you are, there is always hope (Video: <u>bit.ly/ ThereIsHopeForYou</u>). There is hope for you because you have the ability to choose.

As your birthright as a vibrational being of light born into this human form, you *do* have an intuition, a built-in spiritual GPS that is designed to guide you through the ocean of fear and illusion that is life here on earth. But it only works if you work it. Recognize you have a mind, but are not your mind. Like your intuition, your mind is another built-in tool to help you navigate this reality. While it's great to keep you safe, it's not the best guide towards your joy. If you want find your bliss, learn to recognize your mind with all its fears, judgments, and belief systems installed in its operating system. Then realize that your mind and all of its thoughts, projections, illusions, and plans, is different than your intuition - that inner GPS system you can trust to guide you home.

When you are led by the mind, you will seek control and the illusion of safety. When you decide to let your intuition be your guide, when you decide to pay attention to your vibration and commit to raising it through what gives you true pleasure, what you will seek and ultimately find will be something much better and more fulfilling. Perhaps the very thing that you feel you're lacking from where you are now.

It's okay if you don't know how to get there yet. In fact, *it's not your job to know*. Your job is to tune into yourself, look for the things that give you pleasure, and in so doing commit to raising your vibration. That's how you'll find your path. Wherever you're stuck, get on your knees and humbly ask for guidance from whatever your concept is of a power greater than yourself. Then listen and follow when you receive a nudge, a hunch, a push or an opportunity that feels expansive. Even in that space of not knowing of how things will work out, if you're *willing* to listen and to seek, then you already have the key in your hand.

If you're not ready to listen to your intuition because what it says scares you too much, that's okay. Maybe you need to do more research, like I had to do in the desert with Bilal. Whatever you choose is okay. Whatever you're feeling is okay. This is *your* journey. Just know that truth is waiting for you, as it was in the beginning and so shall it be in the end. Your bliss is also waiting for you to decide to start seeking it. And as M would say, *"It's up to you."* Adding with his characteristic shrug over a dusty case of rubies and emeralds, "It's all for learning, anyway."

"Leap and the net will appear"

~ John Burroughs

Chapter 11 - Why Most People Will Never Leave Home

Most people will never leave because they fundamentally don't want to let go of the way they're used to doing things. They want to keep running the same patterns of living because they are deeply entrenched and familiar, and doing the inner and outer work to forge a new path can be too scary and uncomfortable. Many people will never step out of what feels safe and familiar because they are not willing to face that discomfort. They will not be willing do the necessary work to challenge and peel back the accumulated layers of belief systems that have been programmed, trained, traumatized, and educated into them that inform their expectations of what they can and cannot do - belief systems that leave them feeling fearful and easy to manipulate into patterns of consumption, scarcity, and control.

In order to find the bugs in the system - the beliefs that hold us back - sometimes we need to do a whole system reset. That can be a very difficult and uncomfortable process, which most people would rather avoid altogether. So many people would rather keep the things they are complaining about than make the hard choices and necessary sacrifices in order to call in something new - something more aligned with who they really are and what they truly want out of life.

One primary reason I believe so many people stay submerged in the programs and limiting belief systems that keep them down at the bottom of the cage, and not going after their dreams, is that they surround themselves with a certain kind of crab. The kind of crab who is content at the bottom of the cage, content to complain, almost as if they know who they are when they complain. Not complaining would be too uncomfortable, so they dare not let go of something that gives them a sense of identity and purpose.

Most people will stay trapped in a loop of shame, guilt, and a lower vibration. Sure, they are interested in going to do the thing calling them to South Africa, but they are not committed. They are not willing to push themselves past the discomfort of change. Instead, you'll find them every night planted in front of Netflix with a bottle of wine and a bowl of weed, all too satisfied to cut the edges off the stresses of life while also numbing what otherwise might be the potential for their own joy and self-discovery.

In order to go on an adventure like I do, you may need to start doing some rebelling. You may need to start rebelling against the programming of your friends, family, and your own mind that says you can't do it. You may need to start rebelling against a system of thinking, speaking, and behaving that is specifically designed to keep you consuming, working, and running on the hamster wheel but going nowhere.

I'm not saying that anyone should quit their job like me. In fact, I highly encourage you *not* to quit your job. I encourage you not to make any hasty decisions in a moment of inspiration and excitement. What I encourage my friends to do is recognize where they're at. Take some time alone, without all the distractions, and recognize what's going on inside of you. Recognize what systems you've been buying into, where you're putting your energy, and how you distract yourself from the truth calling to you from within. Recognize the games you've been playing to get energy, attention, and feelings of safety, and decide if you want to keep doing things the same, or if you're ready to make a change. If *you* are ready and willing to change.

Most people will never leave home, will never change their lives, because they can't or are unwilling to focus their energy. They have too many leaks in the system. Other things come up and they get distracted and put their energy there. For some - especially women - trying to take care of everyone else and make sure everyone else is okay is energetically taxing and leaves us little for ourselves. Using drugs (prescription or otherwise), alcohol, and other addictive behaviors, we further block our intuition and kill our energy because the edges are too sharp and we don't have a better support system to help us manage our feelings. So we default to the most convenient method, possibly what we learned from our parents, the people around us, and from popular culture that saturates our perspective of reality. Unfortunately for so many, sometimes the easiest thing within reach are opiates, and too many friends have been lost in this kind of dance with life.

But like M said, "It's up to you." What do you want? What are you willing to make sacrifices for? How many more red flags need to stand up and start waving in your face before you recognize the pattern and become willing to take action to stop violating yourself and your truth?

We must learn to protect our energy. We must learn to open our hearts and find the truth that is there. We must learn to challenge what we believe and become willing to peel back the layers of shame, guilt, anger, fear, and accumulated belief systems that aren't ours and aren't serving us. Only then can we become free.

Freedom is the thing waiting for us when we've decided we're going to stop trying to climb the rope and get anywhere. Freedom is the bird that sails over the mountain range, not separate from it, but a part of it. Freedom is the thing calling to us from underneath the oppression and repression, it is the thing that says "Don't give up, I'm still here and I want you." Freedom wants you just as much as you may want her. And like any partner, she needs you to show up. She needs you to wake up early and decide in your heart you're not going to waste your time anymore on meaningless things that keep you small, that keep you playing the same power games and having the same conversations in the places you don't want to be. Freedom believes in you, but do you believe in her? She's waiting for you to look up from the rungs of the ladder of success you've been busy climbing, waiting for you to realize that both ends are on fire and the only way to her is to *let go* and *trust*.

We must learn to stop leaking, killing, and stealing energy.

Most people will never leave, and they'll point the finger outside of themselves. They'll say they can't afford it, they'll say it's not possible, they'll say it's the fault of their job or their boss. The funny thing is that they'll blame their imprisonment on the jail keeper outside of themselves, while they themselves are holding the key in their hand all along.

What if you were holding the key to your freedom all along, but you never realized it? Perhaps you've been too distracted by watching other people's lives on social media, the adventures of fictional characters on your favorite show, the drive for career success, the drama of family and life, other people's projects, or perhaps an endless stream of romantic relationships that keep you focused on someone else?

What if you stay stuck because, in a weird subconscious way, you actually like it? It can be hard to see from the level of the mind that loves to identify things as good or bad, or what should or should not be. Underneath the rules of the mind we can discover a different story. There we can find an addiction to the energy and power dynamics of pushing and pulling with others, like a pump that draws up water from the earth. I realize now in this writing something that M would say to me that I didn't understand at the time, but now I do. In my moments of drama and extreme emotions, he would tell me to "S*top this pumping.*" I didn't know what that meant, but I see now that I was unconsciously using the drama I was creating with the people around me to pump my energy, just like water in a well. I didn't consciously realize it, but a part of me actually *liked* to get my energy this way, even though it often left me angry or in tears.

232

I remember when things were really falling apart with Alex. I was starting to flex new boundaries to protect myself and what I really wanted, instead of just going along with what he wanted. As I started saying no to him, he responded by saying "I don't like you very much anymore." In one instance, when his true colors were rising, I was engaged in a conversation with him that was a back-and-forth story. I wanted him to understand how he hurt me and we were both trying to make each other wrong and in an un-winnable power game.

When I talked to Seulki about it, she called me out with exasperation over this self-imposed drama, telling me to just stop responding to him, to simply stop texting him back. She suggested that I was actually *addicted* to this power game of shame and blame I was playing with him, and that's why I couldn't stop going back for more. If I wasn't addicted to this drama, then why did I keep texting him back, even though it was literally hurting me and robbing me of peace? I had to admit, she was right. I was getting something out of engaging in this drama with him. And I think part of the reason why I kept doing the thing that hurt me, was that unconsciously, I believed I deserved it because I had such low self-esteem.

By engaging in these games, I was getting what I felt like I deserved, so I kept interacting with this person who would give me that kind of energy exchange. That's why, in many regards, we were a perfect match. I felt like a piece of poo on the inside and, subconsciously, I enjoyed the feeling I got as the vampire fed on me, because at least by taking my blood (as in, my energy, time, money, etc.) I felt wanted. Even though it was literally draining me, I continued to play the game because part of me enjoyed it. Crazy, I know.

If It Were Easy, Everyone Would Do It

Ending the cycles of abuse, addiction, self-betrayal, deception, and neglect is no easy task. It requires a strong desire to change and a willingness to end the madness by any means necessary. And that means doing the hardest thing of all: facing ourselves and what we *really* want. For me, in order to find my freedom, I needed to pull back the rug of everything I had hidden away from my conscious mind. I needed to break the many locks and open the door to my own darkness. I needed to go down into that cave and meet myself there.

I needed to find my inner child, crying, scared, feeling rejected, abandoned by her parents, fearful of the world and of being abandoned. I needed to take her into my arms and become the mother I needed all along. I needed to take this little girl in close and tell her that it's alright. That she is loved, that she can do it, that there's hope and she's not alone. I needed to tell her that she's worthy of love. She doesn't need to bring home perfect grades or know what she wants to do with her life. She doesn't need to have the right answers in order to be worthy of love. She is worthy of love just by being herself. Just by being the gift that she is on this planet, without any extra effort or force, without having to prove herself to anyone. Just by being who she is, she is welcome, safe, and loved. There's nowhere to go, there's nothing to do, there's nothing to fix, earn, prove, perform, or achieve. She needs to know that she is lovable, accepted, and enough - exactly as she is.

Most people will not do this work on themselves, and as such will never leave the life they know. They will stay put exactly where they are, playing the same games, feeding on the same ideas and belief systems they've been fed without questioning them. The kind of beliefs that say you need to trade your time for money, show up at the factory every day, keep your head down and don't complain or want anything. But often they *will* complain about it, however they won't *do* anything to change it. They will not *seek* another way. They will keep doing the same work that is killing their body and soul, day in and out, coming home to get high or drunk or fat because it's a relief, but not a pleasure. They will not change because truly they don't want to. Because that low vibration is a comfortable and familiar place to be, and stepping out is too scary, so they'd rather stay on the couch and not take responsibility for their choices, their dreams, or their lives.

Serving Others

I want to make something clear: learning to connect with yourself, taking your power back, consciously directing your energy, and manifesting your dreams does *not* mean not helping others. No. In fact, meaningful service to others is an important part of being happy and whole as we unlock the formula to fulfill our spiritual mission on this earth.

Serving others is an integral part of meaningfully living our lives and finding our bliss. The point is, we must put our water where it will make a difference. Where it will help grow the life that is yearning to know itself. We must find the place where we give because it is enriching and nourishing for us to do so - not giving to others out of guilt, obligation, or a desire to control and manipulate others, which can often be the case with unsafe people or situations.

When we keep giving our energy and gifts to unsafe or unhealthy people - those who do not have respect for our truth nor our boundaries - then we are allowing a violation of something sacred to occur. They may be violating and taking from us, but we are the ones who *allow* it to happen. We are the ones who let it go on, even when it makes us feel uncomfortable because - in a weird way - we feel wanted. And that can better than what we really feel on the inside.

It feels better to allow the vampire to suck away your time, your energy, your love, your intention, and life-force energy, because the alternative can feel worse. Even receiving toxic energy from someone can feel better than receiving no outside energy at all. Often times, we tolerate and endure abuse because it feels better than being left alone with ourselves - especially if we're used to using others to distract ourselves from our own dreams and wounds - and from facing ourselves and the root of our pain. Most people will spend a lifetime avoiding coming back to themselves and to their own pain, to finding and healing the original wound from long ago that became covered in the overgrowth of an unexamined life.

The Story of the Miracle Tree

Once upon a time in Thailand, I had a friend who was a Banyan tree that was over three-hundred years old, and she was very sick. Most of her leaves had fallen off and she lacked a certain vitality, as the branches themselves appeared to be grey and wilted. I cried under this special tree, because at that time I felt like that tree - I felt like I had a sickness inside too.

One day, I heard a silent plea from the tree asking me to help her, so I went to ask permission from the monk. You see, the tree was growing in the courtyard of a very old Buddhist temple where I would come to learn walking meditation. So I went to the monk Olarn and asked him if I could help the tree, and he responded that first I must *help myself*. First I must meditate and take care of my energy before I try to heal anyone else. So I took that as the permission I needed and I came back the next day. Driving up on my motorbike through the red and golden archway of the temple grounds, I saw the sad state of the tree missing her leaves and it filled my heart with sadness. But I also felt hope for her.

So first, I would meditate. I would walk in the meditation hall for two hours, up and down the smooth marble floors of the temple. A golden Buddha waited for me on one side, watching me with eyes that know suffering and the freedom from it. I would walk and watch my busy mind, witnessing the whirlwind of thoughts and try again and again to let them go. Like watching leaves floating down a river, I would witness the dramas that were playing out inside my head and of all the illusions and stories I was telling myself that were not actually real.

For those two hours, I would see the thoughts for what they were: judgments, imaginary conversations, stories, regrets of the past or plans for the future, etc. By beginning to recognize my thoughts, I started to see the ways my thoughts pulled at my emotions and the wellness of my mental state. I would practice recognizing them and coming back to the present moment. No matter how busy my mind was, I would keep bringing my awareness back to the sensation of my feet on the floor. Come back to my breath and to the quiet center within me. Every time my mind would wander like a lost lamb, I would consciously herd it back with each footstep and breath.

After two hours of walking meditation were completed, I went to the well on the temple grounds. I found this hidden well one day by chance, following the nudge of my intuition and a subtle feeling of *"What's over there?"* The structure looked older than the memory of several generations, with crumbling bricks and a modest dark well inside. I swept the stone floor with a waiting broom, then dropped the bucket down into the ancient well. It was a simple well, made of stones fashioned into place by hands from another time, when there was no internet or airplanes or televisions and the propaganda they spew.

Lowering the bucket by a rope into the darkness, I pulled a few times before it submerged and I was able to bring up the humble water. I took the bucket to the small window and leaned out, instinctively pouring the water over my head while saying, "Thank you for washing away what no longer serves me." Again I poured the cold, possibly parasite-infested, and yet oh-so-sacred water over my head and said, "Thank you for cleaning my thoughts. *Thank you for cleaning my energy.*"

I then filled another bucket and took it back to the sickly tree. She looked so majestic and enormous, swallowing up the whole frame of my vision in the distance. As majestic as she was, it was sad to see her like this. The branches missing their leaves was such a sorry sight. I felt deep remorse for that tree, and all the while, the tree was my mirror for how my own heart felt at that time after all the mistakes and disappointments with Labracadabra and Alex. I felt like I was empty of leaves, grey, and almost rotting inside.

When I arrived with the water, I reached out and touched her bark as I would the skin of a lover. I came close and took her in my embrace, or rather, I let the tree take me into hers. On many occasions, I quietly cried when I hugged the tree. I cried because she was sick and I was sad to see her this way. I cried because *I* was sick inside and it hurt to see *me* this way. I cried because it felt we would always be sick, that our leaves would never grow back, and that's just the way things were and would always be. But in the face of the desolation of the ways things might always be, I showed up with the water of my love and started walking around the vast circumference of the tree.

I walked around three times, pouring the healing water at her roots, and I spoke to the tree. I told her that she was beautiful, she was strong, she was worthy, and that I loved her. I told her that I believed in her and that her leaves could grow back. I encouraged her not to give up as I delicately touched her bark. I spent perhaps an hour each time with the tree. I would sweep away the fallen leaves at her feet and pull out the dead branches. The tree was so large I would only do one small section at a time, and then I would sit under her to pray and listen to what she might have to say. I felt a feeling of peace and gratitude then.

I came back to the tree again and again over a period of two weeks. I would first meditate alone in the halls of the monastery, practicing witnessing my thoughts and coming back to my breath and my body in the present moment. After about two hours, I would return to the hidden well of healing water and drop the bucket of my intentions into the darkness and pull up the water. Again, I would pour it over my head in a ritual of absolution. Amidst the pain of having no leaves to shine in the light, I would give thanks for my healing, and the healing of my friend the tree. And again, I would bring this water to my friend and pour it on her roots and tell her she was beautiful, even though she was missing her leaves. Each time, I would proceed to clean away the debris of death collected at her feet.

As I worked through each section on my hands and knees, I made the most surprising discovery. There, hidden amongst the dead leaves of the past, I found ancient relics. Statues that must have been hundreds of years old - gifts from monks and disciples long since deceased. I found faces of wise old sages and of the Buddha himself, glorious in his transcendence of suffering. I found powerful Durga riding her tiger and beautiful Kuan Yin perched on a cloud, carrying a vessel containing the water of life, the purifying water of forgiveness and compassion. I dug into the tree, pulling away the layers of death to find the love and life underneath. I swept the passageway and she became clean again.

As I returned each time I would do more, little by little. Each time I brought her fresh flowers and placed them in her branches I could reach, as if adorning her with precious jewels. I tied ribbons to her many wrists that I had gotten from the shop as I was practicing my own self-love errands I was just starting to adopt. At this time, I was learning a new self-care practice that included going out of my way to give myself flowers, the overflow of which I was now sharing with the tree.

Then, one day, the most surprising thing happened. I was driving along the road on the way back to my house on Coconut Lane that I had moved into after the breakup with Alex. As I passed the red and gold entryway of the temple, something caught my eye. Something I had never seen before. I did a double-take followed by a U-turn, and found myself rolling into the driveway of the temple with my jaw dropped. Tears welled up in me as I raised my eyes to the sky in astonished awe. *She was growing leaves!*

Green leaves like triumphant jewels were sparkling and waving at me in the sunshine. I was speechless. I was in awe. I wished I had taken a photo of her before, but I hadn't because honestly I never expected there would be such a remarkable change. I didn't think such healing was possible from such a state of sickness and desolation. But there she was with leaves that were not there before, and I could barely believe my eyes! It was a testament to the healing power of love, and what happens when we take care of ourselves and each other. This was what happened when I placed the medicine at the root of the wound. You can see a video from that moment of astonishment here: bit.ly/MiracleTreeHealing

So my friends, your tree of life may be sick. It has been neglected. Its leaves have fallen off and it doesn't seem like there's any hope. You could give up. It's true, it's easier not to try. It's easier not to believe, to just give up and deflate your energy in front of the TV or computer screen and not try to change. When we say it's impossible, that it can't be done, it's like giving ourselves a permission slip to fail. It's like giving ourselves the excuse to not take responsibility for stepping up and actually putting energy toward our own healing and joy. It's much easier to stay in the bottom of the cage with the other crabs, but *is that really where you want to be?*

Most People are Not Willing to Believe

Most people will never leave for their adventure because they don't believe it's possible, and they're willing to accept that. They're willing to accept that the leaves are not there and that's the way it will always be. They resign themselves to that belief, as if it were a fact. But I can tell you, I've seen it with my own eyes: the leaves can grow back. But you'll have to show up. You'll have to invest the time in yourself, to take responsibility for your thoughts, your beliefs, and the poison in your own water. You must purify the your thoughts and clean your energy. You must purify your water of yourself with love and the intention to release the poison. Send it back, reject it. You must refuse to continue to allow the violation to occur within your own system.

It's not easy - that's why most people will never do it. Most people will spend their lives avoiding what's down there in the shadow space of themselves. They will be too afraid to face it, so instead they'll distract themselves with work, sex, shopping, or other earthly clamors, like the crabs scuttling around in the bottom of the cage. Crabs too distracted by the gossip and drama of their little society inside the cage that few will ever even stop to look up, to see that the light is there just waiting for the one brave enough to start reaching for it.

If you want to go traveling, it's not just about the places you'll go and the things you'll see. Sure it's incredibly fulfilling to bathe in the cool cascading water of a waterfall reached by paddle boat down a jungle river in Bali, or to swim as a mermaid in the clear blue waters hugging a magical island in Thailand, or to pet wild horses in the open rolling fields of Iceland, or finally to taste the heart opening medicine of cacao in a magical valley in Guatemala.

But more than anything, this is about the journey we take on the *inside*, from darkness and slavery, through the valley of tears, and onwards toward the sunny shores of happiness and freedom just waiting for us to dare to set out and claim it for ourselves.

Most People Will Let Fear Stop Them

Most people will not go. They will not connect with their heart. They will stay hidden under the layers of the mind. They will choose their fears over their freedom. They will not leave behind their homelands with a dream held firmly in their heart, in their hands, and in feet that take the brave steps forward. They will stay home where it feels safe, where they can see all the walls and touch all the edges of their familiar reality, even though it may feel like they are closing in towards death by suffocation.

Most people will not summon their courage to face their monsters with compassion. Most people will not invest the time to show up at the temple to meditate and go through the motions to heal themselves and the tree. They will stay at home and scoff and scorn from their couches that it's not possible. Then they will complain about what they have, about their jobs, their life, and their curdling dissatisfaction. They will complain about it, but then choose to continue on with it. They will follow the same routine and patterns like prisoners working in the same trenches, day in and out. They work the trenches of their own depression and dissatisfaction. *Why?*

Perhaps they believe they deserve to be there. Their mothers and fathers spent their lives in these trenches, so they never thought there was any other way. They're supposed to be in this trench. Perhaps they believe that they are meant to be here and that they are not allowed to leave. Leaving would mean leaving behind a something that feels familiar, safe, and comfortable. Leaving might mean you would have to leave behind your friends and family working alongside you in the trench, and that idea alone is enough to strike terror in the heart.

But the thing is that you can climb out of that trench anytime you choose. First you have to wake up and realize where you are. You might have to appreciate for a moment how familiar it feels there, how well trained these tools you're holding in your hands feel, how in a way it feels *safe* inside the trench. Then ask yourself: is that the kind of "safety" you want? Then, look up and see what's over the edge. There is a light that is there waiting for you, and you must decide if you want it. In order to claim this light, you must reject the trench and all its comforts and familiarities and decide in your heart that it's time to go.

Swim little crab, *swim*.

The other crabs might look up at that point and tell you you're crazy, and that you should get back to work. In fact they'll probably start should-ing all over you, entrenched in their own belief systems of right and wrong, and the way things should be done. As they spew their poison to keep you down, don't listen. Close off the ports and don't let that USB key full of viruses and psychic parasites inside your system. Protect your energy and swim. If they reach for you, keep going. If they tear off your claws, bless them, forgive them. They don't know what they're doing. Give them your compassion for their human suffering. It's only normal they want you to stay in the trench with them. They love you and your energy, and they don't want to be in the trench without you. Love them with all your heart, but decide where you want to be. And then take your precious energy and go there. Move towards the light. Because when you decide to show up with a heart of desire for healing and freedom at the tree of life, and put your love and healing intentions at the root of the wound, the leaves can and will grow back.

Chapter 12: The Way to Freedom

So, *wow*. We've covered some pretty tremendous terrain together. If you've gotten this far, I'm proud of you. And by all means, you're probably still at home sitting on the couch. Wherever you are, my hope is that at some point during this reading you got up, went outside, and sat under a tree.

Sometimes M would do the strangest things with me. Sometimes he would take me to sit under a towering Chinar tree in Kashmir, or out onto an intricately carved and colorfully painted shikara boat on Dal Lake. Sometimes in New Delhi we would go and sit together in an open field near the India Gate monument. He would take me to these places, often against the indignant protestations of my mind that had imaginary important things to do and always, *always* the need to understand. But we would go, and I would follow him to sit in the shade or out on the water. If I could go back, I would gladly do it in a heartbeat. I would close my eyes and try to feel. I would witness my mind endlessly chattering away "What's that? What's this? Why are we doing this? What's this supposed to do? I'm bored. Can we look at Facebook now? How much longer do we have to do this? Why, why, *whyyyy*?"

My mind would whine, and like a patient mother I would smile and bring her in close for a hug that says "I love you." And then I would tell it to wait, that everything is okay, that I need to do this right now, and I will come back to you and all your questions later. But right now, I need to focus on my breathing and the feeling of the water underneath this boat, or the feeling of my bare feet walking across the smooth marble floors of the temple while the golden Buddha smiles at me as I suffer. Perhaps he smiles because he knows I'm the one doing it to myself, or perhaps he smiles because he knows I possess the key to my freedom.

Will I look for that key? Will I look into my heart and see what strength I possess?

The first step to claiming your adventure is looking within your own heart and seeing what's there. If your heart is open and smiling, great. Change nothing and keep this feeling. But if your heart is not smiling, if it's crying in the corner feeling alone and neglected, then it's time to recognize this and decide if you're going to do something about it. Again, you could change nothing and keep this feeling. It's up to you whether you're going to keep your heart in a cage - for you are the judge, jury, and jailer.

That's why the next stage is to decide. Decide from your heart that freedom is what you want and that you're willing to go to any lengths to get it. The *willingness* to change is the key that opens the lock. The willingness to run and jump off the dock into the water even though it feels scary. The willingness to take the time to show up at the temple even though everything feels dead and hopeless and you can't possibly imagine how the leaves will grow back. The willingness to start saying no to others where you always used to say yes. The willingness to start saying yes to yourself in the mirror even when everything feels like a no. The willingness to get uncomfortable, instead of running to the easiest tool you can reach to cut off the fingers and nose of your discomfort. The willingness to look in the mirror, to see yourself in all your pain, and dare to say "I love you. *I believe in you.* I don't know how we're gonna do this, but I trust we'll find a way." This is the step where we ignite the mysterious mechanics of life by setting our intentions, and then throwing the switch in our hearts. We choose our activation, and then we plant the seeds.

Next, we need to ride the winds of change and inspiration to show up with our energy, the water of life purified with our love, and we give it from our hearts to the new seeds we want to grow. Showing up means taking action, like a new fire sparked in the heart, trusting that the seeds are in the sweet embrace of the magical earth. The earth is where things grow without us forcing them out of the soil. They grow naturally without our control, and even better with our love. Love and energy directed through our thoughts, our words, our visualizations, our songs, and through the clear channel of our actions that make our dreams and desires become real.

The next stage is to start feeding ourselves with new information. We become selective about what we consume, and bring new awareness to what inputs we are feeding ourselves. We stop feeding our eyes and mind commonplace junk and start actively directing our useful mind to do research online. *Seek and ye shall find.* We come up with a plan and craft a vision in our minds of what it will be like when we are executing the harvesting of our new crop - the manifestation of our dream. We see the outcome, create a basic structure to support that outcome, and then let it go. We hold the vision and *trust the process.*

The next step is where we practice receiving. This is where we let go of what we thought was possible. We let go of how we thought the answers would come and we let them come in the way only God knows, and only Time will tell. We keep our eyes open to the flow and recognize the coincidences when they appear, like a million invisible hands of God's grace delivering you exactly what you need at exactly the right moment. When the mysterious coincidences arrive, when the window is open, take action. Press record, say yes, show up. Do the scary thing that previously you doubted you could do. However imperfectly, take action and allow the manifestation to arrive.

As we pass through the next portals, we will meet all the ways we hold ourselves back. In order to become truly free, it's a necessary part of the process to walk through the fire so it can burn away what no longer serves us. When we summon our courage we will enter the Cave of Fear and meet the monsters in our minds - the sickness inside that wants you to stay small and trade your long-term happiness for instant relief, the one that avoids facing the pain by any means necessary. Here we will meet our patterns of abuse toward ourselves and others, and we will be faced with a choice. We get to decide whether we want to keep following these same patterns, like a well-worn path traveled by our mothers and fathers. We decide if we are going to follow that path or break off and find ourselves a new path - to write ourselves a *new* story.

This part is best done with support, because going off alone into the wilderness can be hard and scary. Without a guide or a supportive tribe, you might not survive the trials ahead and end up reverting back to familiar ways. If your tribe was a group of crabs happy to scuttle along the bottom of the cage, this is about where you'll want to start looking for a new higher-vibrational group of people who will cheer you on as you swim up toward the light, instead of trying to tear you down. The moral of the story is that both success and failure are an inside job - either way, you're doing it to yourself through the responsibility you take and choices you make, or *don't*. Not actively choosing is *also* a choice.

The key to ending the pattern of abuse is to first recognize that it's happening and then choose to stop engaging in it yourself. Learn to see the ways you hold yourself back. Call out your patterns and make the choice to opt out of the games you've been playing. If you're in an abusive relationship where the other person is using fear, shame, and guilt to manipulate and control your behavior, then that's likely a survival strategy that you're *also* using - both against yourself and others. If you weren't using it, you wouldn't be with a person who mirrors that back to you. This is the time to recognize our dramas, take responsibility for our experience, and stop playing the victim. It's a weird energy game or addiction to keep engaging with an unsafe person in an attempt to make them understand and to be right about how you were wronged by them. If you need someone to understand you and your pain - or my favorite - to understand how they hurt you, then you're screwed. You're screwed because if that's your goal then you're caught in a loop of an un-winnable game like a hamster running in a wheel, running and running, burning all that frantic energy but going absolutely nowhere. You have to decide to step out and stop playing the old games with the wrong people. Stop pumping this drama. Stop texting back, even if you're sure you're in the right. Stop trying to win an un-winnable game that is killing your energy. Surrender. Let go of the old, and decide you want something *new*.

After doing the work to grow, face our fears, recognize and let go of our old self-limiting patterns, believe in and manifest the impossible, we finally catch our flight and step into a new and foreign land. This is where we must learn to surrender and trust that we are exactly where we're meant to be, as we were all along. Here, as much as we may want to speed ahead, we must learn to slow down and breathe. Stop running, jumping, or pumping our energy. Develop a mediation practice, if you haven't already. The sooner you learn to be still and become a compassionate witness of your own experience, the better.

If you're like me, you may find that you can go to a whole new place, but the same patterns and sadness still come up. That's okay, especially since now we're in a space where we can really explore ourselves. The outer journey is a metaphor for the inner journey, and so much healing is possible when we courageously venture forward into the Great Unknown. Here, we learn to trust ourselves and our path. We will face situations that will teach and challenge us. For me, I had to learn how to listen to that little bird of my intuition and start standing up for myself and saying no to others, even if that meant potentially disappointing them or making them angry with me. I needed to stop taking responsibility for other people's emotions and experiences and start taking responsibility for my own. This was how I needed to learn how to protect my energy. I had to learn how to stop trying to please everyone all the time, and instead focus on pleasing myself and cultivate the discipline to raise my own vibration, which is the real healing work.

Ultimately, the real lesson of the journey is the importance of following your bliss. Becoming a sleuth of what gives you real pleasure and raises your vibration is the secret to tapping into the real magic of life. Learning to feel good by following your bliss means to receive energy from an inner resource that is connected to a greater source, rather than engaging in these petty back-and-forth dramas and power games to try to draw energy out by manipulating, controlling, or dominating others - or allowing them to do that to us. By learning to listen to my intuition and pay attention to what makes my heart sing, then daring to follow that golden thread of inner guidance, is how I found the goats of my bliss and my little house in the mountains of Hummingbird Valley.

The Art of Seeing Hummingbirds

Speaking of hummingbirds - if you don't know already - I love them *so* much. Almost as much as I love goats. I love to sit on my little porch and watch them magically hovering in my garden, defying logic and reality with their mystical qualities. But there's a certain art to seeing hummingbirds. Apparently, not everyone can do it. The thing is that it's much harder to see a hummingbird if you're running. If you're constantly busy in your mind and body, you may miss the magical hummingbird hovering right in front of you. The art of seeing hummingbirds requires that you slow down and be still in nature. You must breathe, be present, be quiet, and be patient. Only then does the hummingbird appear, and so too will you have the eyes to see it. And in that fleeting moment it's obvious that magic is real, joy is possible, hope is alive, and there are unseen forces in this reality that we will entirely miss when we stay rushing around at the level of the mind.

The journey never ends. Even though I'm happy to be here in Guatemala, I've only arrived at the next beginning. We must keep doing the work to purify ourselves, to recognize our limiting beliefs and patterns, to wash our thoughts, clean our energy, and come back again and again to our center. There's always work to be done. It's like peeling back an onion - each layer brings its own challenges, lessons, and blessings. Over and over again, we must learn to recognize anything that pulls us back from our center and make the choice to disengage from the all too familiar drama. "Stop this pumping," as M would say.

This is about reclaiming your energy and your power. Stop leaking it, wasting it, killing it. Stop consenting to play the role of martyr, vampire, parasite, or victim. You are not the victim of your life. You, in collaboration with the unseen forces of Spirit, are the Creator. And this creative force hopes you will choose something amazing. It wants that for you. It wants to prosper you, but you must first choose it for yourself. You must allow the flow of love and abundance that is your natural state, and not pinch it off. No one can do that for you, and neither can you do that for anyone else. When you fully embrace this idea, everything will begin to change. The patterns will change and the games can end. But until you do the work - the necessary excavation of self - you will continue to be pursued by a darkness of your own making.

Go Claim What Calls to You

Go traveling if it calls to your heart. If it doesn't, then don't. But ask yourself, what does? Maybe for you it's to start a new business, move to the ocean, or write your book. When you choose to face your fears and follow your heart, there you will find your treasure. It could be as simple as starting finger painting or as drastic as selling your house and starting a dog rescue center. Maybe for you it's to move away from the city you know well, and all the ghosts and bones of the past buried there. Whatever it is for you, cast off the shackles and go claim the thing you truly want, while you still have time. While the breath of life still moves within you. While you still have the chance, before you're lying underground forever.

What's in your heart will be different than mine, or hers, or his, and that's okay. Your job is just to connect to *your* truth and dare to be honest about what it is. Then choose it and take responsibility for what it is you really want to experience in this life. Only you can choose to wake yourself from this slumber and move toward the light. It has been calling to you all along.

Be still and know that there are forces conspiring in your favor, but *you must ask* for their help. Ask for guidance and build a relationship with these energies. Be in conversation with them and share your thoughts, feelings, fears, and dreams, as you would with any trusted friend. Get clear on what you want and dare to ask for it. Then let go. Ask for protection and direction, and trust that while you may not get exactly the thing you want (aka what your mind and ego wants), you will be led into exactly what you need.

This is a process of letting go. Shake off the cobwebs of your expectations and remember you are a being made of energy and vibration and when you commit to raising your vibration, the real miracles of life and abundance begin to unlock. Release the control and energy games that keep you down. Allow the fabric of destiny to weave together to form something new, something that from where you are may seem impossible. Let me tell you, as someone who has stood on that cold, dark hill of doubt and impossibility, it's not true. What's true is that *your life is up to you*.

Stop Playing Old Games

You must choose to stop playing the game that keeps you in a low vibration. The trick to ending this pattern, aside from asking God to help you do so, is to stop engaging in it yourself. Stop pumping the lever of your dramas. Stop texting him or her back. Stop trying to control or convince the other person that you're right and they're wrong. Stop resisting. Step back and take some time for yourself. Ask your Higher Power to show you a different way to do things. Just know that the resistance you offer provides the fuel for the game to continue. Whatever you resist, persists. That doesn't mean give in - you have done nothing wrong. While you may have things from your past or present to acknowledge, you have nothing to apologize for.

Changing yourself means, when it's your turn, opt out. Unsubscribe. Disengage your energy, and in many cases, find a way to remove yourself from the situation. Whether that means finding some other place to live, or just going for a walk to the forest. When in doubt, *sit quietly under a tree and pray*. Learn to sit in the discomfort and ask God to guide your next thoughts.

Deep personal reflection through meditation, prayer, and silence will be required in this process of undoing the poison. Without it, I don't know how you'll get to the truth of your heart. This process takes time. And more importantly, *patience*. Whenever you can, go into nature alone. Turn off your phone and sit quietly. Find the question on your heart and set your intention to receive guidance. Imagine yourself as a tight flower bud. Breathe and settle in your body, and as you take those deep breaths, imagine your tight petals are beginning to relax and fall open. As the petals open, like the fingers of a tightened fist now relaxing to reveal the center, what do you find there?

It Starts With You

In the beginning must be your word, and your word is God. By that I'm referring to the invisible mysterious force of creation that weaves through all things. The force that is guided and directed through your attention, awareness, and intention. Created in the image of this great force, like a hologram a piece is a perfect copy of the whole, so too can we be the weaver of our reality - this precious thing we call life. Through our words, our thoughts, and actions, flows our energy, the water of life that we give to the things we want to grow. As we give us of ourselves and surrender into the mystical force that wishes to prosper us, it also challenges us. Challenges us to grow toward the infinite light available to us crabs, the ultimate source of energy that is ours by birthright. It is up to each one of us to make the choice to activate ourselves and align our inner tools with integrity. In the face of our challenges, we must dare to swim - we must *dare to rise*.

The real adventure, the journey we go on to discover the truth of who we really are, happens when we let go of our old games for control and drama and instead make the choice to listen to our hearts. Connected to the truth of your heart, you will discover that which is aligned with your highest purpose on this earth. But you will have to face yourself and transform as a person to make that discovery. And when you choose to take responsibility for your own transformation, life can and will surprise you.

Whether your dream is to travel the world, or just live a peaceful and happy life, get clear on what you want. Align your mind to work with you, not against you. Learn to mediate. Spend time in nature. Summon your courage. Listen to the voice of your soul. Get on your knees and ask for guidance and support. Surrender to the flow and let go of trying to control what happens. That's not your job. Your job is to learn to trust yourself, to love yourself, to take better care of yourself, to listen for your heart's gentle whispers, and ultimately, to dare to believe your leaves can and will grow back when you show up for yourself with love. And for those who choose to follow the compass of their heart's inner knowingness, true freedom is possible for those of us who dare to believe.

Above all, remember that *you're learning*. You're not always going to get it right, and that's okay. The point is to stay open, be willing to change, seek guidance, ask for help, take action, and have compassion for yourself in the same way you would have compassion for a child just learning to walk. You would not insult or shame an innocent child who falls. You would offer them support and encouragement to get up and try again - and it needs to be the same way with you. You are that innocent child, and above all, you are learning to walk yourself home.

This is it friends, this is your time.

You are the person you've been waiting for.
It was you all along.
And you had the key in your hand the whole time!

You don't need to play small anymore.
It's okay to feel again.
You're allowed to dream again.
Everything you need is already inside of you.

Now is the time to choose.

I dare you to listen to the voice of your soul.
I dare you to face your fears.
I dare you to show up with love at the tree of life.
I dare you to reject the poison inside of you.

Choose to wake up.
Choose for yourself.
Choose to face your shadow.
Choose to transform your pain into power.

Find and follow your bliss.

Go claim your adventure!

You can do it.
I believe in you.

I hope to see you at the top of the mountain.

All the Beloved Known Things

From "All the Beloved Known Things"
by Luke Maguire Armstrong

There is a light that shines at dawn that is not the sunrise.
There is music in the air your ears will not detect.
If you know why the free bird sings,
If you can understand why someone might leave all the
beloved, known things
To follow a preview of a premonition of a spark of the
heart's tugging hopes,
Then you have already been to that place where no one
arrives or leaves.

Why not?
Rise to the occasion of your own possibilities?
Forget the appeasement of unfamiliar natures
To race toward the ancient ecstatisicm
That's been hidden in everyone on the cosmic Easter
egg hunt?

Once you cross the bridge,
You are on the other side.
Once you take a dive,
The water is not able to resist
Engulfing you completely.

It's okay to dream like that
wild-open-hopeful
Assured that will be will be wonderful,
Committed to come alive
It whatever comes your way.

No need to worry about whom to believe.

Notice who's happy.
See whose joy can barely fit in their smile.
See who dances with the dawn.
Whose song lift up the corners of the heart.
Whose closely held serenity leaves them
Unperturbed in the turbulence of preferences and opinions.
Who presence is a gift
Guiding lost starlight home to heart.

Seek.
Seek your heart out sojourner.
Join the party.
Enjoy the feast.
You belong here.
We've been waiting and wondering
When you'd grace us with your possibilities.

Be.
Be well wanderer.
You are as home as you are living in your heart.
And today the ocean inside of you is as calm,
As it is immense, as you are
Fortunate,

And *free*.

Afterword

In this story, I talk a lot about belief systems and what an important role they play in my journey - and in all of our journeys. Beliefs systems are the mental structures we adopt and assume to be the truth. They help us function in our families, societies, and cultures. Belief systems give us our sense of right and wrong, the best way to do things or not do things, and essentially inform the core assumptions of what is "common sense."

They are our understandings of how the world works - understandings that generate our systems of government, religion, economy, and society - which create our patterns for living. They help us uphold moral standards we wish to live by, and they also inform what we believe is possible and what is not. Belief systems are an important part of having a healthy, functioning structure for living. However, they can also become toxic, limiting, and the justification used to crucify one another.

What most humans don't understand is that belief systems are fluid. They are not truth cast in stone, and they can change if we are willing to question them, explore them, and allow them to change as our understanding of ourselves and the world around us changes. The problem arises when we don't see them that way, when we take our beliefs for granted without examination, and then we use that as the measuring stick for reality and the aforementioned crucifixion.

Take, for example, the belief that catalyzed my whole journey to India. My sister told me she was pregnant, and at that time I was operating within a belief system that said once I became a mother, I could not travel. It was a fact to me. I believed it to be true so strongly that it fueled me to make the necessary sacrifices to go traveling - and that's valuable. However, something interesting happened when I got to India. I started meeting mothers traveling with their children! And I mean kids of all ages: babies, toddlers, small people of all sorts. These kids were being exposed to other cultures and ways of living, and I could see they were learning so much and were far better off for this unique education they were receiving at such a young age (Video: bit.ly/TipeeSchoolforKids). It totally blew my mind open, and it showed me quite palpably that what I had believed before, *and would even swear my life on*, was not actually true.

But wait, it gets better.

I encountered one of these courage women, a young woman from Europe traveling India with her five month old baby with whom I shared a rickshaw ride, and I made a video called "The Traveling Mother" (Video: http://bit.ly/TheTravelingMother). I sent this video to my sister, expecting nothing except a good laugh. Instead, what she did totally surprised me. She bought a ticket to India and brought nine month old Alia to India to join me!

My sister, her baby, and I spent the last two weeks of my six-month trip to India together in Kashmir with M. We had an amazing experience together staying on intricately hand-carved houseboats on Dal lake, visiting mosques and other sacred places of worship, and M even did energy work with the baby to help her gain more power and balance. He did all sorts of weird things with her, like placing her at the tip of a shikara boat on Dal Lake. He put her in a tree, on a horse in Pahalgam, and essentially helped her in ways were both terrifying and brilliant. It's a funny and complex story, and maybe one I'll tell in another book someday. My experience with M would need its own book.

My point is that a lot of people watch my videos and wish they could do what I do, but feel they can't do it. Maybe they have kids, maybe they feel they're too old, they have financial difficulties, or maybe they have health problems. I'm not here to tell anyone what they can or cannot do. My only wish is to point out that, *like me,* sometimes what you believe *isn't true*. Sometimes the limitations you feel are firmly set in place to block your way are, in fact, illusions. To each their own. I just know from my own experience that I was living my life within belief systems that were trying their best to hold me back from doing the thing that would make my heart sing.

What if we took those beliefs off? What if we realized we were wearing a sort of helmet, complete with a visor in front of our eyes, that was providing a filter for reality. Looking through this visor, we sensed what is right and wrong, what is possible and impossible, etc. It's like there's an American visor, and each country, religion, political party, and culture has their own - their own moral standards, their own set of customs and rituals that seem true and correct. What if we were to take that helmet off? Who would we be without that filter that has been trained, programmed, and educated into us by family, government, religion, and culture? If we stripped all of those belief systems away, what then could be possible?

"Out beyond ideas of wrongdoing and rightdoing,
there is a field. I'll meet you there."
~ Rumi

My Favorite Prayers

I fiercely rebelled against the concept of God for most of my life. I didn't like the way religion forced upon me this idea of God as an old white man in the sky who was constantly judging and trying to control me. As a young human, this did not resonate with me as something I was willing to believe or surrender myself into. It wasn't until I read "Conversations with God" by Neale Donald Walsch that my defenses cracked open and I finally became willing to acknowledge the presence of the divine in my life.

"God" is such a loaded word for so many people, especially after all the trauma associated with other humans trying to force their beliefs on each other, which comes down to power, control, and the need to be right. I have no interest in trying to control what you believe, or make you wrong if you believe something different than I do. I believe we are each on our own spiritual journey, and each journey will look different, and that's okay. The most important thing is that we return to harmony, to oneness, to love, to the knowing that we're not alone, that we are part of something bigger than ourselves, that there's some kind of universal power influencing us, and that it will help us help ourselves and each other if we are willing to get humble and ask.

Rather than insisting that you believe what I believe, I encourage you to develop your *own* personal relationship with your *own* understanding of a Higher Power, a force that is greater than you, in whatever way that looks like or feels right - for *you*. This is about cultivating your own relationship with the divine, not anyone else's.

Using spoken prayer is a great way to develop that relationship, just like regularly getting on the phone with someone is a great way to build a meaningful and intimate friendship. Personally, for most of my life I had a lot of resistance to prayer, but over the years I've come to understand that humbling myself in prayer is one of the most powerful things I can do to open myself to the flow of universal energy.

I believe that life is not just a series of coincidences and accidents, that there is a greater intelligence and wisdom at play. This power that influences and guides us is the same power that transforms the tiny acorn into the might oak tree. And it wants to do the same for us, if only we'll allow it to work in our lives. To that end, I offer these prayers as a way of opening the connection and being in conversation with the mysterious source of creation that weaves through all things, that knows no gender or limitation, and that wants to help you grow just like the acorn - but only if you'll humble yourself and surrender into the process.

Speak these words or come up with your own. You can't get it wrong. The most important thing is that you speak from your heart with the intention to connect to and build a relationship with the mysterious energy and force of Creation that only wishes to prosper you. And if you're "lucky" like me, then you'll learn to surrender into the direction and guidance that you receive.

CODA 3rd Step Prayer: God, I give to you all I am and all I will be for your healing and direction. Make new this day as I release all my worries and fears knowing that you are by my side. Please help me open myself to your love, to allow your love to heal my wounds and to allow your love to flow through me & from me to those around me. May your will be done this day and always.

Big Book 3rd Step Prayer: God, I offer myself to thee - to build with me and do with me as thy will. Relieve me of the bondage of self that I may better do thy will. Take away my difficulties, that victory over them may bear witness to those I would help of thy love, thy power, and thy way of life. May I do thy will always.

Big Book 7th Step Prayer: My Creator, I am now willing that you should have all of me, good and bad. I pray that you now remove from me every single defect of character which stands in the way of my usefulness to you and my fellows. Grant me strength, as I go from here, to do your bidding.

Father Mother God, I know not what this day is for, nor do I need to know. Remove from me everything I think I know, or thought I knew, so you may teach me anew. Reveal to me how you would extend your love, my eternal treasure, through me, as me, for me, and for all beings across all realms, so that they too may come to know the peace the passes all understanding, and remember their Oneness with their Creator and all of Creation. And make it so that I cannot miss it is your hand leading me. Make it abundantly clear as I step forward into this day, expecting nothing less than miracles.

God, please lead me. Show me the way. I ask that you send me the signs and signals I need, and give me the eyes to see them. Thank you for directing me, protecting me, and correcting me. Thank you for helping me learn something worth teaching to others. Thank you for showing me what I must do, and for leading me to it and through it. Thank you for sending an army of angels to my aid. Thank you for leading me home to the truth of myself.

Thy will, not mine, be done.

NEXT ACTION STEPS

So, you want to embark on your adventure of self-discovery?

Here's a plan I recommend:

1. Learn to meditate and develop a regular daily practice. I recommend 20 mins a day, preferably in the morning. If you have to wake up early, do it. Download the app Insight Timer (https://insighttimer.com/) and explore their guided meditations, or just set a timer and sit quietly and focus on your breath. Alternatively, you can look up your local Transcendental Meditation Center or find meditation meetup groups near you. Find others who can teach and support you to meditate. Remember, it's called a "meditation practice," not a "meditation perfect."
2. Get clear on your destination (desired outcome) and set a date by when you're leaving (or having it).
3. Set a financial goal clear in your mind, somewhere between $3-10K, depending on where you want to go and for how long.
4. Open a free online savings account with Ally Bank (www.allybank.com) or other trusted financial institution.
5. Start working towards your goal and put money in your Adventure Fund.
6. Do some research online about your destination. Search for Facebook groups dedicated to your destination. Create a Pinterest board with *specific* images that inspire you most.
7. Think, speak, and act like it's happening.
8. Buy your ticket!
9. Let go of anything holding you back. When in doubt, get on your knees and ask for signs and guidance.
10. Hold the vision and trust the process! And please, be gentle with yourself. You're in the process of coming home to your true self. It won't be easy, but it'll be *worth it*. And so are you. ☺

Good luck on your adventure!

Acknowledgments and Fist Bumps

There are so many beings and spirits I wish to thank, and without whom this journey, these lessons, and this book would have been possible.

Firstly, I wish to thank the Spirit of this Book, also known as Inspiration, the muses, genius, etc. Whatever you are, thank you for choosing to work with me. I am so grateful for this opportunity to serve you and to work together to bring this message to the world. Thank you for your patience with me and for showing up. Thank you for encouraging me to trust when I felt so confused and demoralized at so many times during this process. Thank you for your love, and the magic of this message.

Next, I wish to thank my parents. Thank you for giving me the gift of my life. For giving me the chance to grow up all over the world. And for pushing me out of the nest. It wasn't the best experience at the time, but it was what I needed to learn how to fly. Thank you for your choices and sacrifices. Thank you for the computer and camera. I love you both very much.

I'd like to give a special shout out thanks to my amazing sister Krystina and my bold and beautiful niece Alia, who inspired my adventure and continue to inspire me every day. I love you both so much and I look forward to many more adventures together in the future.

Next, I would like to thank the angels, spirits, and guides who have been watching over me and helping me on my path. I know it wasn't an easy job, especially when I was so stubborn and difficult. Thank you for directing me, protecting me, and correcting me. I love you all very much.

I would like to thank my teachers, who appeared in many unexpected forms and in unexpected places. Specifically Mustafa and his grandfather, who knew I would write an important book to teach people how to use their energy. Thank you for not giving up on me, especially when I was being a little shit. The other teachers to whom I would like to extend special thanks include, but are not limited to, Buddha, Seulki Koo, Amma Sophia Rose & Monika Nataraj (the leaders of the "She Rises" goddess pilgrimage to Egypt), all my goddess sisters on the Egypt trip, Bilal and the camels, Adam 'Kalari' Phillips, Laoshi, Craig, Weng, Annabelle the goat, Rosie Maria, Charles Quinn, Ben Maitland-Lewis, and pretty much every human being and animal I've ever encountered. Each one of you were my teachers. I love you all.

I would like to thank my family at the farm, Granja Tz'ikin, and my family at Karuna Atitlan. Neal, Jeremy, Adriana, Matt, Josh, Maria, the goats, Mia and Panda the cats, Camilo and Luna the dogs, Kim, Marie, Holy Wow Cacao Matt, AJ, Yasmin, Cat, and Weepy and Little Bear the dogs. You guys held me and continue to hold me and teach me as I go through this massive transition to write this book and continue the process of discovering who I am and how I'm meant to serve others in a healthy way. I love you all so much!

I want to specifically thank Luke Maguire Armstrong who took a chance on me and gave me my home at Karuna Atitlan. Luke, you are my brother. Thank you for recognizing the falcon. Thank you for holding me so many times as I cried in your arms through the not knowing and discomfort of this process of stepping into my dharma. Thank you for the work you have done on yourself and to create our home. Thank you for leading me into silence. Thank you for teaching me new ways to meditate. Thank you for deepening my appreciation for and practice of yoga. Thank you for always being honest with me, especially when it hurts. Thank you for editing this book, for your experience and advice as an author, and for supporting me through each step in the process of birthing this book into the world. Thank you for your work with the kids of the Integral Heart Family. Your commitment and dedication to feeding and caring for these children shows me what it means to be in meaningful service to others. Thank you brother, for this life, and all the others we have shared tea. It's good to keep crossing paths with you and I look forward to discover what the next one holds.

I would like to give a special thanks to my dear friend and herbalist Maria Fernandez. Thank you for being my friend all these years, and for believing in me and this book when I didn't. Thank you for letting me send my mail to your house while I was out of the country, and for helping me handle stuff that was inconvenient. Thank you for teaching me about the healing power of our plant allies, and for equipping me with tinctures that helped me stay healthy and strong on the road. I love you woman! We have so much more growth and adventures ahead.

I would like to extend special thanks to Dr. Angela Lauria and the whole team over at The Author Incubator, the high level coaching program I enrolled in to write this book. Thank you for creating the system, structure, and accountability I needed in order to write a book that makes a difference. I couldn't nor wouldn't have done it without you!

I would like to give special thanks to Matt Rentz, the shining light on the other side of the cave. Thank you for helping me learn what healthy love with a man feels like. Thank you for being willing to communicate honestly and hold space for all my emotions without trying to fix or change them. Thank you for telling me I'm beautiful when I cry. Thank you for flexing healthy boundaries with me and yourself. Thank you for hiking up the mountain with me to listen and be present with me. Thank you for admitting your fears, and hearing mine, so we can work through them together. Thank you for being willing to learn and grow with me. You are a big part of the treasure from this very long journey. I'm grateful and excited to have arrived at a new beginning with you, and I immensely grateful for how much you've taught me and eager to see what new adventures we'll take together. <3

I would like to give a special thanks to our dog Bella, or rather should I say the dog who chose me as her human. Bella teaches me every day what unconditional love is. Thank you for showing me how to never stop loving, no matter how badly I've been hurt. Thank you for showing me how to turn aggressors into playmates. I love you Bella Rose!

A special thanks is to due to my amazing and supportive team of early readers. Thank you for showing up to receive my work and endure its word vomit, cursing, and typos. Thank you for sending in your reviews and just having my back when I needed some friends. You guys are amazing and I love you all.

I would like to extend my deepest gratitude to my audience online. Thank you for being with me! Thank you for allowing me to share my journey with you, and for being open to the lessons therein. Thank you for those who have supported me emotionally and financially, especially when I was going through hard times. Thank you for your views, your comments, your likes, and shares. Thank you for your love, your criticisms, your words of encouragements and for sharing your love, time, and attention with me. I want you to know that when I was at the Solar Cross in Egypt, I made a special prayer for you all and your wellbeing. May you be happy, may you be well, may you be free from suffering. May your hearts be happy and free. Thank you for going on this adventure with me all these years. Here's to many more years of storytelling and adventure yet to come!

I would like to thank the spirit of the lands where I traveled, who held me on this path and allowed my safe passage. I would like to thank the spirits and ancestors in Maryland, New York, California, Massachusetts, New Hampshire, Maine, Thailand, Bali, Egypt, and Guatemala who graciously received me and helped me along my path. I would like to thank the sacred spring at the temple I would visit near Pancoran Hotel in Giyanyar in Bali. Thank you to the healing waters that gave me new life, and for helping Gentle Knowing to emerge. Thank you to Hummingbird Valley, Tzununa, and the Mayan people. Thank you to the spirit of cacao who helped me open my heart and write this book. I love you all so much!

I would like to give special thanks to Isis, Hathor, Sekhmet, Horus, Nefertari, Kali, Sobek my love, and all the other energies and vibrations I encountered in Egypt. I do not understand, and I accept. Thank you for guiding me and helping me release what no longer serves. Thank you for helping me learn how to love myself and to reawaken the divine feminine within me. May she rise within us all.

I would like to thank the recovery community in Bali and especially the hard working folks at the Kembali Recovery Center, who give so much to the community. If you want to find real help to take a good honest look at yourself in a ridiculously beautiful place, look them up. Thank you for holding me with love and compassion as I stepped into the fire to discover who I really am. Thank you for your service.

I wish to thank my energy - my qi. I'm sorry for all the times I hurt, pinched, blocked, numbed, or killed you. I'm sorry for all the times that I didn't give you what you needed from me. I love you very much and I'm so grateful for this journey to discover and align myself with you. Thank you for flowing with me, teaching me, and reaching me.

I wish to thank my mind. You're a good mind and I'm happy to have you on board. Thank you for being so great, in spite of all the mischief and poor mathematical skills. I love you.

I wish to thank my body for carrying me and my soul. I'm sorry for all the times I didn't treat you so well. Thank you for your patience and forgiveness. I love you and I promise to listen to you and take good care of you.

I wish to thank my intuition and other abilities. It's such a pleasure to meet you and to dance with you. Thank you for showing yourselves to me. Thank you for leading me. Thank you for teaching me. I love you. Go team!

I wish to thank the trees. Thank you for your beauty, wisdom, and for teaching me what it means to grow slowly. To send my roots deep into the earth and my leaves high into the sky. Thank you for your medicine.

I wish to thank my plant allies. Thank you for your medicine. Thank you for believing in us, and for helping us heal ourselves and each other. Thank you, sacred teachers.

I wish to thank the medicine, wisdom, and intelligence within the fungi mycelium and grandmother Ayahuasca. Thank you for helping us see the truth. Thank you for healing our hearts, minds, and bodies. Thank you for cleaning what needs to be cleaned, healing what needs to be healed, and teaching what needs to be taught. Thank you for helping us, especially when we humans can be so…human.

I wish to include in this thanks the energies and divine teachers known as Jesus Christ and Mary Magdalene. Thank for planting the seeds of love and leading the way for us. I'm sorry what they did to you both. But it's all for learning, right? Thank you for teaching us about compassion, forgiveness, and real love in the face of total bullshit.

Most of all, I wish to thank my Creator, the Great Spirit, the Great Mystery. Thank you, Mother Father God. Thank you for leading me. Thank you for showing me. Thank you for helping me learn something worth teaching to others. Thank you for putting in me the words to help the people.

Last but not least, I wish to thank myself. *Thank you,* Erica. Gentle Knowing. Zooney. Chakri. Indra. Amrika. Mermaid. Neo. Thank you for accepting the call to this ongoing adventure. Thank you for your courage to face your fears. Thank you for your willingness to step into the cave and meet the monsters there. Thank you for believing, even when it felt impossible. Thank you for being willing to honestly look at yourself, your beliefs, your patterns, and take responsibility for changing them into something more loving. Thank you for doing your shadow work. Thank you for your courage to ask for help. Thank you for your courage to be vulnerable and speak your truth. Thank you for the flowers, the brownies, the time and space to let those healing tears flow. Thank you for the gold Isis ring and the beautiful new clothes. Thank you for how hard you worked to save the money, to learn new skills, to press record every time your hand was shaking. Thank you for waking up early. Thank you for doing your work. Thank you for being willing to invest in yourself when it felt scary. Thank you for everything you had to overcome and show up for in order to write this book. Thank you for trusting, especially in the darkest moments. Thank you for not giving up on your dream. Thank you for being willing to be seen, and to share your experience, strength, and hope with others. *You're the tits, kid.*

About the Author

Erica Derrickson is an adventurer who travels alone as a woman to places like India, Thailand, Bali, Egypt, and Guatemala. Her popular videos online receive millions of views as she authentically shares her adventures with the hope of inspiring others to claim theirs. As a bestselling author, award-winning photographer, actress, mermaid, and social media influencer, she is a bright source of energy and inspiration in the lives of others. She lives in Guatemala where her greatest pleasures are watching hummingbirds and herding goats up the mountain.

You can connect with Erica and view her latest videos and posts at:
Facebook: www.facebook.com/withErica
New Youtube: bit.ly/TheAdventuresOfEricaDerrickson
Old Youtube: https://www.youtube.com/user/ericaderricka
IMDB: http://imdb.to/EricasIMDB
Photography portfolio: www.ericaseye.com
Instagram: @ericaderrickson
Twitter: @ericaseye

About Karuna Atitlan

This book was birthed at Karuna Atitlan, at one of Author Luke Maguire Armstrong's "Writing Your Dreams True" Writers Retreats (IG @WritingYourDreamsTrue).

Karuna is a forest Retreat Center/Conscious Community created by Luke Maguire Armstrong in The Valley of the Hummingbirds above Lake Atitlan, Guatemala. It's a place where birds sing, a brook babbles, and humans who have left the grind create and contemplate.

Karuna is a place for artists, writers, and yogis to live in a supportive community and have the right condition to dive deep into their art or practice. We host supportive retreats and offer ongoing residency programs. We hope to be of service to you as you walk your path.

To inquire about residencies, trainings, and retreats, visit:

www.KarunaAtitlan.com
FB: Karuna Atitlan
IG: @KarunaAtitlan
"All the Beloved Known Things"
http://amzn.to/BelovedKnownThings

Become a Part of The Integral Heart Family

"If you enjoyed this book and want to show your gratitude,
I ask that you please join me to support the children of the
Integral Heart Family." - Erica Derrickson

Something indescribable is the smile of a child's first day of school after being told he or she was too poor to study.

The Integral Heart Family is a school in Guatemala of which Erica is a donor and supporter, as are many of her amazing worldwide network. It is located in Antigua, Guatemala and provides impoverished students with all they need to grow and thrive. Kids come from situations of generational poverty and through what's provided are thriving, getting through school, and reaching their dreams. This program is 100% crowdfunded. The support you provide translates into enabled dreams and inspiring smiles. In helping kids like this, ultimately we are helping us— responding to their need helps us grow our own hearts' capacity to care.

For more information about getting involved and how to join Erica and our family of supporters, please visit:

www.IntegralHeartFoundation.org
Facebook: Integral Heart Family
IG: @IntegralHeartFamily

THE ADVENTURE CONTINUES...

www.facebook.com/withErica

...ARE YOU WITH ME?